Phoenix from the Fire:
A History of Edgewood College

by

Mary Paynter, O.P.

1927 *2002*

EDGEWOOD COLLEGE
SEVENTY-FIFTH ANNIVERSARY

Phoenix from the Fire: A History of Edgewood College

First published 2002

PUBLISHED BY EDGEWOOD COLLEGE
Edgewood College, 1000 Edgewood College Drive, Madison, Wisconsin

Cover image: *Phoenix from the Fire* by Sister Stephanie Stauder, OP

Design: Bay Graphics, Inc., Williams Bay, Wisconsin

ISBN 0-9718106-0-5

Contents

Acknowledgements

*M*y indebtedness to the many people who assisted me in the research and writing of this history of Edgewood College is great. Put simply, it could not have been done without the collaboration of many others. In particular, I am deeply indebted to two of my Dominican sisters. Sister Jean Richter, Archivist of Edgewood College, went far beyond the usual archival research assistance, extending always insightful suggestions, extensive and thoughtful editing, and never-failing patience and encouragement. The generosity of Sister Clemente Davlin of Dominican University in creating the book's index greatly enriched the usefulness of the book for its readers.

The Sinsinawa Dominican Archivists, Sister Marjorie Buttner and Sister Pauline Ingram, graciously helped me as I attempted to pinpoint primary sources in their collection. The Archives and Library of the Wisconsin Historical Society provided valuable materials for the early chapters. The photographs in the book are published with the permission of the Edgewood College Archives, the Wisconsin Historical Society Archives, the Sinsinawa Dominican Archives, the Washburn-Norlands Foundation Archives, the Public Relations Office of Edgewood College, Warner Bros. Publications, Mark Peters, Anna Fox, Julie Sawyer Krier, Eileen Dhooghe-McIltrot, and others. I also wish to acknowledge the encouragement and support of James Ebben, President of Edgewood College.

This history is a brief account that attempts to span more than the 75 years of Edgewood College's existence. It offers the reader highlights from key moments in that history, but necessarily omits far more than it records. Because this book is designed as a popular history, it is not heavily footnoted; however, all sources may be traced in detail in the annotated versions of the manuscript available to readers in the Edgewood College Archives and at the Sinsinawa Dominican Archives.

Mary Paynter, O.P.

Prologue

The story of Edgewood College has a beginning; its end is yet to be told. The narrative has been developed by the many people who loved it and labored on its behalf—sometimes during periods of growth and expansion and other times during great trials and difficulties. The complete story is not contained within this book. That story is made up of all the dreams and struggles and dedicated efforts of the Sinsinawa Dominican Sisters, of the many faculty and staff who served so faithfully through the decades, and of thousands of students.

The writing of history is often a search for connections: links of present with past, of effects and their likely causes, of people and events—all in the context of exploring a past bonded to the present by written records and oral traditions, by photographs and art works, by music and poetry and drama, by living memories. One way of approaching history is through stories, the narratives of human experience. This brief history of Edgewood College focuses on some remarkable stories of some intriguing human beings as well as on critical turning points at key moments in the past.

A narrative pattern emerges in the history of Edgewood: an alternation between shadow and light, between tragedy and recovery, between failure and new birth. Perhaps a good symbol for the Edgewood College story is the phoenix, that mysterious mythical bird perennially reborn out of its own fiery death.

This book is dedicated to all those—Sinsinawa Dominicans and their colleagues—who through the years labored with faith and courage and often against great odds to ensure that Edgewood College would be born, would "rise from the fire" again and again, and would grow and flourish. Because of them, many generations of students have expanded their minds and deepened their hearts by being offered the values of a Catholic, Dominican, liberal education rooted in ideals of compassion, justice, and service to humankind, as well as in the unending questions that seek truth. Most of these valiant teachers, staff, administrators, and trustees are not named in this book, but they are remembered and celebrated in the memories and the lives of colleagues and graduates.

"What's past is prologue," wrote Shakespeare in *The Tempest*, and so the future of Edgewood College may be figured in the memories of its rich heritage. As we celebrate the Diamond Jubilee of Edgewood College, it is time to look back at a remarkable history and recall some of the people who shaped it, and at the same time prepare for the new challenges and opportunities that the future offers us.

TERRIBLE CALAMITY

EDGEWOOD ACADEMY DESTROYED BY FIRE AND TWO LIVES LOST.

MARGERY RICE AND MAGGIE STACK THE VICTIMS.

LITTLE FRANCES HENEBERRY NOW HOVERING BETWEEN LIFE AND DEATH.

NO HOPE AT ALL FOR HER RECOVERY.

Both the Old and New Buildings Are Burned to the Ground—The Three Children Suffer from Suffocation. Narrow Escape of Katie Sweeny and Sister Bertha—Financial Loss Nearly $50,000—History of the Old Villa.

DEAD—
MARGERY RICE, aged 8, of Stevens Point.
MAGGIE STACK, aged 6, of Chicago.

FATALLY INJURED—
FRANCES HENEBERRY, aged 8, of Chicago.

SLIGHTLY INJURED—
SISTER BERTHA.
KATE SWEENY, aged 9, of Michigan.

FINANCIAL LOSS —
NEARLY $50,000; insurance $25,000

The St. Regina academy, at Edgewood Villa, is in ruins—the old and the new buildings—falling victims to flames last night.

Soon after eight o'clock the city was startled by a report that the fire department had received

The scenes presented were distressing in the extreme as people from the city flocked to the scene, and frantically inquired after the particulars, as many of the 28 scholars boarding at the academy belong in this city.

It was a sorry sight also to witness the time-honored old structure tumbling to pieces, while the flames were fiercely lashing the new structure. In less than an hour after the old building was destroyed the flames had full control of the new one, and there was no power to stem their fierceness. The roof was completely destroyed before 12 o'clock midnight, and a terrible crash was heard. At midnight, when the Democrat's reporter left the scene the interior of the new structure was completely destroyed. The exterior

men who had assembled to learn the particulars of the sad accident and to lend aid to the sisters. The jury went into the room where the lifeless bodies of the little ones lay on a cot, side by side. It was a touching sight indeed. Both of the children seemed to be but asleep. One of the bodies showed absolutely no marks to tell how it died, while the other was somewhat blackened by smoke. The jury looked upon them but a minute and adjourned to meet in Justice Wakeley's office at 2 o'clock this afternoon.

LATER AND BETTER DETAILS

From the latest investigations it appears that the fire started either from a defective flue in the attic or from a fireplace. The house very quickly

THE NEW BUILDING WHICH WAS BURNED.

walls were standing, but the transverse walls were very badly damaged, and some of them had fallen.

Chief Engineer Bernard said that had No. 2 fire engine been in the city, it would have been taken out and set at the lake. In that event good work could have been done. But, unfortunately, the engine is in Milwaukee for repairs.

Nearly all the furniture of the academy was saved and safely laid away in the grove of evergreens.

To the firemen and the many others who rendered assistance great credit is due.

The origin of the fire is not known. The sisters reported that the flames were first seen in one of

filled with a dense, black smoke, but the sisters and older girls went heroically to work to save life and property. All the pupils were up and dressed except four—the youngest children in the academy. They were called the "babies," and they had all been put to bed in one room and Sister Bertha was with them, having put them to bed and remained to get them to sleep. One of the children was not entirely well. It is supposed Sister Bertha fell asleep too, but it was evident that she had been awakened and had tried to flee with one of her charges. She was found unconscious upon the floor of the bedroom, with one of the children clasped in her arms. Other sisters rescued her and

CHAPTER ONE

Trial By Fire

A devastating trial by fire could have ended Edgewood's history soon after that history began. During the night of November 16, 1893, little more than ten years after the Dominican Sisters had opened St. Regina Academy in "Edgewood Villa," a tragic fire took the lives of three children, boarders in the Academy, and totally destroyed the Villa and the adjacent, nearly completed new school building.

The next morning, the *Wisconsin State Journal* headlined its front-page story, "Horror in a School," and the opening sentence declared: "The most distressing fire which has ever occurred in this city was the burning of the St. Regina Academy at Edgewood last night." A reporter for the *Madison Democrat* remarked that "the matter of rebuilding is in doubt…. but it is more than probable that the valuable property will not be relinquished, and that ultimately another noble educational institution will be found there." Even in the darkest hours after the fire, hope was alive that a new Edgewood would rise like a phoenix from the ashes.

How had the Sinsinawa Dominican Sisters come to that terrible moment in 1893, not only mourning the tragic deaths of three of their youngest pupils, but also facing a difficult decision about the future of education on the Edgewood property? Indeed, how did they obtain this beautiful estate and villa so early in their own history?[1]

Long before Edgewood College began, the Dominican Sisters of Sinsinawa in 1881 had been given a colonial-style mansion situated on 55 acres on the north shore of Lake Wingra outside the city of Madison, Wisconsin. This beautifully sited property with gardens, vineyards, an exotic tree collection, and trout ponds belonged to the former governor of the state of Wisconsin, Cadwallader Colden Washburn, who had purchased the mansion and its estate from Samuel Marshall, a banker, in 1873. The Edgewood Villa, as it was called, had been built in 1855 by John Ashmead, who

Front page account of the Edgewood fire:
The Madison Democrat   November 17, 1893

Wisconsin Historical Society WHi-1835

Samuel Marshall (1820 – 1907)
founder of the State Bank in Madison
owner of Edgewood Villa and grounds 1857 – 1873

had purchased the land from Leonard J. Farwell, then serving a second term as Wisconsin's governor. A Madison newspaper account of the 1893 fire described the Villa as "of colonial architecture, a facsimile, it is said, of an old home in Philadelphia…. To Mr. Marshall is due the credit of beautifying the grounds and adding, by his excellent views of landscape gardening, to its artistic setting."

Samuel Marshall had acquired the property in the spring of 1857, not long after he had opened the State Bank on Pinckney Street on Madison's capitol square. During the early 1850s, Washburn also opened a bank in Mineral Point, and the two men were business acquaintances. After Washburn was elected governor in November of 1872 he learned that Marshall had decided to move to Milwaukee, where his wife could be close to a Catholic church and where his principal banking interests lay in the Marshall & Ilsley banking firm. Washburn may have seen the opportunity to purchase Edgewood as part of a long range plan to continue his political career based in the capital city. According to the Madison *City Directory* for 1873, the governor's residence during that year was down town at the corner of Gilman and Butler Streets, close to the capitol.

In any case, during his first year as governor, Washburn purchased the property from Marshall in September 1873. Governor Washburn took a special interest in his new country home, continuing the landscaping of the lakeside property begun by Marshall, planting formal gardens, developing trellised grapevines, importing exotic trees and shrubs, stocking fish ponds, and acquiring a herd of Cotswold sheep, according to his daughter Jeannette. She also recalled that "although my father did not spend a great deal of time at Edgewood, as his business called him away frequently, he always was glad to get back and enjoyed the place greatly…. When he bought the place, my father fully expected to be re-elected, and so intended to make Edgewood his home for a number of years."

After November 1873, when Washburn lost the election that would have led to his second term as governor, he decided to turn his attention to the development of his flour-milling business, centered in Minneapolis, and his lumber business, operated from La Crosse, Wisconsin. His political influence was waning, his beloved wife Jeannette had suffered a serious mental disorder many years earlier and was hospitalized in the East, his two daughters were married, and his own health was declining Despite his frequent travels, he resided at times in his Edgewood Villa in Madison, and, at other times in his long established residence in La Crosse.

By 1880, Washburn was a seriously ill man, suffering from kidney disease, and in 1881, he went first to Switzerland and later to Eureka Springs, Arkansas, seeking to regain his health. Perhaps his own illness, coupled with the sad weight of his wife's long

Wisconsin Historical Society WHi-1832

Samuel Marshall opened the first Wisconsin bank incorporated under the Wisconsin banking law of 1852, Pinckney Street, Madison.

Cadwallader Colden Washburn (1818 – 1882) owned Edgewood Villa and grounds 1873 – 1881 before donating the property to the Sinsinawa Dominican Sisters to be used "for educational purposes"

Courtesy: Washburn-Norlands Foundation

mental decline and the realization that his daughters and their families had established homes back East, led him to consider divesting himself of properties that were no longer needed, including his much-loved Edgewood. Certainly he no longer needed a political base in Madison, having been passed over during the 1870s as a candidate for the U.S. Senate.

The question arose: what should he do with the beautiful villa and acreage on the shores of Lake Wingra? His daughter Jeannette said that he had offered to give Edgewood to her, "but I did not want to live in the West—that was before he ever thought of giving it to anyone else." Jeannette may have had some unpleasant memories of Edgewood, too. She and her husband, A. Warren Kelsey, had lived there briefly (and two of their children were born there) in the early 1870s, but the Governor had a troubled relationship with his son-in-law, and in 1874, he threatened to expel them.[2] Various accounts indicate that he offered it to the city of Madison, to the University of Wisconsin (to which he had recently donated the famous Washburn Observatory), and to the State of Wisconsin.[3] All turned him down, probably because the location seemed so far from the city of Madison—after all, it would be some years before the first streetcar line was extended outside the city to the new "suburb" of Wingra Park in 1897.

Finally, in 1881, he found grateful and willing recipients of his generous gift— the Sinsinawa Dominican Sisters. The story of the gift is intriguing. In the St. Clara Convent Annals at Sinsinawa, the entry for May 10, 1881, states:

Feast of St. Antoninus. The Hon. C. C. Washburn, ex-Governor of Wisconsin, deeded his beautiful home, Edgewood Villa, to the Dominican Sisters at Sinsinawa, to be used for educational purposes. Mother M. Emily, accompanied by Sister M. Magdalen and Sister M. Alexius, met the Governor at his country home.

Plans were made for the transfer of Edgewood and for the opening of school in September. We must ever be grateful to this Christian gentleman for his princely gift, and to Rev. Father Pettit, pastor; and Major Nicodemus, Dean of the Military School at the University. These two latter gentlemen, by their loyalty to the Sisters at Madison and their devoted praise of the Sisters' work, did much to influence the Governor's choice of a religious Order to whom the donation would be made.[4]

Washburn's "princely gift" of Edgewood to the Sinsinawa Dominicans undoubtedly came through his acquaintance with the high quality of their educational work at St. Regina Academy, opened by the Sisters in Madison ten years earlier. In April of 1871, the Sisters had purchased a building and three lots running west on Washington Street at the corner of South Henry Street, in the block adjacent to the property given as the site of St. Raphael's church by James Doty, former governor of the state and early Madison land speculator.[5] The pastor of St. Raphael's parish had

"The influences which had shaped his character were simple; he lived in a community of hard-working people who were... most of them descended from soldiers of the Revolution.... His character was formed when he left Maine. In all the rest of his life nobody ever spoke of him without speaking of his honesty and firm common sense.... He felt kindly towards people in distress— towards the Southerners when he had fought and conquered them, towards the Indians whom he saw cheated and despoiled. Much that happened to him in after life, which would have embittered a weaker nature, only mellowed him."
— *Gaillard Hunt*

wanted the Dominican sisters to come and teach in his parish school, and at the same time the sisters saw a good opportunity to open a new academy in Madison, in the shadow of the capitol.

The annals of the Convent of St. Regina record:

The building was not new but was in good condition. For some years previous to the coming of the sisters it had been used as a hotel by a private family. The school rooms, one for girls and one for boys, together with the music rooms took up the best part of the house. The sisters had a kitchen, a dining room, and a dormitory.... The people were most kind.

St. Regina Academy opened in the fall of 1871, with seven founding sisters, including Sister Alexius Duffy as the first prioress. Their first classes, ranging from primary grades through high school, included thirty girls and twelve boys. Times were hard. The purchase price of the property had been $4,000, and the sisters had only $400 for a partial payment. But the debt was paid off in 1876, and the St. Regina convent annals record that in the early years, "the people were most kind and sent vegetables and groceries in abundance. The ladies of the congregation brought their own sewing machines to the convent and made bedding." The young academy quickly flourished and developed a strong reputation for educational excellence. One student who finished eighth grade around 1880 later wrote, "They can say what they like, Sister, about crowded conditions and other handicaps, but we did as well as the best of them in high school and in the university."

Madison was a small city in the early 1870s with a population of about 9000, down from its peak of about 11,000 in 1857. St. Regina Academy, the only Catholic academy in town, located two short blocks from the capitol square, surely attracted public attention, especially since, like most academies of the time, it held annual public examinations. St. Regina Academy was also known for its ecumenical breadth, with the advertisements for the Academy stating firmly: "The religious principles of the pupils are not interfered with." The writer of an 1880 *History of Dane County* also noted that "this school is open to, and is patronized largely by, people of all denominations."

Mr. Bartlett, a Protestant whose children attended St. Regina Academy, was a key element in influencing Governor Washburn to choose the Sinsinawa Dominican sisters as the beneficiaries of his gift. A letter from Sister Serena to Sister Paschala O'Connor explains that "Mr. Bartlett was instrumental in getting the Governor, Mr. Washburn, to attend with him a public examination of the children under Sister Alexius Duffy, who was the Superior. Out of this came the donation of the Governor to the community of his country home which he called Edgewood Villa." A description of that memorable examination time was given in a reminiscence, "Our First Year at Edgewood," by Sister Alexius Duffy, who had a vivid memory of the occasion:

St. Regina Academy,

Cor. Washington Ave. and Henry St.,

Madison, Wis.,_____187__.

The Sisters of the Order of St. Dominic will be prepared to receive pupils, (day scholars and boarders) on the first Wednesday in September.

Every educational advantage afforded. Latin included in the terms of tuition.

Particular attention is paid to the morals and manners of the pupils.

The religious principles of the pupils are not interfered with.

TERMS, PAYABLE IN ADVANCE:

Board and Tuition per Scholastic Year,	$150.00
Music on Piano, per quarter,	12.00
Music on Guitar, per quarter,	6.00
Cultivation of Voice, per quarter,	10.00
French and German, each per quarter,	5.00

DAY SCHOLARS:

Tuition for Senior Class, per quarter,	$10.00
" " Junior " "	8.00
" " Primary " "	6.00

For further particulars address,

SISTERS ST. REGINA ACADEMY,
Cor. Washington Ave. and Henry St.

Sinsinawa Dominican Archives

Will it surprise you to know that Edgewood, the educational Edgewood, became a possibility at a public examination? Glance at this picture: A pretty schoolroom, thirty odd years ago [1870s] in the city of Madison. The room was usually very attractive, but today seated at one end are three clergymen, two University professors, the principal of the Madison high school, and a principal of a select school for boys. What schoolgirl but recognizes that half circle, or needs to be told, "Finals are in progress!"

A ring of the doorbell passed unnoticed until the Sister who answered it appeared at the schoolroom looking so important that the Superior at once went to her. 'Governor Washburn and a friend wish to visit the school and be present at some of the examinations.' If the Superior felt any trepidation she did not show it but at once welcomed the visitors and ushered them into the schoolroom where the Governor was warmly greeted by the examiners and introduced to the students.

Governor Washburn took no part in the examinations; his attitude was that of an interested listener, but very shrewd and alert were the kindly eyes beneath the heavy brows that watched the pupils and teachers.

When other engagements called him away he spoke a few words of praise and encouragement with such evident sincerity that all, but especially the teachers, were delighted. That day a Dominican Edgewood became a probability.

Surely it was this favorable impression of St. Regina Academy that was remembered by the "shrewd and alert" Washburn and reinforced by equally favorable impressions of the educational work of the Dominican sisters given him by Father Pettit, the pastor of St. Raphael church, and the influential Major W. J. L. Nicodemus, Professor of Engineering and Military Tactics at the University, among others. Arrangements for the transfer of the property to the sisters were made in the spring of 1881. The Trustees of the Corporation of St. Clara Female Academy, meeting in special session on May 1, 1881, unanimously voted to accept Governor Washburn's offer "of his beautiful Villa of Edgewood." The deed transferring the property is dated May 26, 1881, signed in New York, and witnessed by Washburn's son-in-law Charles Payson and by George Woodman. The deed describes the property as "a gift…to be used and occupied and given and granted upon the express condition that they shall be used and occupied as a school."

Sister Alexius Duffy, who accompanied Mother Emily Power and Sister Magdalen Madigan to meet with Washburn at Edgewood on May 10, 1881, described the momentous experience:

It was an ideal May day, a fit setting for a gracious deed.… With a stately courtesy all his own, Governor Washburn met us at the foot of the steps, led us to the front porch and thence to the red room, for the beautiful old colonial building, like the White House, had its own color scheme in furnishing. Business concluded, the Governor accompanied us through the house, eagerly discussing the changes that might be made in fitting it for a school.

Then, assisted by his valet, John, for the Governor's health was failing, [he had suffered a stroke earlier that year] we went from group to group of trees on the front lawn. Very beautiful these groups were on this fair May day, the exquisite tints of newly budded trees set off by the deep foliage of the pines. Governor Washburn was a tree lover and at each group had something of interest to point out. The center tree in one is from Japan, its vivid green very effective; of another a cork tree from the Spanish Isles, while the cedar of Lebanon towered gracefully on many parts of the grounds.

From the lawn to the orchard, then through the grove to the fish-ponds. How proud the Governor was of these. He hoped they would give us as much pleasure as they had afforded him.... On our way back to the house we passed the vineyard, another source of pride to our benefactor. On the porch facing Lake Wingra we paused a moment to admire the view, and Governor Washburn, pointing to a tree, a shell-bark hickory that shaded the lawn, said he hoped that unless a real necessity arose we would not let it be cut down; it had many associations for him.

One can only imagine the bittersweet quality experienced by the ailing Washburn as he proudly shared with the sisters the beauties of his country estate, his beloved Edgewood, which he was about to leave for the last time. His own death would come just one year later on May 14, 1882.

Over the course of his truly remarkable life, Cadwallader Colden Washburn had experienced many remarkable triumphs. Born in 1818 in Livermore, Maine, the young man set out for the West at the age of 21, eventually settling in 1842 in Mineral Point, Wisconsin, the main town in the booming mining area of the south-western Wisconsin territory. Nearby, in Galena, Illinois, his brother Elihu established himself in 1840. Cadwallader Washburn opened a law practice in 1842, and quickly became known for his honesty.

In 1844, he joined forces with Cyrus Woodman, also from Maine, who was a land agent for the Boston and Western Land Company. The two men formed a strong partnership that lasted eleven years and an enduring friendship that lasted until Washburn's death. They developed various businesses, such as the production of lead shot at Helena, Wisconsin, and the Wisconsin Mining Company, but one of their most successful ventures was land acquisition, particularly land in northern Wisconsin. They even sought a monopoly of the pine timber in the Upper Mississippi area, and although they did not achieve that goal, they acquired rights to about 200,000 acres of prime timber land. David Atwood, in his eulogy for Washburn, stated that the land company "became widely known throughout the country, and by a system of fair and honest dealing, prompt and energetic action, established the reputation of being a strong, successful, and wealthy one for that early day in the West."[6]

This successful business enterprise was accompanied by the establishment of Washburn and Woodman's Mineral Point Bank on High Street in May 1853, the year after Samuel Marshall opened his State Bank in Madison. The Washburn and Woodman partnership was dissolved amicably in 1855, and the two men remained close throughout their lives. Indeed, Cyrus Woodman seems to have remained Washburn's most trusted friend, regularly corresponding with him and assisting Washburn in drawing up his will not long before his death. Woodman had returned east to Cambridge, Massachusetts, before Washburn moved his residence in 1859 to La Crosse, Wisconsin, where he had established an office in 1853. Seeing great opportunities in the frontier milling business, Washburn with some partners formed the Minneapolis Mill Company in 1856, having secured key water power rights at St. Anthony's Falls. Later he purchased the La Crosse Lumber Company, which turned the timber from his lands in northern Wisconsin into profitable lumber.

Edgewood Villa, ca. 1875

Jeannette Washburn Kelsey, Cadwallader's daughter, wrote to the Dominican Sisters to thank them after they had sent her this photograph:

"I received the picture... of my Father sitting on the familiar old piazza. I took so much trouble arranging everything there—even the bird cage. The chair was rather small for the portly governor!"

Letter (June 6, 1914)
in Sinsinawa Dominican Archives.

Mary Paynter, O.P.

The Washburn and Woodman Bank, 324 High Street, Mineral Point, Wisconsin, opened by the partners Cadwallader Washburn and Cyrus Woodman in 1853; now a private residence

Meanwhile, from 1855 to 1861 Washburn served in the U.S. House of Representatives, a first important step in his long public service career. He represented the second district of Wisconsin, an area that stretched from Dane and Rock counties to the Mississippi and north to Lake Superior. During the same period, his brothers Israel from Maine and Elihu from Illinois also served in the House. The Washburns were known as strong opponents of slavery, and in 1858, Cadwallader and his brother Elihu engaged a southern colleague in a fistfight on the floor of the House over the issue. Cadwallader Washburn's daughter Jeannette recalled her father's version of the incident:

A year or two before the Civil War broke out the feeling between the Northern and the Southern States was very bitter....   One day a discussion arose between my father's brother Elihu and a Southerner named Barksdale; they became very much excited and Barksdale made a lunge in the direction of Elihu. My father, seeing this and thinking his brother in danger, sprang forward and caught Barksdale by the hair and a moment later was staggering backward with the latter's wig, which came off with a jerk in his hand, while the members of the House roared with laughter. I remember as a child seeing a cartoon of this affair. Of course the newspapers were full of it, and the London Punch published a poem in which the scene was vividly described.

The smoldering conflict between north and south was moving toward a more violent level in 1861 when Washburn served as a delegate to the Washington Peace Conference that tried, vainly, to avert a war. Washburn saw what lay ahead. In January 1861 he said in Congress:

I have no special dread in regard to the future of this Republic. Civil war may come—disunion and dissolution may come, but, I pray God to deliver us from both; but, sir, whatever may come, I have an abiding faith in a kind Providence that has ever watched over us, that passing events will be all overruled for good and for the welfare of mankind in this and other lands..... If this union must be dissolved, whether by peaceable secession, or through fire and blood and civil war, we shall have the consolation of knowing that when the conflict is over, those who survive it will be, what they never have been, inhabitants of a free country.

During the Civil War, Washburn served as commanding officer of the Second Regiment of the Wisconsin Volunteer Cavalry and left the Union Army in 1865 with the rank of major general, his appointment document signed by Abraham Lincoln. Karel Bicha indicates that Washburn's role as a field commander "had never been markedly successful....As an astute businessman, however, he brought important administrative skills to an army in which these skills were often conspicuously lacking. On one occasion U.S. Grant called him 'one of the best administrative officers we have.'"[7] At a memorial service for Washburn after his death, David Atwood pointed out that "his military record, like that in all public positions he has held, was excellent, evincing determined courage and will power, directed by strong common sense."

His compassion was evident, too, and he was fully aware of the sufferings inflicted on the "rebels" by the war. On March 18, 1863, General Washburn wrote to his twelve-year-old daughter Nettie (Jeannette), warning against any romanticizing of war:

Major-General Cadwallader C. Washburn, with his officers, in camp during the Civil War. Washburn is seated in front row, far ~~left~~. right

You, my dear, who are living so pleasantly and quietly at home, have little idea of the misery and unhappiness that war brings. Just imagine ten or twenty thousand rude men coming into La Crosse some morning and taking possession of the town, going into houses of the people and helping themselves to whatever they want, burning houses, killing cattle, hogs, sheep, chickens, and almost everything they see, destroying furniture—and you will have a pretty good idea of the march of an army through the county. The people here are paying dearly for their wickedness in trying to destroy our government.

After the war, Washburn returned to La Crosse, to the supervision of his business interests there and in Minneapolis, and again he was elected to Congress for two terms. In 1871, when his last term as a U.S. Representative ended, many people urged him to run for Governor of Wisconsin against a formidable opponent, the Honorable James R. Doolittle, considered a superb orator. Debates in various cities and towns of Wisconsin were held, and David Atwood recalled that "while Mr. Doolittle may have possessed more of the graces of the finished orator than did Mr. Washburn, the latter was able to present the largest array of facts in support of the positions he assumed, in a straight-forward manner, and in strong and plain language for which he was proverbial." Whether or not Washburn won the debates is not clear; however, he did win the election and was inaugurated as Governor of Wisconsin on the first Monday in January 1872.

From his earliest days, the life of Cadwallader Washburn seemed destined for unmitigated triumphs—as an elected member of Congress, as Governor of the state of Wisconsin, as a U.S. general, as President of the Wisconsin State Historical Society, as recipient of an honorary doctor of laws degree from the University of Wisconsin, and as a remarkably successful business entrepreneur whose estate, after his death, was valued at between two and three million dollars—an enormous sum in that era.

Yet before his death in 1882 Cadwallader Washburn also experienced tragedy and failures. Long before the terrible Edgewood fire of 1893, the generous donor of the Edgewood Villa had himself been "tried by fire." His trials had been in the three areas most significant in his life: business, politics, and family.

Although remarkably successful as a businessman, he had suffered several near catastrophes. The first came after the country's severe economic depression of 1857-58. In 1858, Washburn wrote to Cyrus Woodman that he suffered under a terrible burden, a load that weighed him down "worse than the pack of Bunyan's pilgrim." A few years later, he wrote again to Woodman, "If, however, I ever again get caught as I was in 1857, you may kick me high nor a kite." His absence from his business enterprises while serving in Congress and, later, in the Civil War, coupled with the difficult economic period in the country, nearly brought him to disaster. In 1863, he could neither pay his taxes nor meet his obligations to creditors. In fact, he was only saved from bankruptcy because of the immunity he enjoyed as a military officer during the Civil War. He recovered quickly, however, and rebuilt his fortunes through his land and timber businesses and especially his Minneapolis milling interests.

Like many other lumber barons in Wisconsin, Washburn suffered from the periodic forest fires which ravaged the pineries of the north woods. Portions of these timber lands, including those in the Black River and Chippewa River areas—where he had large holdings—were consumed in the regularly recurring fires of the 1860s and 1870s. During the month before Washburn was elected governor of Wisconsin, a disastrous fire ravaged the north woods. During the summer and fall of 1871, a severe drought and heat spell had turned the Wisconsin forests to dry tinder, and fires throughout the northern part of the state broke out sporadically. In early October, at the same time as the great Chicago fire which leveled a large portion of that city, an even more disastrous fire broke out in the northeastern counties of Wisconsin near Green Bay, destroying farms, towns and forests across an extensive area and killing nearly 1,200 people. In January of 1872, during his first annual address to the Wisconsin legislature, Governor Washburn spoke feelingly of that disaster, known to history as the Peshtigo fire:

During the last days of September, and the first days of October, the northeast part of the State was overrun by extensive fires, destroying much property, and causing great distress, but nothing compared to what was soon to follow, for, on the 8th and 9th of October, a conflagration, unparalleled in the world's history, swept over portions of the counties of Oconto, Brown, Door, and Kewaunee, consuming all before it.... By this conflagration, it is estimated that over a thousand persons lost their lives....

What Washburn did not mention were the business losses to Wisconsin timber barons like himself, although the worst of the fire losses in September and October of 1871 were not on his properties but in the northeastern counties of the state. It is a measure of the character of the man that his primary concern in the face of this disaster was to care for the people who were most severely affected. His only request to the legislature was for the authority "through which the amount now subject to my order may be so disposed of as to give the most relief [to the people in the burnt-out counties]."

The news of a far more terrible disaster to strike his personal business interests came seven years later. Washburn with others had formed the Washburn Crosby Company in Minneapolis, a successful flour milling company that became the main source of Washburn's wealth and was eventually to become the General Mills Corporation. The company's rapid growth and prosperity led to the building of new mills, including a large one called "Washburn A," which manufactured 1200 barrels of flour a day. During the night of May 2, 1878, when Washburn was at his Edgewood Villa alone except for one or two servants, toward midnight a man from the Madison telegraph office brought the news of a terrible fire and explosion in the Minneapolis Washburn mills. William Edgar provides a vivid description of the catastrophe:

Front page description of the destruction of the Washburn mills, *St. Paul Daily Globe*, May 3, 1878.

All day the mills ran as usual; by evening the weather had grown warmer and it was rather close inside the mills. At six o'clock the day crew had quit, and the smaller night shift was on duty. Without preliminary warning, there came a sudden frightful explosion, like the sound of a great cannon; the roof of the Washburn A mill rose hundreds of feet into the air, followed instantly by a sheet of flame. Other explosions occurred almost at the same time.... Every window in the neighborhood was broken and even on Summit Avenue in Saint Paul, miles away, panes of glass were shattered....

The citizens of Minneapolis at first thought that an earthquake had occurred and hurried from their houses to seek safety in the streets; they saw flames rising from the milling district and rushed thither in excited crowds.... When dawn came the fire was out and a vast heap of smoldering, smoking ruins was all that remained of the Washburn A and five other flour mills.... Beneath these ruins lay what was left, if anything recognizable, of eighteen men, who composed the ill-fated night crews.[8]

Washburn's daughter Jeannette later wrote to Sister Fidelia at Edgewood that, after reading the telegram that told him of the catastrophic fire in his mills, "deep in debt, disappointed due to the loss of the [senatorial] election, he returned to bed, lay down and went through a tremendous struggle, but he pulled himself together," and the next day went to keep an appointment with the University Regents to discuss the erection of an observatory building he had promised to provide for the campus. Most remarkably, when Governor Washburn entered the meeting at the University, as William Edgar describes it, he appeared to one of the Regents,

calm and impassive, showing no indication, either in his face or manner, that he was disturbed by what had happened. When the Regent expressed his surprise at the governor's presence after the great disaster that had befallen his property during the previous night,

"Without preliminary warning, there came a sudden frightful explosion, like the sound of a great cannon; the roof of the Washburn A mill rose hundreds of feet into the air, followed instantly by a sheet of flame."

Washburn quietly said that while the loss in property was large, it was of no consequence in comparison with the loss of life that it involved; the thought of this saddened him.[9]

After the meeting, Washburn left immediately for Minneapolis where, as Edgar says,

there was much to do. First of all the families of those who had been killed must be provided for. A fund was immediately raised for their relief, to which Governor Washburn contributed generously. The men out of employment were given work in building the new mill…. On May 4, two days after the disaster, he personally marked out the lines for its foundation.

As was characteristic of the man, Washburn's first and deepest concern was for the human beings who had suffered in the calamity, and secondly, his indomitable spirit led him at once to begin anew, to raise a new and better mill from the fire's ashes, a mill that would use the latest European equipment and that would soon produce the high quality flour known as the "Gold Medal" brand.

Besides encountering challenging business losses and recovering from them, Washburn also endured several wrenching political setbacks.

Although he was ultimately successful in the gubernatorial campaign of 1871, Washburn had lost the Republican nomination for governor in 1865 to General Lucius Fairchild, another Civil War veteran: "the popular general [Fairchild] with his empty sleeve conspicuously pinned across his breast, proved a satisfying vote getter.

Wisconsin Historical Society WHi-1826

The Washburn Observatory, 1880, University of Wisconsin.

His alliances successfully stood off the challenge for the nomination from another general, C. C. Washburn."[10]

After Washburn's successful run in 1871, the next gubernatorial election in November of 1873 proved an unexpected loss for the Republican party and a surprising disappointment to the Governor who had anticipated serving a second term. Nesbit and Thompson call the 1873 election a "debacle," and they suggest a number of reasons, two of which involved Washburn's actions as governor: his recommendation and signing of "a stringent liquor control bill, known as the Graham Law, which drove the Protestant Germans back into the Democratic fold," and his veto of a railroad bridge measure.[11] In his eulogy for Washburn, a former mayor of Madison and prominent Republican newspaper publisher, David Atwood remarked that

owing to a combination of circumstances over which he [Washburn] had no control—the various factions of monopoly and anti-monopoly, of temperance and anti-temperance, and several other distracting elements were arrayed against him—his opponent, William R. Taylor, was elected, to the surprise of the people generally. In this defeat of Governor Washburn the people were the greatest losers.

Never attaining election to the U.S. Senate was another political disappointment deeply felt by Washburn, who had come close to nomination several times, beginning in 1861. David Atwood recalled that Washburn

doubtless had a very strong desire to become a member of the United States Senate; and, in this ambition, he was backed, on several occasions, by a strong array of friends.... but it seemed decreed that this ambition should not be gratified; that he should not become a member of the United States Senate, a position he apparently desired above all others.

His last opportunity to become a U.S. Senator came in the election of 1875, when Senator Matthew Carpenter's term expired. Nesbit and Thompson explain that the incumbent had "become a controversial figure.... Matt enjoyed the good things of life with open gusto and defended the ripe scandals of the Senate and the Grant administration with too much candor." Carpenter had been successful in opposing Washburn for Republican senatorial candidacy in 1868. Washburn was a potentially strong candidate in 1874, but he had "no use for Keyes [the state chairman of the Republican party] and the Madison cabal," and, according to Nesbit and Thompson, the large

Reform-Democratic minority finally joined the [Republican] holdouts in voting for a Republican long-shot who was innocuous enough to be acceptable to the Democrats. This was how Angus Cameron, a railroad attorney from La Crosse, became a United States senator, to his considerable surprise. The important contest had been between Carpenter and C. C. Washburn, but the Democrats were not foolish enough to advance the fortunes of a Republican as prominent as Washburn.[12]

Washburn was also deeply interested in the senatorial campaign of 1879, although he did not formally enter it. He opposed the candidacies of Carpenter and Keyes vigorously, and Nesbit and Thompson suggest that Washburn even considered supporting a fellow lumber baron and former congressman Philetus Sawyer, but decided against that course, perhaps because "Sawyer was barely literate and a figure of great fun to the opposition press."[13] After ninety ballots and a long deadlock during the party's nomination process, the party's chairman Keyes withdrew in favor of Carpenter who won the election. It was clear that Washburn's long political career and influence on Republican politics was finished.

Undoubtedly the greatest and longest trial of Washburn's life, felt more keenly than any political or business setbacks, was enduring the long illness of his beloved wife Jeannette. Jeannette Garr was one of fourteen children of Elizabeth Sinclair Garr and Andrew Sheffield Garr, a noted attorney in New York City. Jeannette Garr came west in the 1840s to visit her sister who was married to the lawyer Mortimer Jackson and living in Mineral Point. There Jeannette Garr married Cadwallader Washburn on January 1, 1849, when both were thirty years old. Their first daughter, Jeannette (Nettie) Garr Washburn, was born in 1850, and a second daughter, Frances (Fanny), was born in 1852. After the birth of their first daughter, Mrs. Washburn showed evidence of mental illness, and Cadwallader took her to New York in an attempt to find doctors who could treat her. In 1851, Elihu Washburne wrote to their brother Sidney that "Cad got home [from New York] two or three days ago with his wife and I am sorry to learn that she is far from being well." She did not improve, and in 1852, Washburn arranged for Jeannette to be cared for in the Quaker-founded Bloomingdale Asylum in New York. Later she was placed in an institution in Brookline, Massachusetts, where she remained until her death at age ninety in 1909. The two little girls were reared by Washburn's parents back at the family home in Livermore, Maine, during their childhood. After Washburn's mother's death in 1861, an aunt cared for them, and then Washburn placed them in boarding schools in Boston, bringing them home to La Crosse during school vacation periods. As the eldest daughter, Jeannette, later remarked, in a letter to Sister Fidelia, "We were not at Edgewood as children."

Professor Butler, in his eulogy for Cadwallader Washburn, spoke of the tragic illness of his wife: "A ghost haunted his home. The behavior of Washburn all through the thirty years which it pleased Heaven to make his life bitter with this great sorrow, I cannot but admire beyond all the rest of his life." On the same occasion, David Atwood declared:

In all this time of sadness, she has been tenderly cared for, in the best possible manner, by her devoted husband. Nothing that money could provide to alleviate her terrible malady has been left undone. His wealth has been liberally bestowed in seeking her comfort; and in his will, the most ample provision is made for her future support.

While the last will and testament of Cadwallader Washburn provided generous bequests for his two daughters and their families and for many other relatives and friends, the greatest amount was set aside to provide for Jeannette's care. The terms of the will speak volumes about Washburn's enduring and generous love for his wife:

I direct my executors to bear constantly in mind the wants of my wife, and to set aside, use, and expend whatever moneys may be necessary, consistently with her condition, to provide for her comfort and physical health; and I place no limit upon the sums which they may spend for the purposes indicated.

Cadwallader Washburn was clearly a person who, through thick and thin, lived out the motto of the Washburn family, *Persevera deoque confide*, translated colloquially by his own father as "Stick and Hang," and by others as "Persevere and trust in God." His daughter Jeannette wrote to Sister Fidelia that the Washburns

Edgewood College Archives

Portraits of Jeannette Garr Washburn and Cadwallader C. Washburn

all had the Washborne grit which has ever been a family characteristic and carried them and their descendants through dangers and vicissitudes innumerable. My own grandfather used to say that the motto of his family was "stick and hang," which may have been a liberal translation of the "Persevera deoque confide" found on the family crest; at any rate they all appear to have adopted it.

That remarkable ability to persevere, to hang in, even in the face of seemingly insurmountable circumstances was a basic quality of the Governor, that "great giver," as he was once admiringly described by the Dominican sisters of Edgewood. Perhaps it was providential rather than coincidental that some of those very qualities that many admired in Cadwallader C. Washburn are to be re-discovered in the history of Edgewood and in the lives of the sisters who taught there. After the tragic Edgewood Villa fire of November 16, 1893, the sisters faced the question of the school's future, determined to "stick and hang." Washburn's desire, expressed in his deed of gift, that his beloved Edgewood property would always be a setting for education, a princely gift to generations of students in the years ahead, was reaffirmed in the sisters' decision to rebuild. A new Edgewood was to rise from the ashes.

[For the State Journal.]

ADISON, WISCONSIN.

pot on earth be found
the soul with sorrows smitten,
ed sore in strife unequal,
e that knows no sequel
eat and failure, written
tablet mem'ry reads
heart that weeps and bleeds?
within earth's bound,
adison is found.

pot on earth be found,
remorse, hard-hearted sinner,
is lust and vice can fetter,
im good or somewhat better,
im back as a beginner
path of virtue sweet,
e trod with youthful feet?
s bells here gently chime:
r, cease from lust and crime."

pot on earth be found,
two foes by chance are meeting,
o each in love surrender,
s hand of friendship tender,
arm, with warm hearts beating,
nt each other peace,
thereto by nature's pleas,
om earth and air resound?
ll Madison is found.

pot on earth be found,
a lovely youth and maiden,
ed by that imp most stupid,
in ancient ballads Cupid,
th heavy sorrows laden,
nce their sorrows leave,
ir hopes forlorn retrieve?
Madison they heal
deep wounds and true love seal.

n, most lovely gem,
our thousand cities peerless,
e that lately budded,
a with diamonds studded!
in morning dews, but tearless,
lovely, pure and bright
morning glory's light
a cities' fairest queen,
robe of summer green!

the midday sun its rays
upon the crowded cities,
them into a Sahara,
ns into pools of Marah,
by maidens sing their ditties,
cool and lovely shade

THE FALL TERM
Of the Day School at
St. Regina Convent,
Will Commence
MONDAY, SEPT. 5th.

Every educational advantage is afforded the pupils. The removal of the Boarding School to Edgewood will not in any way change the course of study heretofore pursued Music on Piano, Guitar and Zither, as also Vocal Music, on the same terms as formerly.

DOMINICAN SISTERS,
870au30t1w St. Regina Convent, Madison, Wis.

St. Regina Academy.
11TH YEAR.

THE SISTERS IN CHARGE OF this Academy have been enabled, by the generous gift of ex-Governor Washburn, to offer t is year increased advantages to its patrons This donation consists of his handsome residence and sixty acres of land just outside the limits of Madison. The residence known as

EDGEWOOD VILLA.

Is large and commodious, furnished with all modern improvements. The grounds surrounding it are tastefully laid out and embellished with a great variety of trees, flowers and shrubs. A beautiful grove, adorned with artificial fish ponds, and sloping to

Lake Wingra,

Affords a delightful recreation ground for the pupils. Art has united with Nature in making this one of the most favored spots in the North west, and health must favor the student who seeks its shelter.

Terms of Tuition.

Board and Tuition, per scholastic year, including washing, bedding and instructions in plain and ornamental needle-work $165 00
Music on Piano, per quarter............. 12 00
Music on Harp   do 15 00
Music on Guitar, do 8 00
Music on Zither, do 8 00
Music on Organ, do 12 00
Cultivation of Voice, per quarter 10 00
Painting in Oils, per quarter 12 00
Crayon, per quarter.................... 10 00
French, German and Italian, each per quarter 5 00
Latin and Drawing included in terms of tuition.

The Fall Term will commence the first Monday of September.

For further particulars, address
SISTER SUPERIOR,
St. Regina Academy,
795jy30daw4m Edgewood, Madison, Wis.

W. I. AYRES,
148 Main Street,

HOOLEY O

Thursday Ev
. . . S P
The Madison S
Repr
ORIGINAL NI
Will produce in its
greatest dramatic

HAZEL

This charming Com
Second Year of conse
Company, has by far
LONGEST R
And has been witness
HAZEL KIRKE is f
HAZEL KIRKE is r
HAZEL KIRKE is
HAZEL KIRKE ap
HAZEL KIRKE goe
HAZEL KIRKE the
Seats can be secure
tore, Tuesday at
eats, 31 00; reserved
864atg29d4t

Your houses thorough
the pas
BOYI
Durable

CHAPTER TWO

From Academy to College *1881-1929*

*T*he sisters moved quickly to open a school in the Edgewood Villa. By August 1881 the first ads were appearing in the Madison newspapers, announcing the September opening of St. Regina Academy in its new location on the Edgewood property, while stating that instruction in music—including piano, guitar, zither, and vocal—would still be continued at the "day school" building, now named St. Regina Convent, at its West Washington Street location. On August 30, 1881, the *Wisconsin State Journal* carried a large ad for the new St. Regina Academy at Edgewood:

> *The Sisters in charge of this academy have been enabled, by the generous gift of ex-Governor Washburn, to offer this year increased advantages to its patrons. This donation consists of his handsome residence and sixty acres of land just outside the limits of Madison. The residence, known as Edgewood Villa, is large and commodious, with all modern improvements. The grounds surrounding it are tastefully laid out and embellished with a great variety of trees, flowers, and shrubs. A beautiful grove, adorned with artificial fish ponds, and sloping to Lake Wingra, affords a delightful recreation ground for the pupils. Art has united with Nature in making this one of the most favored spots in the Northwest, and health must favor the student who seeks its shelter.*

The newspaper advertisement explained that board and tuition for the year, "including washing, bedding, and instruction in plain and ornamental needlework, Latin, and drawing," as well as the other academic subjects, was $165.00. Music lessons on the piano, harp, guitar, zither, organ, and "cultivation of the voice," as well as oil painting, cost extra, ranging from $8 to $12 a quarter.

On September 5, 1881, Governor Washburn's Villa at Edgewood welcomed its first sixteen boarding and day students; eight Dominican sisters also lived there with the boarding students. During their first year at Edgewood, the sisters experienced some setbacks as well as successes. Friends of the sisters were generous in helping the new venture get underway, and the annalist dutifully and gratefully recorded gifts of goods and money received. However, Sister Alexius Duffy, one of the first fifteen

Advertisement for St. Regina Academy at Edgewood, and announcement of continuation of programs at St. Regina Convent. August 30, 1881 – *The Wisconsin State Journal*

News of Governor Washburn's gift of his Edgewood property to the Sisters of St. Dominic, Sinsinawa Mound, to be used as "an educational institution" May 11, 1881 — *The Wisconsin State Journal*

sisters at Edgewood, later recalled that, among the trials of the first year, "a pupil, Theresa White, died, and Governor Washburn's rowboat was stolen" (though, disguised with a fresh coat of paint by its new "owner," it was soon spotted on Lake Wingra again), while "twelve trees were toppled in a storm and two fine Jersey cows were lost." President Garfield had been shot in July of 1881, not long before the new school opened, and the front pages of the Madison newspapers throughout the summer and into the fall carried reports of his struggle to survive. The sisters, with the rest of the nation, agonized over the attempted assassination, and mourned when the President died on September 19, 1881.

But a worse blow was yet to come. On May 15, 1882, near the end of that memorable first school year at Edgewood and almost exactly one year after Mother Emily with Sister Magdalen and Sister Alexius had come from Sinsinawa to meet Governor Washburn on the steps of his Villa to receive his gift of the estate, news arrived of Washburn's death on May 14 in Eureka Springs, Arkansas, where he had gone for treatment in hope of recovering his health.

The sisters of Edgewood, like other citizens of Wisconsin, were shocked and saddened by the news. The convent annalist wrote that when the sisters got word of the death of Governor Washburn, prayers were immediately said to "the Great Friend of our great friend." Washburn had written to the Edgewood sisters on March 22, 1882, expressing his delight in their first year's accomplishments and promising a visit when he returned to Wisconsin: "I am much pleased to know that you are progressing so well at Edgewood and that your school promises to be popular and useful. The place is beautiful, and I never had a doubt that you would make a success of it, and that it would be no dishonor to me." But instead of planning a happy welcoming ceremony honoring their benefactor's anticipated return, the sisters with heavy hearts arranged instead to send a simple floral funeral tribute to honor Washburn's memory.

The six-car funeral train that bore his remains moved in stately procession from Chicago through Wisconsin to LaCrosse, Washburn's home, for the burial. The reporter for the *Wisconsin State Journal*, in his lengthy front page story "Dust to Dust," covering the train's gradual progress across the state, wrote:

The very handsomest train that ever pulled out of the great Union depot of Chicago is that on which we are speeding northward this cloudless morning [May 17].... In the Minneapolis car, jealously guarded by the young soldiers of the Lake Cities, lay in their beautiful casket and covered with floral emblems, the mortal remains of our ex-Governor and General. The car itself is of sombre hue and heavily draped in black.... With all honor the remains were received last evening in Chicago, and a soldierly band of veterans of the Grand Army appeared with their drums and colors and beautiful flowers.

The intention had been to return at once to La Crosse, but the Governor desired that his people along the line might have an opportunity of seeing the honors rendered their old chief, and, at his request, the plan was changed.... On the way, demonstrations of respect were made at Watertown, where the military were drawn up in line on the depot platform and a large concourse of people were assembled. At Portage a large number of citizens were gathered, and a dirge was played by the Portage band.

Mourners arrived by special train from Minneapolis for the funeral, and relatives, friends, and guests poured into LaCrosse from all parts of Wisconsin and the nation to attend the lying-in-state in the rotunda of the courthouse and the funeral services which attracted several thousand people standing on the courthouse grounds and in the streets nearby. Among the many elaborate floral tributes sent from distant places, the *Wisconsin State Journal* reporter took special note of one small bouquet:

Two years ago [sic], ex-Governor Washburn presented his charming suburban villa, "Edgewood," near the confines of Madison, to the Dominican Sisters as a school for girls. The sisters, as a modest, but lovely, touching and fragrant tribute to their lion-hearted benefactor, sent a beautiful floral design which appeared on the coffin of the distinguished dead, as the remains lay in state at the court house last night and to-day. It is a pillow of white lillies, with a crown of white roses over it. This sweet tribute of regard, while unpretentious of itself, was admired both for its severely simple beauty and because of the associations connected with it.

The same issue of the newspaper recorded the fact that "the Sisters of the St. Regina Academy, to whom was donated the beautiful property of Edgewood, by ex-Gov. C. C. Washburn, have appropriately draped the villa, in sorrow for the death of its generous donor."

"Dust to Dust" – *The Wisconsin State Journal*
Front page account of the funeral train's passage through Wisconsin to LaCrosse, where Cadwallader Washburn's funeral was held with great ceremony on May 18, 1882.

These were but the first tributes to "their lion-hearted benefactor" that the sisters of Edgewood would make. The tradition soon developed of celebrating a special "Washburn Day" at Edgewood each June.

During the next few years the Academy at Edgewood grew and developed steadily. The student body increased during the decade of the 1880s, and although the school was small, the students were lively. A faculty member of that period, Sister Charles Borromeo Stevens, later wrote:

It was a real Italian villa, on the shore of a Wisconsin lake, an embryo academy…. The children left no one in doubt as to their sense of their own importance. Their faces were turned toward the sunrise regions of higher education…. Suddenly they became interested in politics. "The twins," non-Catholics, daughters of an assemblyman, were the leaders. One was a Democrat and the other a Republican. The latter had no followers. The former came [to the principal] accompanied by certain deputies, to present their views

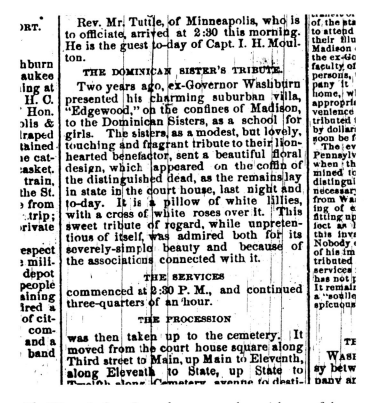

Rev. Mr. Tuttle, of Minneapolis, who is to officiate, arrived at 2:30 this morning. He is the guest to-day of Capt. I. H. Moulton.

THE DOMINICAN SISTER'S TRIBUTE.

Two years ago, ex-Governor Washburn presented his charming suburban villa, "Edgewood," on the confines of Madison, to the Dominican Sisters, as a school for girls. The sisters, as a modest, but lovely, touching and fragrant tribute to their lion-hearted benefactor, sent a beautiful floral design, which appeared on the coffin of the distinguished dead, as the remains lay in state in the court house, last night and to-day. It is a pillow of white lillies, with a cross of white roses over it. This sweet tribute of regard, while unpretentious of itself, was admired both for its severely-simple beauty and because of the associations connected with it.

THE SERVICES

commenced at 2:30 P. M., and continued three-quarters of an hour.

THE PROCESSION

was then taken up to the cemetery. It moved from the court house square along Third street to Main, up Main to Eleventh, along Eleventh to State, up State to

The Wisconsin State Journal reporter took special note of the small funeral bouquet which was placed prominently on the Washburn casket – a "sweet tribute of regard" from the Dominican sisters of Edgewood.

as to the propriety of letting President Cleveland [a Democrat, then in his first term of office] know what a highly commendable school was flourishing on the Republican soil of Wisconsin. Some one inquired how they proposed to enlighten him. Well, they thought a letter was the proper thing.

The letter was duly written by one of themselves. It contained the information that all the pupils in the school, but one, were Democrats, and a request was made for Mrs. Cleveland's picture. The important missive was mailed, and we [the sisters] supposed that would be the last of it, but in a few days there came a great square envelope, and on it was engraved in raised blue letters, "Executive Mansion." Within it was a congratulatory answer to their letter, and a photograph of Mrs. Cleveland. They [the young students] were two inches taller the next day and proudly exulted over the Juniors and Seniors.[1]

One might wonder what would have been Cadwallader Washburn's reaction to the political leanings of the young Democrats at Edgewood, since he was always a stalwart Republican leader. Perhaps he would have enjoyed the irony of that single brave but lonely Republican holdout among the young students at his beloved Edgewood.

In October 1883, a year after Washburn's death, his son-in-law A. Warren Kelsey was in Madison, and, after visiting Edgewood, he reported in a newsy letter addressed to his young daughter Mabel: "There are now twenty-one girls being educated there, and nine sisters looking after them." Some things were not so well kept up, Kelsey noted, adding that "the front door bell would not ring and the trees had grown so I could scarcely drive the covered carriage round the circle in front of the house." However, Jeannette's husband was warmly received by the sisters and offered "milk and doughnuts," and he told Mabel that some day "Mama must certainly make a pilgrimage to Madison." That pilgrimage eventually took place, when Jeannette and her husband returned to visit Edgewood in 1890.

The pressures of steady growth soon led the sisters to begin plans for a new school building adjacent to the Edgewood Villa. A. Warren Kelsey's 1883 letter stated that "they like the place very much and think it will have to be enlarged it is so popular." In 1888, Sister Charles Borromeo began a process of correspondence with the Washburn heirs to secure quitclaim deeds to the property, a necessary step preliminary to obtaining loans for construction of the new school building. During 1889, while she was in charge of Edgewood, Sister Borromeo completed obtaining the quitclaim deeds, and loans were arranged. The architect was G. S. Mansfield of Freeport, Illinois, and a contract for construction was signed in June 1893 with W. J. McAlpine of Dixon, Illinois, for a four-story, pressed brick building. The granite cornerstone, inscribed with the date, 1893, and a single word, "*Veritas*" (Truth), was laid, and construction rapidly proceeded.

When school began in September of 1893, fifteen sisters and twenty-eight boarding students were crowded into the living quarters of the Villa. One can imagine the excited anticipation of both students and sisters during the fall of 1893 as the new building quickly took shape. Then, suddenly, about 8 p.m. on Thursday, November 16, while the sisters and older students were celebrating the sister superior's feast day on the Villa's first floor, someone smelled smoke.

Two sisters rushed to the top floor to awaken the "minims," the four youngest boarders, who had been put to bed earlier. They tried several times to enter the room where the children were sleeping but were driven back, nearly overcome by smoke. The *Wisconsin State Journal* reporter who came to the scene described the catastrophic situation:

The most distressing fire which has ever occurred in the city, so far as loss of life is concerned, was the burning of the St. Regina academy at Edgewood last night. Two little girls [Maggie Stack, 6, and Margery Rice, 8] who yesterday were full of life and happiness, are today hushed in the embrace of death, victims of the stifling smoke which overcame them in their sleep and gave them no chance to escape from their fate. The large and handsome buildings, one just ready for occupancy, are a mass of charred ruins, with only the foundations and a few walls left standing.

A third child, Frances Henneberry, also overcome with smoke, was rescued and taken to St. Regina Convent downtown where Dr. Philip Fox tried to save her;

View of the Edgewood Villa front porch, with some Academy students on the drive (ca. 1891)

Students of St. Regina Academy on the Edgewood Villa steps, in 1892, the year before the fire. The youngest students, in white pinafores, are "minims"; probably pictured here are at least two of the children who perished in the 1893 fire.

however, she died the next day. Sister Bertha McCarthy, who had attempted to rescue the little girls, was herself overcome by smoke but survived as did the fourth minim, Katie Sweeney.

What must have been the sense of devastation and near despair felt by the Edgewood sisters that terrible November night when the temperature dipped below freezing and the city received a dusting of snow? With the Madison fire department helpless to stop the raging fire, the sisters with firemen and neighbors could only try to rescue furniture and pianos, books and school equipment from the Villa. The *Madison Democrat* reported:

The department was prompt in answering, and Chief Engineer Bernard dispatched the hook and ladder truck, with a large supply of hands, to the scene.... The hook and ladder boys and scores of others did all in their power to save the new and handsome structure, which was near completion, but to no avail.... The fire was beyond control in the old building before the department arrived, but the firemen say they could easily have saved the new building if they had had an engine [water pump] or even a chemical.

News article on the inquest held after the Edgewood fire, with testimony from Dr. Philip Fox, Sister Bertha McCarthy, and others. The Madison Democrat

The nearby stone carriage house, built in 1864 by Samuel Marshall, survived the fire as did the more distant barn and a chaplain's cottage nearby. The *Wisconsin State Journal* reporter opined that "whether or not they will rebuild has not yet been considered by the sisters, their entire attention being devoted to caring for the little ones, but one of them this morning expressed doubts as to the school being rebuilt." Yet the *Madison Democrat* reporter concluded his article about the tragedy by saying, "It is the general belief that a larger and a better school will soon rise upon the site where now there is nothing but smoking ruins." The latter view proved prophetic.

Friends of the sisters in Madison rallied to assist them, quickly organizing a benefit concert at the Fuller Opera House on the capitol square the night of November 28. The next day's *Madison Democrat* reported a most successful evening:

The Dominican sisters, of Edgewood Villa, are between $350 and $400 better off by reason of the benefit concert last evening. The opera house was jammed to standing room long before the first number was presented. Those who took part were the Misses Donovan, Reuter, and Bruske, and Messrs. Silber, Findorf, Donovan, Simpson, Prof. Chas. Nitschke, and J. D. Purcell. Prof. Lueders' orchestra and the Standard Male Quartette rendered splendid numbers. The accompanists were Prof. F. A. Parker, J. S. Smith, Mrs. Janette Ainsworth, Fred Silber and Prof. Sired. All services were, of course, kindly donated.

The warm local support was welcomed, but the struggle to obtain insurance monies was daunting, and the total amount of insurance on both buildings only amounted to $24,000, while the construction costs for the burned "new" school alone had been $32,000. Nevertheless, the sisters— perhaps aware of the Washburn motto, *Persevera deoque confide* (Persevere and trust in God)— quickly determined that a new Edgewood would rise from the ashes. Rebuilding began almost at once, and the new Academy opened the following year on September 5, 1894.

In July of 1895, an Iowa visitor to Edgewood, Mrs. Mary Jones Hay, wrote an article for the Dubuque newspaper, saying,

Undaunted by the fire of a year ago, which destroyed the old manor house and first building erected here, the sisters immediately set about retrieving their loss, and now have a handsome three-story and basement structure of Milwaukee brick with cut stone trimmings. It is of the Gothic style of architecture, of a noble and generous design.... and every modern convenience, including electric lighting, has been embraced.

She noted that a plank walk extended from the gate of the Academy grounds, exiting toward what is now Madison Street, to the terminus of the "electric cars," half way toward the city, near Camp Randall, "thus affording those who are not afraid of a little pedestrian exercise a pleasant method of reaching this delightful spot." The

which the children slept. He said that it would have taken but a short time in a dense smoke to cause death.

Dr. Philip Fox, of Madison, was then sworn and testified that he was called to Edgewood seminary Thursday night and arrived about 9 o'clock. He found two children dead, apparently from suffocation. There was no mark on one, but on the other there was a bruise on an arm and on the forehead, apparently caused by a fall or by coming into contact with some hard substance. It would take from five to ten minutes to cause death by suffocation. A sister told him of her efforts to rescue the children. The doctor said that the case is so clear that there is really nothing to say in a coroner's examination. He stated that the injured sisters are nearly fully recovered and that little Miss Hennebery, whose recovery was not looked for, is better. At noon he said he had no hopes of her recovery, but he heard shortly before coming to the coroner's that she had regained consciousness.

Sister Mary Bertha, the sister who was in the room with the children who were killed, was the next witness. She resided at Edgewood and held the position of sindica, and did the buy-...

was adjourn[ed] The full jur[y] rendered a v[erdict] [sin]gle Stack an[d] their deaths [Novem]ber 16, 1893, [at ...] p. m., at Ed[gewood] town of Mad[ison] by being ac[tually] smoke in said [...] sumed by fire

The jurors [were] Charles O. [...] C. H. Whela[n] W. W. Youn[g]

Sister Berth[a ...] ly in rescu[ing ...] getting along out of plac[e ...] yesterday, ho[...] difficulty that [...] office.

Sister Mar[y ...] who was ill [...] and suffered very much b[...] The report [...] wood had a [...] Mitchell bank [...] the least foun[...] Little Marge[...] who met her [...]

Courtesy of Anna Fox

Dr. Philip Fox, a prominent Madison physician, rushed to Edgewood the night of the fire to care for the injured students and sisters. He testified at the inquest that he had found two children dead of smoke inhalation when he arrived at Edgewood about 9 p.m. while the fire was still raging. He cared for the other two children at St. Regina Convent, near the capitol square, where the survivors were taken that night, and he was able to save one of the "minims," though a third child died the next day.

writer knew the Dominican sisters well, because their St. Clara Academy was built on Sinsinawa Mound, near Dubuque, a property her own father, George Wallace Jones, had once owned and mined and which he had later sold to Father Samuel Mazzuchelli.

Thus, in a year after the devastating fire, visitors were admiring the "new Edgewood," erected at a cost of $36,719.00, and over forty students had returned for the first semester of classes in the new academy building. The name of the school had been changed from St. Regina Academy to Sacred Heart Academy, perhaps as a sign of the fresh beginning as well as a reflection of a popular Catholic devotion of the nineteenth century. Other improvements were under way, as well. During the 1894-95 school year, the "stone barn" which Samuel Marshall had built was remodeled into a laundry, sewing room, and bakery. In the following year, a telephone line was installed, and the sisters contributed $200 toward a project for extending the electric car line to Wingra Park. The new extension had its first run on August 9, 1896, and Edgewood no longer seemed so "far away" from the city of Madison. The sisters, however, still relied on their horse and buggy for transportation, and a surprise gift of a fine carriage was presented to them in 1897, paid for by subscriptions of "friends of Edgewood," including Dr. Philip Fox, the generous physician who had cared for children and sisters immediately after the 1893 fire and in subsequent years.

The new building facilitated growth, and by 1897 Edgewood had about sixty students and sixteen sisters. More improvements were recorded in the annals in successive years: electric bells and fixtures, window screens, and a refrigerator in 1896-97; a gas engine to supply water "when the windmill is out of order" in 1902-03; connection to city water, "a great blessing," in 1904-05, at a cost of $300; a new rectory for the chaplain, costing $2,700, in 1903-04, and moving the old "cottage" to the rear of the lot; a large addition to the Academy building, costing $16,000, in 1908-09; and connection to the public sewer system on Vilas street in 1910-11, at a cost of $200.

Civic matters affected Edgewood in various ways. One early aim of the Madison Park and Pleasure Drive Association was to have rustic carriage drives around all of the Madison lakes, including Wingra. The Association was a private but powerful group of influential Madisonians, led by John M. Olin, and including Daniel K. Tenney, Thomas E. Brittingham, and William F. Vilas—all names familiar to those who would frequent Madison's future park system. As David Mollenhoff describes them, these were "the movers and shakers of their day....the top slice of Madison's pyramid of wealth, persons who could afford buggies and horses and whom merchants then called 'the carriage trade.'"[2] The Edgewood convent annalist recorded in 1903 that "for many years there had been a question of our granting permission to have the Pleasure Drive run through our property from Edgewood Avenue to Woodrow Street" along Lake Wingra. Finally, but with reservations, it seemed necessary to accede to the wishes of the Association,

---

A BENEFIT FOR EDGEWOOD.

An Excellent Program of Music Now Being Arranged.

Steps were taken yesterday towards arranging a benefit program for the Edgewood sisters who lost their entire possessions in the late terrible fire. A splendid program is being arranged and will be given at the Fuller Opera house, Tuesday evening, November 28.

JAMES WHITCOMB RILEY.

William Dean Howels the novelist, pays this graceful compliment to James Whitcomb Riley: "The fact is our

The citizens of Madison rallied to support the Dominican Sisters after the tragic Edgewood fire. One public effort was a benefit music concert held at the Fuller Opera House on November 28, 1893, twelve days after the fire.
The Madison Democrat

The new Academy building, now housing the re-named Sacred Heart Academy and the sisters' convent, was completed in September of 1894. A wooden summer house was erected near the Jefferson Street side of the campus.

Edgewood's agreement on March 18, 1905, with John Olin, representing the Association, was described by the annalist, who noted that the Association would keep up the fences and that any dead trees would be cut into cord wood for the sisters' use. A passage under the road for the sisters' cows to get to the water was also assured. The matter was not entirely settled, however, for some decades later the sisters attempted to reclaim the road.

Having their own produce and milk still provided significant savings for the sisters, but in 1907-08 taxes were assessed, and the annalist stated ruefully that although some of the Edgewood property was exempt, "we shall pay taxes on 12 acres of the farm." This was not the first time taxes had presented a problem to the sisters. Soon after they had purchased the St. Regina Academy property in 1871 and believing the property exempt from taxes, they found to their dismay that "the City had sold it for taxes due to Mr. Donohue. Mr. Philip Barry, the brother of our Sister Athanasius, bought it back for twelve dollars and gave it to the Sisters."[3]

Perhaps the most exciting new educational development in the 1890s was the sisters' knowledge that the Congregation was exploring the opening of a college at

Academy students on the front porch of the "new" building, about 1900, dressed in their Sunday best.

Sinsinawa. Already in the 1890s the well-established St. Clara Female Academy at Sinsinawa Mound was offering "post-graduate courses" such as ethics, logic, astronomy, philology, and period courses in history to its senior academy students. The annals at St. Clara Convent record that Dr. Maurice Egan, and "other of our scholarly friends" urged the sisters to offer college-level courses. The *St. Clara Academy Catalogue* of 1898 outlined a plan for post-graduate study, and in August of 1899, Mother Emily Power and Sister Benedicta Kennedy came to Edgewood to confer with Professor Knowlton of the University of Wisconsin regarding the plan for the college curriculum at Sinsinawa.

On April 25, 1901, the Board of Trustees of St. Clara Female Academy (Mother Emily Power and the sisters of her Council) adopted resolutions to change the corporate name to "St. Clara College," thus amending the corporate charters of 1868 and 1882 to declare that the institution thenceforth was "to have and exercise all powers and authority possessed by Colleges of the State of Wisconsin, in granting diplomas, degrees or distinctions for proficiency in the arts and sciences to students of said College and others whom it desires to honor."

Thus began a long history of higher education in the Sinsinawa Dominican tradition of teaching and sponsoring educational institutions. Here were planted the seeds of Rosary College— later Dominican University—in Illinois, the Institut des Hautes Etudes in Switzerland, the Rosary College Graduate School of Fine Arts in Florence, Italy, and, in 1927, Edgewood College in Madison, Wisconsin.

This gradual evolution from private academy to college mirrored a trend in American education. Many colleges and universities had developed from strong foundations laid by years of excellence as secondary academic institutions. Another important educational trend of the nineteenth century was the establishment of colleges for women. Single sex colleges were the norm, and the development of Catholic colleges and universities in this country naturally followed a pattern of religious orders of men—such as the Jesuits or Benedictines— founding colleges for men, and religious orders of women—such as the Franciscans or Dominicans— establishing colleges for women. The Sinsinawa Dominicans' plan to establish their first college in the 1890s was a part of these trends in the history of higher education in the United States.

The Sinsinawa Dominican sisters, with both a tradition of educational excellence in their schools and academies and a heritage of strong educational training of the sisters themselves, thus began a new century with the opening of St. Clara College at Sinsinawa in 1901 as a first step in their development of higher education institutions.

By 1913, the sisters were considering relocation of St. Clara College to an urban area. The nineteenth century tradition of situating residential colleges in rural or small town settings was fading, and the sisters recognized the need for establishing their college in an urban environment. Various sites where the sisters already staffed schools or owned property were considered—Omaha, Denver, Chicago, Milwaukee, and Madison. In January of 1914, Mother Samuel Coughlin sent sisters to Madison and Milwaukee to consider sites in those locations where the sisters had long been established as teachers in grade and high schools. Mother Samuel and her Council studied the Edgewood property in Madison carefully, since it offered many advantages, especially with its proximity to the University of Wisconsin and its extensive and beautiful grounds. They had decided to employ the famous American architect Ralph Adams Cram to design the new college,[4] and one of Cram's associates, Mr. Hoyle, visited the Edgewood site in July 1915. No reason why the Edgewood site was rejected is recorded. The focus of site selection after 1915 moved to the Chicago metropolitan area where property was purchased in River Forest, and Cram developed his designs for the college—to be opened in 1922 with a new name—Rosary College.

Despite the fact that Edgewood was not selected as the new college site, the beginnings of higher education there were already well under way. As early as 1902 and 1903, the Edgewood annals report that both sisters and academy students were attending lectures at the University of Wisconsin, among them four lectures "on Grecian art," six lectures on "Intellectual Leaders of the Middle Ages," and a

Courtesy of Anna Fox

Dr. Philip R. Fox, known as "Doctor Rod," successfully brought Academy students and sisters through a serious outbreak of the "Spanish influenza" epidemic in the fall of 1918.

three-lecture series on Shakespeare given by Sydney Lee of London. Attendance at university lectures became a regular feature of early twentieth century study for senior academy students as well as sisters at Edgewood.

The hope of opening a college at Edgewood dimmed with the decision to build in the Chicago area after 1915. Soon, the war years would challenge the Edgewood sisters and students in many ways, but tragedy suddenly loomed in late October and early November of 1918 when the dreaded Spanish influenza swept Edgewood, and forty students were seriously stricken at one time. However, the ministrations of Dr. Philip R. Fox (known as "Doctor Rod" to distinguish him from his father who had cared for the sisters and students the night of the 1893 tragic fire) proved effective, and, with the fervent prayers of the sisters, no student or sister died. In gratitude for their deliverance, Edgewood sisters and students had a Lourdes grotto built on the slope of the hillside behind the academy, and it became a favorite place of pilgrimage. Perhaps not all the students who, in later years, would pause at the grotto could remember its reason for being there, but each student in succeeding years brought her own devotion and special needs to Our Lady. In 1932, one of the college students, Mary Hortense Crowley, wrote of the shrine in *The Conifer*, a student magazine:

> *Down at the edge of the sloping grove*
> *On a lonely, serene Edgewood path,*
> *Shielded from winds by arch of gray*
> *And from the storms' relentless wrath,*
> *Stands the Virgin in white and blue....*

And in the same issue another college student, Mary Wendorf, wrote:

> *Reminiscent of wayside shrines where travelers paused for a few moments of silent meditation, Edgewood possesses a beautiful grotto constructed of cobble stones in the form of a Gothic arch under which stands the statue of our Blessed Mother Mary. Before this miniature altar is a construction of concrete upon which one might kneel to say a few prayers. At each side and also along the front are flowers arranged in the manner of an old fashioned garden.*

The Edgewood annalist noted that in September of 1918 school had opened "with an enrollment that impressed upon us the necessity of soon providing new buildings for the accommodation of our ever-increasing attendance." Along with hopes for a new building to meet the pressing need for more space for academy students came a renewed dream of opening a college at Edgewood. When Mother Samuel and her council decided to move ahead with the new Edgewood building, they turned to the grandson of their "great friend," to Albert Kelsey, Philadelphia architect and son of Governor Washburn's daughter Jeannette Washburn Kelsey. Undoubtedly the Edgewood sisters had spoken of their needs to Jeannette when she and her daughter Kate visited Edgewood in 1916. Jeannette herself had suggested to the Edgewood sisters, two years earlier, that they should contact her son Albert, a well-known Philadelphia architect, as they planned for a new building.

In 1918, Sister Bertha McCarthy invited Albert Kelsey to visit Edgewood and discuss plans for a building. Clearly, hopes were being revived for opening a college at Edgewood, because on March 19, 1919, Mother Samuel wrote to Albert Kelsey, "I see great possibilities here for the development of a high school and perhaps a junior college later." Late in November 1919, Sister Theodosius Kiernan and Sister Bertha McCarthy traveled to Philadelphia to discuss the blue prints and architectural drawings he had sent earlier. The Edgewood annals record that "the sisters were graciously received by him and his parents at their home, and a satisfactory understanding regarding several details was reached."

Kelsey's plans were spectacular, involving an extensive three-story building on the hilltop, running parallel to Monroe Street, crowned with a ten-story tower that would dominate the west-side skyline of Madison, and finished with elaborate terracotta trim. Although beautiful, the plans called for expensive construction costs. Action on the plans for a new Edgewood moved slowly, because the Congregation was involved at this time in a fund-raising campaign for the new Rosary College in Illinois, itself a costly undertaking designed by another famous architect, Ralph Adams Cram.

The steadily growing enrollment pressures on the academy increased year by year, and by the end of 1921, the boarding "minims" (below sixth grade level) had to be dropped because of over-crowding. By September of 1924, the annalist noted that "the enrollment was so large that old and discarded desks were put to use again. Mother Samuel was so pleased with our steady increase of day pupils that she and Sister Richard [Congregation Finance Officer] came to Edgewood in November to take up the matter of building."

In April of the following spring, Mother Samuel and her Council "unanimously decided to engage Mr. Albert Kelsey, Philadelphia, Pa., to be the architect." On May 11, 1925, Albert Kelsey came to Madison and the sisters again discussed the proposed building plans with him, "seeking to view the project from every angle." The key "angle" was financial. The sisters had decided they "could not go beyond an expense of three hundred thousand dollars, so Mr. Kelsey was obliged to modify the plan." Although Kelsey did modify his architectural plan, the "low" contract bids came in at $449,601.90—far more than had been anticipated by the sisters. Groundbreaking for the new building was held on November 4, 1925, with J. H. Findorff as general contractor. Construction moved slowly, but the building was finally ready for occupancy on February 23, 1927. The dramatic tower was never added, but at the same time that the new building design was being finalized, a definite plan for a junior college at Edgewood was being discussed as well.

On April 6, 1927, a few weeks after the opening of the new building, Mother Samuel Coughlin, Sister Thomas Aquinas O'Neill (President of Rosary College), and Sister Grace James (Principal of Edgewood High School and Prioress of the convent)

Edgewood College Archives

The Lady of Lourdes Grotto, with a group of Academy students (minims through high school age) at a May crowning ceremony in 1924. Ann Russell (center, rear) crowned the statue of Mary.

The plan for the new building at Edgewood was designed in 1919 by Albert Kelsey, grandson of Governor Washburn and noted Philadelphia architect. It was to house both a high school and a junior college, and Kelsey included in his architectural sketch his concept of a ten-story "skyscraper" central tower which would be crowned by a statue.

met with Dr. Glenn Frank, President of the University of Wisconsin, to discuss the sisters' intention to open a junior college at Edgewood. The annalist recorded the fact that "the President very graciously encouraged our undertaking." The very next day Mother Samuel met Archbishop Messmer in Milwaukee, and he, too, gave his blessing to the new venture.

Recruitment of members of the college's first freshman class began in earnest. During the summer of 1927, sisters canvassed the southern half of Wisconsin seeking potential students for both the high school and the new junior college, and the annalist noted that "even in our limited territory the results were most gratifying." A brochure was distributed proclaiming, "The Sinsinawa Dominican Sisters, now conducting Rosary College, River Forest, Illinois, announce the opening of Edgewood Junior College, a new college for women at Madison, Wisconsin – now ready for freshman and sophomore registration." Actually, only freshmen were accepted for the first year of operation, and with her excitement indicated by an exclamation point, the Edgewood annalist recorded on July 12, 1927: "First College fee received! Ten dollars matriculation fee was paid by Mrs. Grady of Oregon, Wisconsin, for her daughter, Elizabeth Ann."

On September 14, 1927, Edgewood Junior College officially opened with an enrollment of twelve women—nine boarders, and three day students; five more day students joined them for the second semester. Not only new students arrived at Edgewood Junior College that year, new sisters arrived as well, as the annalist recorded: "Sister Marie Aileen came from Rosary College to be Dean and taught English and speech. Sister Alicia from Omaha was appointed Registrar and taught history and religion. Sister Bonaventure from Rosary College taught science and mathematics, and Sister Grace James taught French." Sister Grace James also served as the nominal president of the college in its first year, as well as being principal of the high school and prioress of the convent of sisters. Other faculty members taught both high school and college courses.

The curriculum of the two-year program offered a strong liberal arts program: mathematics, English, art history, music, philosophy, speech, religion, biology, French, Latin, Greek, and German. Costs for students were modest, as the announcement brochure had promised, "a resident student can meet her necessary expenses at this college for less than $600 a year," while a year's tuition for day students was $150.

Most resident college students were lodged in "the Tower," a single floor above the central part of the three-story new building and the only part of the more grandiose tower structure planned by Kelsey that was actually completed. A few students were lodged in the old academy building. One or two sisters also slept in the Tower area, keeping an eye on what went on there. After all, this was the roaring twenties and a boom time, with few foreseeing the economic collapse that lay just around the corner.

That first college year of 1927-28 was a heady time in America. It was the Jazz Age, and Al Jolson's *The Jazz Singer*, the first "talkie," was being shown in movie theaters. Clara Bow and Gary Cooper were a favorite movie duo in two major films of 1927—*It* and *Wings*—while Charlie Chaplin's films were perennial hits. During the summer of 1927 the long-drawn-out Sacco-Vanzetti trial was concluded, and the two were executed in August amidst controversy. The Eighteenth Amendment to the U.S. Constitution made drinking a daring and clandestine experience of the twenties. Babe Ruth was the Sultan of Swat, belting a record 60 home runs during the 1927 season, while Charles Lindbergh soloed across the Atlantic, becoming America's darling in May 1927. In 1928 Al Smith was the first Catholic nominee to run for President of the United States, and although Herbert Hoover defeated him, it seemed to many that Catholicism in America had finally come of age.

This was an era of famous women, too. Amelia Earhart soon rivaled Lindbergh as a hero of the new air age, soloing to Europe in June 1928. Sigrid Undset won the Nobel prize in world literature in 1927, primarily for her series of historical novels, *Kristin Lavransdatter*. In 1928 Willa Cather published her novel, *Death Comes for the Archbishop*, and she was becoming well-established in the ranks of major American writers. In France, Nadia Boulanger was shaping her reputation as a teacher of music composition—though no one at Edgewood College in 1927 would have guessed that one day she would come to be a guest teacher and lecturer on the college campus. Similarly, Helen Hayes was becoming known as one of America's great actresses on Broadway and in films, and soon Edgewood students would get to meet her on campus when she visited her former teacher and friend, the dean of the college, Sister Marie Aileen Klein. Georgia O'Keeffe, who as a youngster had studied briefly with Edgewood academy art teachers, was emerging in New York City as one of the great American painters of her generation, selling one of the giant flower paintings for $25,000 in 1928. It was an exciting time to be a young college woman.

That first year was an auspicious beginning, and the second year opened in September 1928 with an enrollment of fourteen freshmen and eight sophomores. In October the convent annalist wrote that "we were able to meet the semi-annual interest payment—ten thousand dollars—by using the first receipts." The debt on the new building, though scaled back from Kelsey's original plan, was still a costly burden to the sisters, but in 1928 the hopes of steady growth and a strong American economy seemed to ease that burden.

In June of 1929, the first seven graduates of the junior college received their Associate of Arts degrees. A brief description of that first college commencement in the old chapel was recorded by the Edgewood annalist: "The graduates, dressed in white and wearing white veils, marched up the middle aisle and took places at the front.... The Reverend Raymond Mahoney gave the address and the Reverend P. B. Knox presented the diplomas."

And what of those pioneers, the first graduates of Edgewood College? One, Margaret Whittet, graduated from the University of Wisconsin, taught classes at Edgewood High School, and later was employed for many years with the State Department of Health and Social Services. Another, Marcella Schumacher, earned an M.A. in political science at the University of Wisconsin, worked in St. Louis, married, and taught music. Catherine Cleary taught school after earning her B.A. from the University of Wisconsin, with majors in French and English. Bernadine Ternes entered the Sinsinawa Dominican Congregation and taught in Dominican high schools as Sister Leonette, after receiving advanced degrees. A glance at some of the first graduates and at what they did after leaving Edgewood College indicates the quality of the education they received which prepared them well for future study and valuable careers.

The realization that the first graduates were enrolled successfully in university studies or were pursuing careers in business or teaching must have provided a strong spirit of optimism among faculty and students alike as Edgewood Junior College began its third year in September of 1929. There was already much to be proud of, though at Halloween some prankster (or several) painted the sisters' cows red, green, and yellow. As Sister Jude Green later remembered: "That contributed, as no other argument did, to convince the sisters who liked the Edgewood-produced dairy products, to get rid of those cows. Other sisters, especially the college faculty, had been determined to have those cows gotten rid of, in order to have a more sophisticated college campus." This "sophistication" was not achieved until the following year, as the convent annalist noted in October of 1930: "The last of the cows were sold." Probably the sale was due more to pressure from the neighbors of Edgewood than from the college faculty, for the annalist added the reason for the cows' removal— "because of the proximity of Madison homes to the grazing land."

The bright blue days of October were abruptly darkened for the sisters, the students, and their families, and, indeed, for the nation and the world. After the boom years of the twenties, the stock market crash of Black Tuesday, October 29, 1929, stunned the country. Its full effects would only gradually be revealed in the new year of 1930, but the devastating aftermath experienced during the early thirties would present a new trial by fire to the Edgewood community as it struggled to survive the Great Depression.

BROTHER, CAN YOU SPARE A DIME?

Words by
E.Y. HARBURG

Music by
JAY GORNEY

CHAPTER THREE

Surviving The Great Depression *1930-1939*

The shock of Black Tuesday deepened gradually in the ensuing months and years of the 1930s. The fledgling college that had begun with such promise now faced another trial by fire—this time, a struggle to survive, a struggle shared by students and their families as well as by the Dominican sisters. Unemployment rates soared, and one after another, banks failed. The song "Brother, Can You Spare A Dime?" echoed the tragic reality faced by millions of people. In November of 1932, Franklin Delano Roosevelt was elected president of the United States, and gradually he inaugurated sweeping federal programs to restore the nation's economy and lift its people's hopes.

In order to construct the new building at Edgewood in the late 1920s, the Sinsinawa Dominicans had incurred a debt of $450,000. This, coupled with the Congregation's already large burden of indebtedness for recent construction at Rosary College and Trinity High School, meant that the 1930s would be a time of nearly desperate effort to maintain these schools as well as to pay the interest on loans that had been taken out earlier. Throughout the decade, letters back and forth between Sister Richard Barden, finance officer of the Congregation, and Sister Ricarda Shanahan, business officer at Edgewood, reveal a constant need to "juggle" funds in order to meet payment deadlines or to shift loans to institutions offering lower interest rates. During 1933-34, for example, the total income for all three Edgewood schools was $65,212.97, and the total expenses were $64,512.60, including $25,000 due on loan interest.

Sister Mary De Ricci Fitzgerald, Vicaress for Mother Samuel, was keenly interested in Edgewood, as her diaries and letters reveal. Even before the Wall Street crash in 1929, the Edgewood sisters were considering the sale of some of their land in order to meet the payments on the recent building loans. On February 8, 1928, Sister De Ricci noted in her diary that "Mr. Leo Crowley called on Mother Samuel at Edgewood today. He is interested in a proposition to sell some of the land on Edgewood property. I hope very little, if any, be sold."[1] About the same time, Sister

"Brother, Can You Spare a Dime?" by E. Y. Harburg and Jay Gorney
© 1932 (Renewed) Warner Bros., Inc.

Sister Mary De Ricci Fitzgerald, O.P. Vicaress of the Congregation Even during the Depression years, she was a strong supporter of the dream to create a senior college at Edgewood.

Grace James, president of the new college and prioress, wrote to Mother Samuel, saying, "Have you thought any further of the property here, as suggested by Mr. Crowley? I am trying to sell the Woodrow Street lots, but so far we can't get our price."[2] The matter of selling some of the property was still under consideration during the following year, with Sister De Ricci noting in her diary for April 30, 1929, "I hope this sale is never made. It is the choicest corner of the property."

In early May 1929, however, Sister De Ricci was sent by Mother Samuel to Edgewood to meet with the sisters there and to confer with advisers about the impending sale. In spite of her own misgivings, she noted in her diary that "for the most part the sisters at Edgewood favor the sale. It helps to take care of next year's finances on the bonded debt." On May 9, 1929, Mother Samuel and her Council approved the sale of some land at the southeast corner of the Edgewood property to Leo Crowley, a long-time friend and benefactor, for $20,000— the equivalent of one year's interest on the debt for the new building. Twelve years earlier the Edgewood sisters had considered the sale of some of the property, as evidenced in a letter from Jeannette Washburn Kelsey to Sister Fidelia in 1917, a year after she had visited Edgewood. The daughter of Governor Washburn had approved the idea then, saying, "In regard to selling some acres of the Edgewood estate, I think the idea a very good one if you are in need of money, and the sisters must do exactly as they think best."

In 1931-32, thirty-seven college students were enrolled, an increase of 50% over the previous year, but during the Depression years of the thirties, the number of junior college students fell to an average of thirty to thirty-five students each year. In order to make continued attendance possible for their students, the sisters provided their own "New Deal," drastically cutting tuition, at times lowering it to $30 a semester.

In spite of the belt-tightening experienced in the early thirties, the Edgewood sisters decided to celebrate with solemnity the Golden Jubilee anniversary of Governor Washburn's generous gift. A pageant involving all the students on the Edgewood campus, from the youngest in the kindergarten to the oldest in the college, was held on the terrace in front of the new building on May 31, 1931. The pageant and the jubilee were duly noted by articles in *The Chicago Tribune* and the Milwaukee newspapers, as well as by the Madison publications. A full description of the pageant was given by the college dean, Sister Marie Aileen Klein, who herself wrote, directed, and produced the grand affair:

At the gate, the present Governor [Robert La Follette] was heralded by buglers and drummers. Across the wide greensward came the student representing Governor Washburn to welcome Governor La Follette to the former executive grounds. First were pictured the old Indian days at Edgewood....In the next episode the living Flowers and dancing Butterflies greeted the first settlers, Mr. and Mrs. Ashmead, in 1855. This was succeeded, as in life, by the Wedding March, after the Dryads lured the tree-lover, Samuel Marshall, future Milwaukee banker, and his young bride to Edgewood in 1857. General Sherman was entertained at a garden party, where the Minuet was danced, and where a little [student] impersonating Elizabeth Marshall, first child born at the Villa, made a presentation of an old-fashioned bouquet to the General....[The Washburn era was re-enacted before] all waved a farewell to the beloved Governor even while the symbolic figures of Studies accompanied the children to the new school...[the fire scenes then

Several Dominican sisters saying goodbye to Jeannette Washburn Kelsey and her daughter Kate Kelsey, as they leave Edgewood in Father Hengell's motor car, headed for Madison's Park Hotel. Father Henry Hengell was the first college chaplain. Note his Wisconsin motor car license number: 150.

Cadwallader C. Washburn's daughter, Jeannette Washburn Kelsey, in front of Sacred Heart Academy, during her visit to Edgewood in June 1916.

followed]. Later the Postmen's Song and the Windmill Fantasy recalled the episodes of the first mail by carrier, and the replacing of the pumps and windmills by city water.   The college gave Echoes of the World War in Color, Rhythm, and Sound through a symbolic rally and the formation of a tent out of the red and white scarves and the singing of Tenting Tonight; lastly Taps and Assembly... [more ensued until the grand finale]. After the crowning of Alma Mater by Alumnae, the 600 participants in the pageant were massed in colorful array at the magnificent portal, and they, with the audience, raised the hearts of all to the Giver of all good gifts.[3]

A week later, the annual Washburn Day banquet was held on June 7, 1931, and Dr. Annette Washburn, niece of the Governor, was the guest of honor. Dr. Washburn was in neuropsychiatric practice at Madison's Wisconsin General Hospital, and she was the first woman to be appointed a full professor in the University Medical School. The annalist recalled that at the 1931 Washburn Day banquet "she gave a very interesting sketch of the Washburn family, tracing its history from the days of William the Conqueror."   The tradition of gratefully remembering Governor Washburn, was regularly continued in this June celebration each year, and Dr. Annette Washburn was often the main speaker.

Much earlier Jeannette Washburn Kelsey, the governor's daughter, had been invited to attend, and although she was not able to come, she sent a talk about her father that was read on her behalf at the dinner in 1913. She and her daughter Kate visited Edgewood in 1916, and the Edgewood convent annals record that in subsequent years Jeannette would send special gifts in memory of her father to be distributed each Washburn Day as prizes to students.

Elizabeth Marshall, Samuel Marshall's daughter, who had been born and baptized in the Edgewood Villa, was another visitor, friend, and benefactor through the years until her death in 1940. She had provided the commemorative plaque which was placed on the north wall of Marshall Hall in 1915, honoring her father.

These living connections with the early history of Edgewood remained important to sisters and students through the years, although in June of 1932 the annalist recorded regretfully that "the Washburn banquet, usually held on the first Sunday in June, was this year cancelled." That June, the Archbishop of Milwaukee had asked that "all pleasures, even the most legitimate," be cancelled by all in the archdiocese, and that the month be a time "devoted to prayer and penance for the relief of the great depression."

Whatever the discouragements of those years, college students of the thirties made their own fun. Some later recalled their Edgewood experiences vividly:

These were Depression times, and some of the students, to help pay their way, did manual labor around the classrooms and dorm area, right along with the sisters. But we surely had good times. We could see most of Madison from the roof of the Tower, the high school sports beckoned us many evenings, and we could go downtown for ten cents on the bus. Sister Marie Aileen gave us a key to get back into the building; we never had to sign out, either! Christmas time brought a party and a dance to which we invited our brothers and friends from home. Oh, yes, we got into a bit of mischief, using the fire escape for an exit or a good place to have a cigarette. We were active in sports, too.[4]

In the 30s none of us had any money. We listened to the radio a lot. Sometimes we joined the nuns in the parlor when Father Coughlin spoke... and we listened to the news every night when the Lindbergh baby was kidnapped—it was shocking.

Naturally classes were the main part of our lives, but some Friday nights we'd go to the movies, walking up to the Square.... Admission was a quarter, but we also had enough to stop at the Chocolate Shop for a hot fudge sundae and then walked off the calories on the way back to Edgewood.

We sun-bathed on the roof of the Tower, studied out there on warm days, had impromptu parties, looked up at the stars, watched beautiful sunsets and storms come up from the west. Once we flew kites from the roof.[5]

All shared the financial limitations on recreation in those days, but they also remembered "good times" shared with close friends and with the sisters. As one alumna described college life: "We were a small class, delightfully immature. The world was our oyster.... being young provided us with all the highs we needed." A few stretched the limits, with one alumna recalling that at times "we were very daring—we sneaked cigarettes in the laundry, drank 3.2 beer on State Street, and when we didn't have dates we would turn on the phonograph in the 'rec room' and practice the Dip and the Big Apple with each other."[6]

These early years at the college were challenging for the sisters. For one thing, the administration of the college changed quickly. In 1927-28, Sister Grace James was president, followed the next year by Sister Laurentina Boyle and, in 1934, by Sister Marie Francis Barden. This third president of the College later remarked about those beginnings, "Sister Laurentina and I were never referred to as 'President.'

Several members of the class of 1935—Edgewood Junior College: Janice McGeever, Lucille Hammersley, Cleo Dougherty, Dorothy Carpenter, Elizabeth Erbe, Jean Dunwiddie

I was always teaching a full program, and really we started out with nothing at all—no building and no classrooms of our own, no nothing!" She added wryly, "The less said the better for the early years of Edgewood College."[7]   However, in the same letter, Sister Marie Francis also remembered that "scholastically the school rated well—the girls went on to the University and did well there." She recalled that she "never heard any griping" from the students, adding, "I think that they were happy and satisfied."   These early presidents served primarily as principals of the high school and prioresses of the convent—no easy burdens—and most of the concerns of the junior college were the responsibility of the deans, like Sister Marie Aileen, who were the *de facto* chief administrators as well as college teachers.

The struggles of the Dominican sisters, most of whom taught full programs and wore multiple "hats" in both high school and college in those early years, were not apparent to their students. Student memories of those early difficult days were fond and appreciative. For the young women who ventured to enroll in the fledgling junior college in the Depression years, they were good if trying times. The small population of the college did not daunt them, as is evident from what Margaret Whittet, one of the members of the first class, wrote for a 1927 student skit: "I think that I shall never see a freshman class as small as we." And although the college students had their own dining room and separate living quarters in the "Tower," they shared the chapel, library, and labs with the high school students at various times during the day. In spite of the limitations, one of them later remarked, "But we did learn how to study. It seemed so much easier at the University after those two years at Edgewood."[8]

The college students had their own special celebrations on College Day and at other times during the year, and they acted in plays, such as Molière's *The Imaginary Invalid* or Shakespeare's *Love's Labour's Lost* – ambitious projects guided by the dean, Sister Marie Aileen, mentor and former teacher of Helen Hayes, whose visits to Edgewood were exciting events for the students in those years. A student production of a Molière play won first place in the Wisconsin state-wide dramatic competition of 1933—so the collegians had much to be proud of. Students also wrote for and published their own magazine, *The Conifer*.

The sisters who were their teachers became the students' mentors and friends. The first advertising brochure for the junior college had promised that "intelligent and sympathetic personal guidance of the students... is the chief advantage of the small private college." This "intelligent and sympathetic" guidance was evident again and again as graduates remembered their years at Edgewood. One incident is typical: Sister Jude Green, a science teacher at the college in the thirties, recalled that about two-thirds of the students took her course in college chemistry. She wrote:

One evening I was busily washing equipment and dishes in my lab sink. A college girl came into the lab. She was crying, and said, 'I'm lonesome.' I dried my hands and arms, took off my black rubber apron, and we went together to the apple orchard, beyond the red barn, and walked arm in arm, and the tears were finally replaced with happy smiles. Later there was an office to clean and an academy study hall to supervise. Those laboratory dishes got done about 10:30 p.m.[9]

Cast of As You Like It, directed by Sister Marie Aileen Klein, 1935.

The sisters' days were full ones, but their beloved Founder's priorities guided them. Before his death in 1864, Father Samuel Mazzuchelli had told his sisters, as they were opening their first academies, that they should always strive "to make the school as much like home as possible." The phrase *in loco parentis* may not have been the accurate phrase to describe the relationships between faculty and students in those days, but the caring relationships established at Edgewood brightened the dark and trying years of the Great Depression and lasted for many years afterwards in the memories of alumnae. One member of the class of 1938 later said, "I have always been happy that I was a graduate of Edgewood Junior College, and the two years are remembered fondly.... I recall Sister Marie Aileen's great interest in each of us, along with Sister Jude's and Sister Audrey's support."[10]

Music was another vital part of Edgewood's students' lives during the thirties.

A gifted concert pianist, Sister Amanda Courtaux, was on the faculty. One sister there during those years later remembered that "when she played in her music room, I often hid in the dark of the small room next door—just to listen. She gave a recital in May of 1931 [undoubtedly part of Edgewood's golden jubilee celebrations that month], and each spring when she traveled to Europe, she told me she almost always presented the [ship's] passengers with a recital."[11]

Sister Amanda was an intriguing personality on the Edgewood campus. A French citizen, born on the island of Mauritius, and an accomplished musician from her youth, Marie Mathilde Courtaux had been honored by receiving the highest prize granted by the Paris Conservatory and had been decorated by the French Government with the Rosette of *Officier d'Academie*. During wartime, she had moved to Fribourg, Switzerland, and was living with the Dominican Sisters at the Villa des Fougères, a branch of Rosary College. In the fall of 1920, she met there with Mother Samuel Coughlin to discuss becoming a Dominican sister, a desire fulfilled when she entered the Sinsinawa community in 1921 at the age of 62. She taught piano at Edgewood from 1924 to 1932, and academy and college students recalled her French accent, her short stature, and her superb gifts as a pianist while also ruefully noting that they tried in vain to meet her expectations.

Another remarkable pianist, teacher, and composer, Sister Mary Edward Blackwell, came to Edgewood in 1939. Sister Edward had been studying in Europe during the 1930s—first on scholarship with Ottorino Respighi in Rome and later, after his death, with Igor Stravinsky and Nadia Boulanger in Paris—both of whom would come to visit her at Edgewood, much as Helen Hayes came to visit Sister Marie Aileen Klein. Students recalled Sister Edward's strong personality, her broad appreciation of the arts, and the stories of her remarkable European experiences. They also observed that, like Sister Amanda before her, Sister Edward's expectations were often beyond their capacity. During the thirties other music teachers at Edgewood offered courses in piano, harp and voice, and choral participation was expected of almost all of the college students.

Another unforgettable faculty member was Elizabeth Du Bois, physical education teacher at the college in 1934-35 and 1935-36. She had won a gold medal in the 1000 meters speed skating race and a silver in the 500 meters race during the 1932 Olympic Games at Lake Placid, N.Y. At that time, women's speed skating was an "exhibition event," not yet an official part of the Winter Games. For the

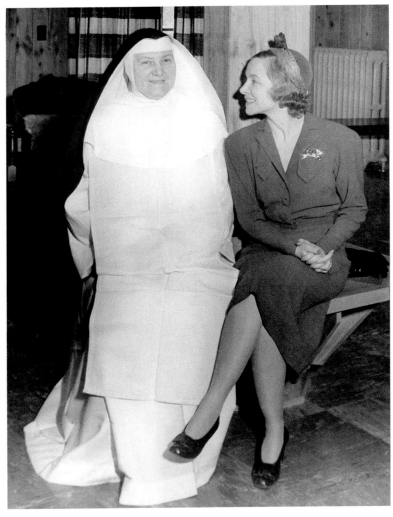

Sister Marie Aileen Klein and Helen Hayes.

Edgewood College women of the 1930s having an Olympian medalist as their instructor must have been exciting. The convent annalist recorded the fact that Elizabeth Du Bois was the first to organize an "athletic association," and that she "not only was very popular among the girls, but was generous and helpful to every sister.... She was an Olympic speed skater and thus attracted much attention on the Vilas Park lagoon, when she chaperoned the boarders on their skating trips." Later she entered the Sinsinawa Dominicans, becoming Sister Vincent.

It seems clear from the evidence given in reminiscences of graduates and former faculty members that Sister Marie Aileen Klein, college dean from 1927 to 1940, was the key figure in the success of the college's first difficult decade of existence. Her skills of administration as well as of teaching, her remarkable gifts as director of theater productions, as well as her strong personality and capacity for friendship—all provided a solid basis for weathering the storms of the thirties. One sister who was completing graduate studies at the University of Wisconsin and living at Edgewood in the early thirties remembered "the strong personality of Sister Marie Aileen, dean, whose days and nights were devoted to the young students."[12] A member of the class of 1936 said:

Helen Hayes once said of her mentor:

"There is always one teacher you meet in your lifetime who inspires you. That is Sister Marie Aileen in my case. She poured theater into me....It was a joy to be in her classroom."

Sister Marie Aileen, our dean, I believe had the most influence in my life. She taught me to appreciate good literature and theater, an appreciation I have treasured all my life. One of the highlights of those days was when she took all her drama students to see Mary, Queen of Scots, *starring Helen Hayes. We all went backstage afterwards to be introduced to her and get her autograph. What a thrill!*[13]

Another Edgewood student had a vivid memory of Sister Marie Aileen performing her "deanly" role:

I was dating a boy from my hometown, so I went home on weekends and took a lot of razzing from my friends. When he would drive me back on Sunday nights and we would 'linger' in the lower hallway, Sister Marie Aileen would invariably drop her large ring of keys down the stairwell and hit my friend on the head![14]

The dean's disciplinary measures apparently did not discourage the young suitor—the couple later married, and both served their country during World War II, he in the Army and she in the Signal Corps.

Another graduate said, "Who could forget our darling Sister Marie Aileen? She hated the habit and always said that she would speak to God about having to wear all that cumbersome paraphernalia, as soon as she got to heaven. Obviously she was very persuasive!" A sister faculty member of the thirties recalled that when Sister Marie Aileen celebrated her silver jubilee, "she seemed not to want the students to know about it,"—perhaps because it would have given them a hint of her age—so the convent jubilee was not held until after classes were finished in June.[15]

When a new wing was added to the building in 1938, the former gymnasium was remodeled as an auditorium, and it was used by both high school and college as the site of dances, assemblies, and dramatic performances. The first college production directed by Sister Marie Aileen in the newly remodeled auditorium featured scenes from *Victoria Regina*, the play made famous on Broadway and on tour by the starring role of her former pupil, Helen Hayes. In March of that year, Helen Hayes had performed in the play at the Parkway Theater in downtown Madison, and had been a guest at the college. Those students who had seen and visited with Hayes must have striven mightily to emulate the dynamic star in their own amateur production.

Under Sister Marie Aileen's strong leadership, with the hard work of an overburdened but devoted faculty, and with a small but enthusiastic succession of students, Edgewood Junior College survived the economic trials of the thirties. Harbingers of war were darkening Europe in the late thirties, but in 1938 the Edgewood annalist recorded only a local sorrow:

On November 7 occurred the death of Fanny, who was a familiar figure around Edgewood for the past thirty years. This old white horse will be missed by her partner, Joe; by the sisters, whom she has so faithfully served; and by the students, who often were seen carrying sweets or apples to her.

Although the sisters' cows had been sold in 1930, the late thirties still offered a bucolic atmosphere to students, with horses, barns and barn cats, chickens, gardens, an apple orchard, and an expanse of wooded grounds near Lake Wingra.

Greater awareness of the original inhabitants of the area was created when, in May 1939, students and sisters were excited by the archaeological dig of the Native American mounds on the property undertaken by WPA workers under the direction of Dr. Charles Brown, of the State Historical Society, a person active in the preservation of mounds in the Madison area. He told the sisters that some skeletons found in the small conical mounds "were probably 800 to 1000 years old." Much earlier, in 1919, the History Department of the Madison Women's Club had placed a bronze marker near the large bird effigy mound on the southwest corner of the property, near Woodrow Street. In all, twelve or thirteen mounds or their vestiges remain on the Edgewood grounds.

The oak savannas and the wooded ridges around Madison's lakes had been home to various indigenous peoples some of whom had created the many mounds in the area[16] long before James Doty envisioned a capital city on the isthmus or before John Ashmead built his colonial-style home on the hilltop overlooking Lake Wingra. The Dotys and the Marshalls and the Washburns were relative late comers to these grounds, and Native American people still moved through the Lake Wingra vicinity during the late nineteenth century. The word "Wingra" is itself a Ho-Chunk

(Winnebago) word meaning "duck." The area abounded in wild fowl during the migrating seasons and, with fish and deer at hand and with the wild rice that grew in the lake, the early people were provided with abundant food supplies. As wars and government treaties pushed the native inhabitants away from bountiful sites desired by the white settlers, including the Four Lakes area, the Native American mounds were neglected or destroyed by later arrivals who had no idea of their sacred qualities. However, even in the early twentieth century, the sisters and students at Edgewood appreciated the rich heritage that was still evident in the many mounds near the shores of Lake Wingra, a sensitivity acknowledged by Charles Brown, Curator of the Wisconsin Archeological Society, in a letter of May 14, 1908:

The Wisconsin Archeological Society has learned through Father Hengell [chaplain at Edgewood] of your kind decision, at its suggestion, to permanently preserve in the interest of history and education the several fine effigy and linear Indian earthworks on your beautiful grounds at Edgewood Villa. The Society desires that I express to you its own grateful appreciation of this act, which it also believes will when made generally known set an excellent example of deserved interest and thoughtfulness to other private owners who have been less careful of similar memorials on their own premises.

Another dimension of Edgewood's past history was kept alive for successive generations of students through the thirties by Elizabeth Marshall, daughter of Samuel Marshall who owned the Edgewood property from 1857 to 1873. During Elizabeth's lifetime, she was invited regularly to share her memories of Edgewood, especially of the old Villa where she was born. Once, when she was speaking to the alumnae association in the early 1930s, she brought to life those long-ago days:

I will ask you to step with me into the past when the stately old mansion, some years later destroyed by fire, yet stood on these beautiful, spacious grounds, and in which I

Edgewood Villa in Samuel Marshall's time there: 1857 – 1873.
Samuel Marshall began the early landscaping of the grounds. His daughter Elizabeth fondly recalled her happy childhood at Edgewood during the 1860s, including a visit by General William T. Sherman.

Edgewood College Archives

Plaque placed on Marshall Hall in 1915 by Elizabeth Marshall to commemorate her father and his family's life at Edgewood. Marshall Hall is the only building from the Marshall-Washburn era that still remains on the Edgewood campus

Edgewood College Archives

passed the early days of my life.   In approaching the Academy one sees the beautiful and stately trees that were planted by my father and this is the sight that most vividly recalls the Edgewood of olden days.... As a babe I lay in my carriage out on these beautiful grounds, my protector a faithful Newfoundland dog.... I can recall that with my brothers we played at saying Mass.... Seated beside my cherished mother, I received my first lessons in sewing, and under the same fond guidance I learned to print my letters....   I can recall with what delight I romped through these grounds, and ran down through the woods to the shore of the Lake to watch my elders either boating or fishing. I was also very fond of visiting the poultry yard and watching the chickens. I took advantage of the famous garden that was a joy and pride to my father, picking the fruits and flowers.

When General Sherman visited Madison in the fall of 1865, he was the guest of my parents at Edgewood, and I was favored by being allowed to sit on his knee.

Vividly comes to mind the first wedding I ever attended, when one who was loved as a sister was married in the front parlor. I can yet see the wedding party at breakfast in the dining room, where the table cloth was caught up at the four corners with bunches of flowers. Afterward the guests assembled on the front veranda and bade God-speed to the bride and groom as they drove off from the old home.[17]

When Elizabeth Marshall died in 1940 in Milwaukee, the last direct link with the early history of Edgewood was gone. Memories of that early history with its joys and sorrows would be recalled in stories passed to new generations of faculty and students, and in the still-standing stone building of 1864. But a new historical moment was about to occur at Edgewood.

As the nation slowly recovered from the Great Depression, and only a decade after the establishment of Edgewood Junior College, the Dominican sisters began taking steps toward significant expansion. While the situation in Europe moved ever closer to the brink of a new and terrible world war, plans were underway for developing a senior college at Edgewood.

CHAPTER FOUR

A Senior College Begins *1940-1949*

*I*n June 1940 France fell to Hitler's invading armies. The distant reverberations of war began to sound ever closer to the United States in the fall of 1940 as Edgewood College began its first four year baccalaureate degree program. The academic year began under the direction of a new dean, Sister Dunstan Tucker, and a new registrar, Sister Eunice Joy. A new president, Sister Rose Catherine Leonard, like her predecessors, served primarily as prioress of the convent and principal of the high school. More than a decade would pass before a "president" of the College would actually function in that role alone. The addition of ten sister students, released from full-time teaching posts in various schools staffed by the Dominicans, brought the total enrollment that fall to sixty. Eighteen more sister students came in the fall of 1941 to complete their degree study. The following spring, fifteen years after the founding of the junior college at Edgewood, the first students—twenty-five in all— received Bachelor of Science in Education degrees in June of 1942. A new era had begun.

What was the impetus for the development of the four-year degree program at Edgewood? Its possibility had been glimpsed twenty-five years earlier in the serious consideration of Edgewood as the site for the relocation of St. Clara College. After 1915, when this dream faded, the focus was on developing a two-year liberal arts junior college—a prospect made possible with the addition of a spacious new building on the Edgewood campus in the late twenties.

During the thirties, the Sinsinawa Dominicans wanted to provide a program of studies leading to a bachelor's degree for the more rapid professional preparation of their elementary school teachers. While many of the sisters in the elementary schools had completed degree studies, mainly through long years of summer and evening sessions at colleges and universities, others had not. The key person urging

Edgewood College Archives

A very tall Uncle Sam, complete with red and white striped trousers, blue tails, and stovepipe hat and carrying the Stars and Stripes, was Grand Marshal at the College Winter Ball held in January 1942, only a few weeks after the U.S. entered World War II.

the development of the senior college at Edgewood was Sister Mary De Ricci Fitzgerald, member of the General Council since 1913 and supervisor of the education of the Sinsinawa Dominican sisters since 1930. As the Congregation historian, Sister Eva McCarty, points out: "Serving in this capacity, Sister De Ricci was untiring in planning for the study of the sisters, both in extension courses during the school year and in summer, and in visiting the mission schools to observe teaching."[1] She was assisted in her supervisory work by several experienced sisters, including Sisters Joan Smith and Dunstan Tucker, both of whom would later become key administrators at Edgewood College, one as registrar, the other as dean.

By 1930 Sinsinawa Dominican teachers were studying at Illinois State Normal University in Bloomington, at the University of Illinois at Champaign-Urbana, and at Wisconsin State Teachers Colleges at Oshkosh and Milwaukee,[2] while during the twenties and thirties, and even earlier, other sisters pursued graduate studies at the University of Wisconsin, Columbia University, Catholic University of America, Fordham University, Yale, and the University of Chicago, as well as at European centers of art and music in Italy and France. This was not new in the history of the Congregation, for Sisters Catherine Wall and Angelico Dolan had studied art in Europe from 1903 to 1906, and Sisters Hyacintha Finney and Chrysostom Borstadt had pursued music studies in Europe from 1905 to 1907. Two sisters were sent to Harvard for the summer of 1906; two more were sent to Washington University for the school year 1908 – 1909; and two sisters attended the University of Chicago in l907 – 1908.[3]

A program to prepare teachers for secondary education had been developed at Rosary College in Illinois by the mid-thirties. Sister De Ricci then turned her concerns to the accelerated professional preparation of Dominican elementary school teachers. At the time it was unusual for sister school teachers to be given a semester or a year off to study; most degrees were earned slowly by attendance at summer sessions or after-school courses, or by extension work. So the assignment of ten sisters to full-time study at Edgewood in September of 1940, followed by eighteen more the next fall, was a remarkable and far-sighted step.

The purpose and curriculum of the new senior college in 1940 had been expanded from the original Associate of Arts degree program. Extensive planning had been done collaboratively by Sister De Ricci, Sister Joan and Sister Dunstan, community supervisors of teachers, and Sister Fidelis Sullivan, registrar of Rosary College.

The college catalog for 1941-42 stated the newly defined purposes and objectives:

Edgewood College is a four-year standard institution. It comprises a Junior College and a Senior College. The purpose of the first two years is to give each student a general acquaintance with the finest in history, culture, and traditions of the past. Courses are planned to include a thorough study of the social sciences in order that the student may be enabled to solve the problems presented by contemporary civilization in the light of Christian principles.

The purpose of the Senior College is to prepare qualified teachers for Art, Kindergarten-Primary and elementary schools and for Commerce in secondary schools.

A totally renovated Marshall Hall opened in February 1942 as a residence for the college students, and served as the first uniquely collegiate building on the Edgewood campus.

To fulfill these objectives the College proposes to lead the student to an understanding of the nature of the child and to a realization that education is the complete development of the individual. Realizing that thorough knowledge in subject matter is essential, the College fosters high scholastic standards. Effective teaching techniques are built up through carefully directed teaching.

Toward the end of the first year of the senior college's existence, representatives from the Wisconsin Department of Public Instruction and from the University of Wisconsin were invited to evaluate the four-year program. In the following year the new Edgewood baccalaureate program was formally recognized by both the Wisconsin DPI and the University. Broader recognition was also being sought, as indicated in the first official college reports made to the Department of Education (Universities, Colleges, and Professional Schools Division) of the National Catholic Welfare Conference. Along with the usual statistics, Sister Eunice Joy, the registrar, stated in the NCWC report for 1940: "In 1940-41, a transition year to a Four Year Teachers' Training School for Women, we are preparing for senior accreditation by the North Central Educational Association."

The senior college grew slowly but steadily during the 1940s. The two-year Associate of Arts program continued, while the four-year baccalaureate program was limited to the preparation of teachers, offering a major only in education. In 1942, a kindergarten-primary major was added under the direction of Sister Mary Rosary

Corrigan. The business department, headed by Sister Alexius Wagner, was given state accreditation for the education of high school business teachers in 1943, becoming the first Edgewood College department to prepare students for secondary school teaching.

The Sinsinawa Dominicans had been involved in education from the days of their foundation in the 1840s—whether teaching in public schools, in their early history, or in parish or private schools. Their founder, Father Samuel Mazzuchelli, had stressed quality of preparation and excellence in the teaching process, and from the earliest years he had encouraged the study of music, art, languages, and science in the sisters' schools. The Dominicans' General Chapter of 1925 reminded all the Sinsinawa sisters of the need for professional improvement, of courtesy and loyalty among school staff members, the strict prohibition of corporal punishment, and concern for the students' welfare.   Not only Chapters of the Congregation, but the frequent letters sent by Mother Samuel and Sister De Ricci to all the sisters during this period, as well as the suggestions and visits of school supervisors, reinforced these ideals of good teaching. Excellence in teaching was the continuing hallmark of Sinsinawa Dominican schools.

The new focus of the senior college at Edgewood on teacher preparation was thus a natural one for the sisters. The curriculum of the first two years remained firmly based on the liberal arts core of the Associate of Arts program, while the junior and senior years were devoted to the professional preparation of kindergarten, primary, and elementary school teachers, and high school teachers of business. The program was designed not only to provide an excellent education for the Dominican sisters who would teach in schools from California to New York, and from Minneapolis to Mobile, but also for those lay women who chose to attend the senior college.   Sister Mary Rosary Corrigan, whose leadership from 1942 established a remarkably creative and influential kindergarten program at Edgewood, recalled the first lay student in her new program:

> Olivette Kennedy, a junior in the College, signed up for the new major. In addition to her regular courses, she was involved in observing in the kindergarten and first grade [at Edgewood's campus school]. During her senior year she did her student teaching on campus at the kindergarten and first grade levels. She graduated in June 1944 and proudly accepted a position teaching in the Mauston Public Schools.[4]

The entrance of the United States into World War II shook Edgewood faculty and students, along with the rest of the country, many of whom had hoped to remain "on the sidelines" as war raged in Europe and in Asia. One student recalled the fateful day when the illusion of isolationism was shattered:

> December 7, 1941, when Pearl Harbor was bombed, was a Sunday, and we were all studying for finals coming up. But nobody could study that evening. We stayed up and listened to the radio and took turns praying in the chapel.[5]

In the Edgewood chapel during the war years, prayers could be mixed with tears and anxiety, awaiting news of and letters from brothers and boyfriends, relatives and hometown heroes away in Europe or the Pacific. It was difficult to keep one's mind on studies when war news filled the newspapers and the radio waves. One graduate recalled,

We all gathered around the radio on the nights when President Roosevelt gave his fireside chats. We were intensely patriotic and everyone learned to knit and made khaki-colored socks for the brave fighting men. Everyone had a brother or a cousin in the war and we exchanged addresses and acquired a list of pen-pals and wrote friendly letters to soldiers. We felt we were doing our bit—and, besides, it was romantic, too.[6]

The sisters, too, had relatives at the front and their prayers joined with those of the students for the safety of loved ones and the end to the war. One week after the Pearl Harbor bombing, Mother Samuel wrote to all the sisters: "Our best contribution to the defense of our four freedoms will be a self-sacrificing spirit and the keeping of the two great commandments of love of God and love of our neighbor." The Dominican community also had anxious moments after the outbreak of the war in Europe about the fate of four of their sisters in Switzerland at the Villa des Fougères. Two of the sisters in Fribourg, Sisters Andreas Goetz and Paulina Coughlin, had sailed home from Europe in June 1940. However, the two others— Sisters Rodolpha Rudolph and Marie Louise Oughton— remained for two more years, finally arriving in New York on the *Grottingholm* on June 1, 1942. One can only imagine the relief of their Dominican sisters when news came of their safe return.

Sacred Heart Chapel was an important place of private and communal prayer on campus for students and sisters. The concerns of the war years brought many to the old chapel with its beautiful stained glass windows and oak pews.

An alumna who was at Edgewood College during the war years recalled that "there weren't too many dates, although a few of us had friends among the airmen stationed at Truax Field."[7] One 1942 editorial in the college newspaper, *The Tower Torch*, written shortly after the U.S. entered the war, proclaimed that "the draft affects after-school pastimes of Edgewoodites.... Fewer and fewer dates will be available."[8] The annual winter formal dance that same winter of 1942 attracted one hundred couples—its theme being "Victory," and its grand marshal a tall Uncle Sam. The draft had not yet had its full impact on college-age men, although photos of that dance show some men in uniform. By May of 1943, however, a writer in the college newspaper indicated a more somber mood among the Edgewood college women:

Gradually, though, the conversation changed to the more vital news—news of the latest 'post-office-address' in Frisco or the shocking tragedy of the death of a friend in the service less than a year. Even the records failed to cheer the atmosphere. Songs such as, 'You'd Be So Nice to Come Home To' and 'Don't Get Around Much Anymore' are just too realistic…. The peaceful serenity of the home town was not comforting—the shadows of all those old friends walked with you and your thoughts marched along with them. Questions, fears, hopes, and prayers all passed through your mind. But the only one that gave you any peace was prayer.[9]

The social life of the young women at Edgewood during the war years was often limited to parties on campus, despite the flu epidemic and the effects of coffee and sugar rationing, spontaneous get-togethers in the "rec room," or to correspondence with young men away at military bases or at APO addresses around the world, as well as walks along the shores of Lake Wingra or excursions to movies down town. The years 1940 and 1941 offered great film-going, with openings of John Ford's *The Grapes of Wrath* and *How Green Was My Valley*, Charlie Chaplin's *The Great Dictator*, John Huston's *The Maltese Falcon*, Disney's *Fantasia*, and Orson Welles' *Citizen Kane*, while the college newspaper listed Humphrey Bogart, Spencer Tracy, Katherine Hepburn and Greer Garson among the students' favorite stars, with Jack Benny topping the list of favorite radio programs. *The Tower Torch*, college newspaper of the forties, also noted that students' activities included bowling on Friday nights, listening to records (Harry James, Count Basie, Woody Herman, Hoagy Carmichael, and Duke Ellington were favorites in the winter of 1942), or visiting Monroe Street drugstores for a coke or an ice cream soda.

Some students volunteered as U.S.O. hostesses meeting socially with service men. One unit was formed at Edgewood College, under the direction of Mrs. Lyons, housemother in Marshall Hall since the fall of 1942, while another group met on Sundays at nearby Blessed Sacrament parish. Strict rules prevailed, and students were told that "hostesses must come to the party and leave the party unescorted by service men," and they "must agree not to smoke on the dance floor and not to drink hard liquor while on duty."[10] Since Edgewood College students were forbidden to drink alcoholic beverages either on or off-campus, this latter requirement should not have surprised them. Other students considered joining the WAACS or WAVES or WAFS or SPARS, the women's branches of U.S. military units, and a WAVES recruiting officer visited the campus in the fall of 1942. *The Tower Torch* regularly reported the names of alumnae who had joined the women's military units or who were working in war-related services.

During the war years, "victory gardens" were a must for any homeowner with land, and Edgewood's acres offered extensive opportunities,

Edgewood College Archives

Marshall Hall residents enjoyed canasta and bridge games, as well as listening to radio programs and phonograph records in their leisure moments during the 1940s.

as the convent annalist noted in 1943: "Edgewood had a large victory garden. The sisters from St. Raphael's, St. Patrick's, and Blessed Sacrament convents also had gardens on the Edgewood farm," as did a number of neighbors from the vicinity. The college student newspaper also ran a feature article on "Victory Gardens" in its March 1943 issue.

Student activities during the 40s were largely on-campus, although drama students presented three plays on WIBA, a Madison radio station, in April 1943, under the direction of Sister Marie Aileen. Many students participated in the college music programs such as the Glee Club or one of the two Schola groups. Sister Justinia Kress was director of all choral groups from 1945 to 1958, and, like the administrators of the College, she wore a number of hats during the forties, directing several Glee Clubs in the high school and college, teaching Fundamentals of Music, the Teaching of Music, and a course on Liturgical Music in the College, along with demonstration teaching and supervising of student teachers in the campus grade school. Sister Justinia later said that "the days at Edgewood were wonderful ones, even though very difficult. What I remember most are the wonderful young women I worked with and the spirit of the faculty as we struggled through the growth process."[11]

Madison was established as a new diocese in January of 1946, with the Most Reverend William P. O'Connor as its first bishop. He knew the Dominican Sisters well, having been their student at St. John's High School in Milwaukee. The new bishop quickly established close ties with Edgewood, and he was often present at graduations and ceremonies on the Edgewood campus. He invited the college students to provide a Diocesan Broadcast Choir, under Sister Justinia's direction, in 1946 when a Madison radio station, WKOW, began carrying "The Madison Catholic Hour" weekly. The choir members also gave concerts during the year, including one each Christmas time for Bishop O'Connor of Madison at his home on Lake Mendota.

During the 1940s Sister Edward Blackwell not only taught music but also offered a special course in "Fine Arts" that was remembered vividly by college students. One, who was a student in 1947, recalled that Sister Edward "gave us a sense of beauty and a taste for the arts.... but most importantly, I remember her—a woman of great refinement, charm, and understanding. I don't believe that her students could ever forget her."[12]

Music was always important at Edgewood, but the forties brought added excitement to the campus with the presence of world-famous musicians Nadia Boulanger and Igor Stravinsky. During the summer of 1943 Nadia Boulanger, renowned French teacher of composition, came to Edgewood to teach about forty Dominican sisters who were music teachers, and to be "the sisters' house guest for the summer."[13] The annalist noted that "each Wednesday evening she gave a concert-lecture which was open to the Madison public. Many of the members of the music department of the University of Wisconsin attended; they expressed much appreciation to Edgewood for the opportunity to hear Mlle Boulanger." This exciting summer music program was repeated the following summer, in 1944, when Boulanger returned to Edgewood to work with twelve sister music teachers. During the second summer she gave two public concerts—on July 30 and August 2,

The student choir performed on radio station WKOW for the "Madison Catholic Hour" during the 1940s and 1950s. Sister Justinia Kress directed the choral music during these years.

performing and discussing works by Bach, Brahms, Milhaud, Fauré, and Stravinsky. On August 2, she presented the world premiere of Stravinsky's *Sonata for Two Pianos*. The renowned teacher also directed a choir in singing Palestrina's *Missa Brevis* at Mass on St. Dominic's Day, August 4. These visits by Boulanger were due to her friendship with Sister Edward, who had been her student in Paris. The link with Sister Edward also resulted in the visit of Igor Stravinsky, her teacher and friend, to Edgewood in January of 1944. He presented a public lecture-concert entitled "Composing, Performing, Listening," on January 23.

Sister Edward's friendships with Boulanger and Stravinsky, begun when she was a student in Europe in the 1930s, continued until the deaths of both famous musicians. In a way, Sister Edward's musical friendships paralleled Sister Marie Aileen's friendship with Helen Hayes—and in both cases, the visits of world-renowned artists to campus not only enriched the educational climate of Edgewood but also provided an unforgettable experience for those students who were privileged to meet Hayes or Boulanger or Stravinsky.

In 1941, the construction of a separate laundry building and boiler house enabled the college to convert the old stone carriage house into Marshall Hall, a residence with twenty-eight bedrooms and several common rooms for the college students. Marshall Hall was the first of the distinctively collegiate buildings on

Nadia Boulanger and Sister Edward Blackwell on the Edgewood campus in the summer of 1944.

campus. Up until the completion of its renovation and occupancy in February 1942, college students had to share facilities in both the "old" and "new" buildings with the students of the other two schools. The population of the college steadily increased, and had the war not intervened more building would undoubtedly have been done, since classroom and living space was growing severely limited. However, building plans were put on hold, awaiting the end of the war and better times ahead.

The move of college residents into the renovated Marshall Hall in February of 1942 helped develop a new *esprit de corps* among all students, since day students also now had a new place to "hang out," in lounges and the Marshall "rec room" as well as in resident students' living quarters. When Helen Hayes visited Sister Marie Aileen in February 1942, she also met with the college students in their Marshall Hall "rec room" where she gave autographs to all who asked. On leaving, "Miss Hayes' parting words to the girls were that she envied them their beautiful new home," wrote the *Tower Torch* reporter proudly.

On April 12, 1945, when Madison newspaper extra editions announced President Franklin Roosevelt's sudden death, classes were cancelled at Edgewood, and students and faculty alike joined the nation in mourning the death of the President. Not long afterwards, on May 8, 1945, the end of the war in Europe, "VE Day," was celebrated on campus with special prayer services, and all of Edgewood joined the nation in jubilant rejoicing With the surrender of Japan in August of 1945, the post-war era and the nuclear age had begun.

In September of 1945, seventy-eight students were enrolled in the college, with forty-two residents packed into limited spaces. Although double-decker beds had been placed in Marshall Hall rooms, the "increased number of resident college students necessitated the use of the Tower, redecorated and newly furnished."[14] When Sister Joan Smith replaced Sister Eunice Joy as registrar in September of 1946, ninety-one students were enrolled in the college, and the annalist explained that due to lack of space some applicants had to be turned down that fall. At a meeting of the administrative officers of the college, October 4, 1946, a key problem surfaced:

Edgewood College Archives

Sister Marie Aileen Klein and Helen Hayes with college students in Marshall Hall, February 1942.

"Before the meeting began, Sister Mary Hope said that she could not possibly take care of the business of the college and at the same time be principal of the high school.... She could not do justice to either if she attempted to do both. She said that she had given all the college responsibilities to Sister Dunstan [the dean].... Therefore, any matters relating to the college would have to be taken up with Sister Dunstan."   As that meeting continued, the minutes record that "Sister Dunstan reported a message she had received that day from Sister De Ricci asking her to get in contact with Mr. Flad to see how much progress he was making for the plans for the new college building." Sister De Ricci continued to press for completion of these plans as the space situation grew worse in the fall of 1947, when 110 college students were enrolled. Even with the increased space added with the renovation of Marshall Hall, and with the use of the Tower as a student residence, college students still competed for classroom space with high school and campus school students in the old academy and the newer building.

Although through the years the largest groups of college students were from Wisconsin and Illinois, a broader dimension was added in 1948, when two Chinese students from Shanghai, and two Latin American students—one from Cali, Colombia, and the other from Arequipa, Peru—were enrolled. In that year, 106 women were enrolled in the college, fifty-six of whom were residents, necessitating the conversion of the former chaplain's residence at the corner of Jefferson Street and Edgewood Avenue into a "dormitory which has been called Washburn Hall," housing nine students and two sisters—this in a small four-bedroom house whose kitchen, living and dining rooms were converted to bedrooms. At this point, only three areas of the Edgewood campus were uniquely "collegiate"—Marshall Hall, Washburn Hall, and the Tower—and all were overflowing. Further enrollment growth of the college was limited, as Sister Joan Smith, the registrar, noted in a letter of December 1948:

> *Our growth has not been rapid, due primarily to two factors: we lack space to accommodate more resident students, and the State University in the same city is more attractive to day students. We have our plans all ready to build but have hesitated because of high costs and difficulty in getting materials.*[15]

The plans mentioned here were ones developed by architect John Flad and Associates in 1946 when the Congregation had approved planning for a new college building, but projected construction costs for the new college building totaled nearly a million dollars—while total college income in 1948 was only $40,218.60. Extensive fund-raising would be needed, and the annalist records that "the school year 1948 – 1949 was ushered in by the launching of an Edgewood School Building Fund Drive." During 1947 and 1948, Sisters De Ricci, Dunstan, and Joan met frequently with Mother Samuel, Leo T. Crowley, Bishop O'Connor, and John Flad, among others, regarding the need for a Madison area fund-drive. In November of 1948, Sister De Ricci launched her own fund drive, writing to all the sisters of the congregation regarding the Madison fund drive effort. She encouraged each sister to make an individual donation of $1.00, returning a booklet of slips, each of which offered a chance to win an "exquisite eider down coverlet" that had been given to her.[16]

While the need for new buildings was a dominant concern of the 1940s, other issues regarding the college remained. Many of the faculty still taught both college

Angus McVicar
Wisconsin Historical Society   WHi-2256

The Edgewood Drive, West End,   January 19, 1945.

The temporary closing of Edgewood's "Park and Pleasure Drive"
in January 1945 was an attempt by the Dominican Sisters to recover the
private use of the road by closing it to motor car and truck traffic.

In a 1904 agreement between St. Clara College—the Dominican Sisters'
corporate name and thus the owner of the Edgewood property— and the
Madison Park and Pleasure Drive Association, the road was opened for
public use strictly as a "pleasure drive" with the fencing and upkeep first
the Association's and later the city's responsibility.

The dispute over use of the drive went to a city court in January of 1946,
and the decision, not favorable to Edgewood, was handed down in April of
that year. Subsequent court appeals were made, but in vain, and the road
remained open to public access, with the city agreeing to keep the road
and fences in good condition and to post signs prohibiting truck traffic.

and high school courses during the day, while the multiple roles taken by the nominal college presidents, Sister Rose Catherine Leonard (1939-44) and Sister Mary Hope O'Brien (1944-50) meant that focused leadership and strong impetus to future development of the college was not possible, although the deans—Sister Marie Aileen Klein and Sister Dunstan Tucker—tried to carry that burden. As one person later recalled, when Sister Joan Smith came to Edgewood as registrar in 1946, the outlook for the college "was almost enough to discourage the bravest heart."[17]

Although Sister De Ricci and the administrators of the college were determined to strengthen the senior college,[18] continued growth was obviously impossible without new buildings. Questions of laboratory space and of library facilities and collections were pressing matters for a college that was seeking North Central Association accreditation.[19] New leadership was also needed in order to sustain and extend the fund-raising initiatives crucial for expansion and growth. As the 1940s ended, Edgewood College faced a challenging moment, another turning point in its history.

CHAPTER FIVE

Growth and Expansion *1950-1968*

The year 1950 will always be remembered in Edgewood College's history as a critical turning point. Sister De Ricci Fitzgerald's death in February 1950 signaled the departure of one of Edgewood College's strongest supporters among the administrators of the Dominican congregation. Much of the correspondence between Edgewood College officials and the congregation, from the establishment of the college in 1927 through the thirties and forties, had been directed to and from Sister De Ricci. Her tireless efforts first to establish and then to strengthen Edgewood College were remarkable. Not only would she be greatly missed, but also the centennial General Chapter in June 1949 had brought a new administration with the election of Sister Mary Evelyn Murphy as Mother General, after forty years of leadership by Sister Mary Samuel Coughlin and Sister De Ricci. Surely the sisters at Edgewood must have wondered how the new congregation administrators would respond to Edgewood's pressing needs for buildings, for financial support, for faculty, and especially for new leadership.

The response was not long in coming. The new Mother General, Sister Mary Evelyn Murphy, visited the Edgewood campus on June 10, 1950, and spoke to all the sisters saying, "My own attitude toward the college has changed within the past year. Now I can see, as I couldn't in the past, a definite need for a college such as Edgewood is intended to be." She went on to indicate what she saw as a three-fold direction for the college—the preparation of excellent teachers (both religious and lay), the combination of liberal arts education with professional education, and the building of a new elementary school as a practice and demonstration school connected with the teacher education program of the college.[1] Her words reassured the Edgewood sisters about her commitment to their cause. Now, with the wholehearted support of the congregation's new leaders, Edgewood College could move forward.

Edgewood College Archives

From an Old Building to a New Campus
In the early 1950s, college students and staff used the old Sacred Heart Academy building, but soon new construction began, and a college campus took shape during the decade with De Ricci Hall as the academic center.

More significantly, these congregation leaders soon appointed a new president of the college—Sister Mary Nona McGreal. On August 24, 1950, she joined the out-going dean, Sister Mary Dunstan; the new dean, Sister Jane Frances Weber; the registrar, Sister Joan Smith; and Sister Mary Rosary Corrigan, head of the Department of Education, in a meeting that would mark a new era in the history of Edgewood College. The minutes of that first meeting of the college administrators with their new president state that the discussion centered around "the pressing need for expansion," "prospects for enrollment," and the academic program. The most telling sentences of those minutes, however, record the fact that "the enthusiasm of the President created an atmosphere of greater optimism for the future. She said, 'Edgewood has great possibilities and we shall develop them.'"[2]

The record of the years of Sister Nona's administration—between 1950 and 1968—is a remarkable one. Her vision for Edgewood College and her ability as a leader on all levels enabled the college to "begin again," to move to a level of accomplishment that few thought possible. At the age of thirty-seven, she began her administration as the first real president of Edgewood College, the first person to serve full-time in that role and to devote her energies to the direction and development of the college. This is not to underestimate the leadership and direction given by the deans who served before her—Sister Marie Aileen Klein and Sister Dunstan Tucker. Nor is it to underestimate the team who worked with her in the formative years of the 1950s—Sister Joan Smith, Sister Jane Frances Weber, and Sister Mary Rosary Corrigan.   Nonetheless, during the first fifty years of the college's existence, no single person had a greater role in the expansion and development of Edgewood College than Sister Mary Nona McGreal.

In less than a month after her arrival, the minutes of the college administrators' meeting record their discussion of a revised college program, "a curriculum for the education of teachers on Christian social principles," the placing of "theology at the core and basis of the curriculum," the need for new faculty, the re-vitalization of student life on campus with the aim of helping students "develop scholarship and Christian living ideals," and the immediate need for physical expansion—"a new separate college building, a new elementary school."[3] An ambitious agenda, but the leadership team was in place to make the dream a reality.

During that first semester, the fall of 1950, Sister Nona and her team faced severe obstacles. Only three administrators and three faculty members served full-time on the college staff with fifteen part-time faculty, most of whom taught both in the college and the high school. The "Edgewood Building Fund" drive begun in 1948 and aimed at raising $100,000 had ground to a halt, while the plans for a new college building costing nearly one million dollars had been put on hold. Resident students were overflowing existing residence space, the faculty were few and over-burdened, the possibility of national accreditation seemed remote, and the Dominican congregation was itself in the midst of other extensive building plans— St. Dominic Villa in Dubuque had just been completed and the Fine Arts Building at Rosary College had just been begun. On the Edgewood campus, the offices of principal of the high school, principal of the grade school, and president of the college had finally been separated in 1950, but Sister Nona still served as the prioress or superior of all the sisters on campus, a situation not resolved until 1955. This

Edgewood College Archives

Sister Mary Nona McGreal, O.P. President of Edgewood College from 1950 to 1968; Ph.D., Catholic University of America.

complex situation involving three schools as well as a large religious community inevitably gave rise at times to internal conflicts of interest.

Sister Nona's eighteen years as president of Edgewood College are difficult to summarize. One may single out, however, six areas of critical importance:

- creating the college campus, through an extensive building program
- enlarging and strengthening the faculty
- obtaining national accreditation and recognition for educational excellence
- shaping a stronger curriculum
- establishing a new corporate structure and a lay board of advisors
- increasing student enrollment while developing a diverse student body.

Creation of a College Campus

In her 1967 report, *XVI Years of Growth*, Sister Nona provided an overview of her creation of the college campus, saying "the campus environment, while not the most essential element, is an important factor in the study and daily life of the college community." She then noted that until the beginning of her term as president, "a large part of the land remained unused," this being the farm, orchard, pasture, and wooded acres on the southern and western parts of the fifty-five acres given by Governor Washburn. It was in this direction, then, that she set her sights on building a new Edgewood College campus.

In 1950 space was severely limited for all three educational institutions at Edgewood. For this reason, the "Edgewood Building Fund Drive" brochure issued in September of 1948 stated that "all three levels of Catholic education—grade

Edgewood College Archives

Planning a New College Campus
Sister Mary Nona McGreal, president, points out the features of the new Regina Hall and St. Joseph Chapel and Library to her administrative colleagues: Sister Calasancta Wright, business officer; Sister Joan Smith, registrar; Sister Cajetan Spelman, dean of sister students; and Sister Jane Frances Weber, dean.

school, high school, and college—will be provided with more room and greater facilities." Potential donors were further told that "expansion of the high school and grade school facilities, along with those of the college, will give Edgewood a complete, well-rounded program." With this in mind, and with limited funds, Sister Nona acted quickly to move toward erecting the first new building: the Edgewood Campus School.[4]

At a meeting on Sunday, September 30, 1951, Sister Nona, Sister Joan, and Sister Jane Frances determined to take action regarding "the advisability and possibility of building an elementary school for Edgewood College." Later that same day, the three sisters met with the architect for the newly constructed Queen of Peace school on Madison's west side. During the discussion, Sister Nona explained the situation:

Edgewood needs more space: the high school, the grade school, the college are crowded and need more room. We had a program for building a college, and work was to have begun in July 1948, but this fell through. Since we have not the money to build a college, we have thought of erecting a new grade school and putting many of the college classes in the old building [where the grades had been].

As Edgewood moved to implement this decision, the original estimate of about $200,000 for the building was seen to be inadequate, and the figure of $300,000 was projected as more realistic. Another fund drive was begun in 1952, as construction began.

Not only did the new Campus School provide an excellent facility for its young students, but the vacated space in the old Sacred Heart Academy building enabled relocation of college classrooms and offices into this area—a helpful move, though not an entirely satisfactory solution since even the president's office had to be used at times during the day for small classes.

To increase college enrollment, more residence space was desperately needed, so in 1953, a loan was obtained from the Sinsinawa Dominican congregation to build an addition to Marshall Hall, a connected residence wing called "Marshall Junior." This was evidently seen as a limited solution rather than a long range plan, because during 1954 the college administrators and faculty were engaged in an extensive study of the plan for a new large residence hall.

The next actual building, however, was designed to meet the need for college science laboratories and classrooms. Mazzuchelli Biological Station was the first college building to be constructed on the "new campus," directly on the shore of Lake Wingra, while plans were under way for building a student residence, Regina Hall. It was hoped that a new government low-interest loan program for college student housing might be obtained to make possible the construction of this new dormitory. Lewis Siberz, who had been the Campus School architect, was engaged again to develop plans for the residence hall. In September 1955, Sister Nona informed the administrators of the college that Bishop O'Connor had called

to say that he was signing papers approving the erection of the projected college buildings.... including the science building which is to be called the Samuel Mazzuchelli Biological Station and the college dormitory to be known as Regina Mundi Hall.... The Bishop said that he wanted the College here in Madison and that he will give it his moral support.

A related concern was that if the Mazzuchelli Biological Station on Lake Wingra were not quickly erected, the college might be in danger of losing its rights to the property on the lake side of the Edgewood Drive.[5]

During the fall of 1955, many meetings were held to discuss the proposed buildings—not only the Mazzuchelli Biological Station and the new student residence hall with attached chapel, but also a new classroom and administrative office building, as well as library space, a fine arts building, a gymnasium, and a residence for the sister faculty. The evolving plans and specific college needs were continually being discussed during this period with Sister Mary Benedicta Larkin, who had been elected as Mother General of the Sinsinawa Dominicans in the General Chapter of July 1955, and with the college faculty.

Sister Nona and the other administrators drew up a Campus Master Plan in their meeting of November 8, 1955, agreeing on the following:

It was the consensus that

1. The proposed dormitory be constructed as planned near the campus school, directly in front of the new parking lot, facing Lake Wingra and the science building.

2. The chapel be built west of the dormitory and adjacent to it, underneath which would be a large room which would serve temporarily as a cafeteria and assembly room for the campus school.

3. Another dormitory be built, when needed, on the opposite side of the chapel, which would serve as a residence for the sisters.

4. The classroom building be built near Woodrow Avenue and the new road that leads through the property to the parking lot.

5. The administration and library building would be placed near Woodrow and just south of the classroom building.

6. The fine arts building for the departments of music, art, and speech, including a little theater, would be built in the southwest corner of the property bounded by Woodrow and the Lake Drive. An auditorium could be added to this building.

7. The faculty house would be west of the fine arts building and near the chapel.

8. The gymnasium would be near the parking lot and would take care of the needs of the college and the campus school.

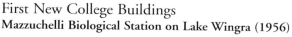

Edgewood College Archives

Edgewood College Archives

First New College Buildings
Mazzuchelli Biological Station on Lake Wingra (1956)   **Regina Hall (1957)**

This extensive master plan, drawn up when no college building had actually been constructed on the southwest acres of the Edgewood property, is evidence of the remarkable visionary quality of Sister Nona's leadership. Like the great architect and city planner Daniel Burnham, her perception was— "Make no little plans, they have no magic."

In 1956, the Mazzuchelli Biological Station was built on the lake shore, followed over the next nine years by Regina Hall (1957), St. Joseph Chapel and Library (1958), De Ricci Hall (1960), the Gymnasium (1961), and Weber Hall Apartments (1965). In subsequent years, more elements of a Campus Master Plan would be added, but by the conclusion of Sister Nona's presidency in 1968, a nearly complete college campus had been established.

Enlarging and Strengthening the Faculty

While energy and time were being expended on building a college campus, the essential purpose of the college as a Dominican institution of higher education was being strengthened, especially in the areas of faculty development and related curricular enhancement.

When Sister Nona first took office as president in 1950, the college had three administrators: president, dean, and registrar—with the first two regularly teaching part-time. Only three faculty members were full-time teachers in the college, while the fifteen other college faculty members were part-time, with most of these teaching also in the high school. Sister Nona saw that just as the college needed a separate campus with its own physical facilities, a separate college faculty with full-time members was also a sine qua non for a healthy future.

Edgewood College Archives

College Campus— by 1965

Her efforts at building the faculty are evident in both the correspondence exchanged with the Congregation officials at the Motherhouse and in the additions of both sister and lay faculty each year. Before 1950, the faculty was almost entirely staffed by Sinsinawa Dominican sisters. While a few lay women had been employed as part-time faculty before Sister Nona's presidency, the proportion of lay faculty quickly increased. In 1955, the college had five full-time sister administrators (two of whom also taught part-time), fifteen full-time and ten part-time faculty, including nine lay teachers. The first full-time male lay faculty member, Robert Young, was hired for the academic year 1955-56. By 1960, ten years into her presidency, Sister Nona had increased the full-time faculty to twenty-six, including three lay women and two lay men, with ten part-time faculty, half of whom were lay. By 1967-68, in Sister Nona's final year as president, there were thirty-two lay men and women serving among the forty-two full-time and nineteen part-time faculty.

In the fall of 1963, four new full-time lay faculty were hired who were to spend the rest of their academic careers at Edgewood, becoming pillars of the faculty community: Jewell Fitzgerald in theater, Daniel James Guilfoil in philosophy, Michael Lybarger in history, and Joseph Schmiedicke in education. The first lay department chairpersons were elected by their departments in 1964: Daniel James Guilfoil, philosophy, and Kenneth Stofflet, mathematics. The first lay members in administrative offices were Greta Shetney in public relations, Jeanne Mikulec in admissions and student loans, and Wilma Sanks in student aid. John Butler was appointed director of public relations in 1966 and director of development in 1968, becoming the first lay member of the administrative team.

One important aspect of enlarging the faculty during Sister Nona's administration was the encouragement of a more diverse collegial body. Mary Pothen, a native of India who was completing doctoral studies at the University of Wisconsin, taught in the social science department at Edgewood during 1954-55 and served as housemother at Washburn House, a student residence on Jefferson Street. The first African-American faculty member, Sharon Wexler, joined the foreign language department in 1956, while she was completing her doctorate in French. In 1957, she was promoted to assistant professor, remaining at the college until 1960. At this time, there were fewer than 1,500 African-Americans in Madison, and discrimination was still commonly experienced.[6]

During the early 1960s, as more lay faculty and staff joined the Edgewood community, the administration recognized the need to provide them with a living wage and group hospital and medical co-pay insurance; yet at the same time the concomitant need to raise tuition was evident.[7] Student tuition remained in the lower

Edgewood College Archives

Sharon Wexler teaching French
During the late fifties, Sister Catherine Moran and Sharon Wexler were the full-time members of the foreign language department, the former teaching Spanish and the latter French. Here the students are using the latest "language lab" audio equipment.

quartile for Wisconsin private colleges throughout this period, while the administration struggled to keep the college affordable while balancing increasing costs.

Throughout these years, the Dominican sister administrators, staff, and faculty received only stipends (basic living expenses), while the differential between the stipend and the normal salary at the appropriate rank was put on the college books as Dominican "contributed services." These contributed services remained the largest annual support amounts for the college throughout the 1950s and 1960s. For example, in 1960-1961, the contributed services of the Dominican sisters was $179,610, while gifts and grants from government or all other sources equaled only $26,128. In 1967-1968, the contributed services amounted to $289,250, while gifts and grants from other sources equaled $64,310.[8]

The separation of the college and high school faculties was nearly complete in 1954-1955. This separation, which had been requested by both Sister Nona and by the principal of the high school, enabled each faculty to focus on its own distinctive mission and direction. In the summer of 1954, the college administrators planned the first of the three-day August "Faculty Seminars," which were to have two purposes: "to open up the organization of the college for discussion, exploring its weaknesses and its points of strength," and "to create *esprit de corps*."[9] Sister Nona's aims were clear—first, to engage the faculty and staff in "creating a college" by involving them regularly in discussion of issues and directions, and, second, to build a vital community at Edgewood College. When De Ricci hall was being planned, Sister Nona suggested having "study teams [of faculty and staff] as we did when planning the Campus School," adding that these teams should visit other colleges, see the latest institutional structures, and assess needs for classroom sizes and furnishings.[10]

Also by 1954 plans were underway to establish academic rank and appropriate salary schedules for all faculty, using criteria based on national research for colleges and universities focusing on teacher education.[11] The president had appointed the first department chairs, but she quickly moved to have department members elect their chair, a position to be rotated among the members every two years. Similarly, by 1956, the administration decided to have the faculty elect a member to serve on the administrative team. By 1957, two elected faculty members joined the administrators on the Administrative Council, whose purpose was "to advise the President."

Another aspect of strengthening the faculty was ensuring the quality of teaching and scholarship. One dimension of that concern involved the paucity of advanced degrees held by faculty and administrators. In 1950, during Sister Nona's first year, three of the six full-time administrators/faculty held doctoral degrees, and none of the part-time faculty did. By 1968, twenty-three of the faculty held doctorates or comparable advanced degrees, such as the J.D., S.T.D., or M.F.A, and fourteen more were at doctoral candidacy status.

As the college faculty grew in numbers, Sister Nona's desire to create a strong *esprit de corps* led to the creation of some faculty meetings just for exchange and socializing among the faculty, and the holding of faculty suppers with spouses of faculty as guests. In 1962, the administration offered spouses of full-time lay faculty the opportunity to take courses for credit without tuition expense, and, later, faculty children were offered this benefit. Because most of the administrators and faculty had offices and taught in De Ricci Hall, gatherings around the single coffee urn on the second floor facilitated conversation and generated inter-disciplinary interchange on a familiar basis, including the postman who regularly dropped in after morning mail delivery.

Obtaining Accreditation

Formal accreditation was absolutely necessary for advancing the college to a position of recognized educational quality.   In 1940, when the four-year degree program began, Edgewood College sought accreditation by the University of Wisconsin as a teachers college offering a Bachelor of Science degree.   In the spring of 1942, before the first bachelor's degrees were awarded, the University's recognition was given. Also in 1942, the Wisconsin Department of Public Instruction declared that "as an accredited institution, the College graduates are eligible for state licensing and the commercial curriculum is approved."[12]   During 1950, the college applied for and obtained affiliation with the Catholic University of America, through its Committee on Affiliation and Extension.

Edgewood College Archives

Conversations and Coffee
Faculty, staff, and administrators met to discuss news, politics, academic policies and ideas, and occasionally to bet on when Lake Wingra would freeze—all while crowded into the tiny faculty/staff "kitchenette" near the De Ricci mail boxes.

Joe Schmiedicke (education) makes a point while Jim Guilfoil (philosophy) asks "what is the meaning of it all" and Sister Mariam Yaeger (psychology) analyzes the discussion.

Broader recognition became a pressing concern, and plans were considered in the 1940s to prepare for accreditation by the North Central Association of Colleges and Secondary Schools. However, officials at the college and in the congregation recognized that the existing limitations then—lack of physical facilities, an inadequate library collection, and joint appointments of faculty to both high school and college teaching— precluded any hope of successfully applying for regional accreditation.

During her first year in office, on March 22, 1951, Sister Nona, together with the dean Sister Jane Frances, and the registrar Sister Joan, met with Dr. H.A. Pochmann, chairman of the College Accreditation Committee of the University of Wisconsin, to consult about the type of degrees the college should give in the light of preparing for North Central Association accreditation. The minutes of that meeting record the conversation:

Our problem is: Should we work toward being a liberal arts college offering a B.A. degree for preparing teachers, or as a teachers college offering a B.S. degree as we have been doing? We explained that we were working toward accreditation by the North Central Association of Colleges and Universities, and we were asking his advice.... When asked what we would have to do in order to offer a B. A. degree, Dr. Pochmann said that we would probably need eight or nine 'good strong majors'... strong in content.[13]

The discussion concluded with the agreement that continuing to concentrate on the preparation of teachers and offering the Bachelor of Science degree was the most feasible route to go in seeking North Central accreditation.

Plans for a self-study, using the criteria of institutional excellence outlined by the North Central Association, were initially discussed by members of the administration in September of 1954. In January 1956, concern about application for accreditation from the North Central Association, along with the lingering question of offering a Bachelor of Arts degree, surfaced with more urgency in the discussions between the college's administrative officers and the officials of the congregation.[14] In late January, Mother Benedicta Larkin and her council wrote to Sister Nona saying that Edgewood College should go ahead and make application to the North Central Association as a teachers college, offering the Bachelor of Science degree, but that the college should continue to expand its programs and at a later date consider the matter of adding more liberal arts majors.

In early September 1956, faculty committees were set up to prepare the comprehensive self-study needed to apply for North Central Association accreditation. The examining team came to campus in January 1958, and the official accreditation approval letter was joyfully received at Edgewood in March of 1958. The report of the examining team was laudatory, pointing to many distinctive strengths:

Good administrator-teacher relationships pay excellent dividends in useful ideas and esprit de corps....   The president is a remarkably able leader and does in fact integrate the work of the institution without discouraging the contributions of others....

Of the 372 students graduated, 151 have done graduate work in 28 universities. No graduate of Edgewood has been denied admission to a graduate school....

Professional education... is imaginatively conceived, carefully executed, and constitutes a kind of pioneering venture....   It has the merit of avoiding fragmentation and needless repetition.[15]

The examiners were further impressed by the "total single-minded dedication of the faculty to their work as scholars and teachers," though they noted that relatively few held doctorates, and recommended that this lack be remedied. Other recommendations suggested that more liberal arts majors be developed for students who were preparing to teach in high schools, that more upper-level courses in the arts and sciences be offered, that more faculty be employed, and that the physical plant be expanded [at this time, De Ricci hall and the gymnasium were being planned but had not been built]. During the ten years between this initial accreditation and the time of the next North Central self-study in 1967, those recommendations would all be implemented.

In 1959, Edgewood College became a member of the Association of American Colleges, and began to prepare to apply for accreditation by the National Council for the Accreditation of Teacher Education. An NCATE team visited the college in January 1961, but the application for accreditation was "deferred." In February 1962, a second visit was made, and Edgewood College received NCATE accreditation the following June. In 1963 the college was approved for membership in the American Association of University Women.

During 1966-67 the college community again was engaged in an extensive self-study in preparation for the North Central Association re-accreditation process. The ten-year period between NCA self-studies was a time of remarkable growth and development in all areas of the college. After the visitors came to campus in May of 1967 and made their report, the formal notice of approval of Edgewood College for another ten-year period was received from the North Central Association in August of 1967.

Shaping a Stronger Curriculum

The mission of the senior college, begun ten years before Sister Nona' presidency, was to create an excellent elementary teacher professional education program strongly based on a liberal arts preparation during the first two years of college. Sister Nona vigorously assumed direction of this mission and quickly moved to enlarge and strengthen it.

In the college catalogs from 1951 through 1958, the following "aims and ideals" were proposed:

Edgewood College aims to give each student a general acquaintance with the culture and traditions of the past to enable her to solve contemporary problems in the light of Christian principles. Realizing that knowledge of subject matter is essential, a well balanced program of studies is offered under the guidance of trained teachers, and high scholastic standards are fostered. Opportunities are provided for the cultivation of moral integrity and the virtues of Catholic womanhood that the student may make her contribution to the times in which she lives.

The language of half a century ago may sound somewhat stilted to contemporary ears, but the goals of providing students with preparation for making "a contribution" to society, developing moral integrity, as well as attaining educational excellence are ones consistent with Edgewood's traditions.   In their 1958 report, the review team for the North Central Association accreditation visit had stated:

The purposes of the College are highly integrative and are quite appropriate to both staff and clientele. They are strongly supported by the faculty, are well understood and positively endorsed by the students, and are plainly matters of dynamic influence throughout the program of the College.

Edgewood College Archives

"It All Fits Together"
Greta Shetney, Sister Nona, and Sister Joan stand near a diagram of Edgewood College's integrated curriculum, divided into six divisions: Theology and Philosophy, Social Sciences, Fine Arts, Language / Literature, and Natural Science / Mathematics, clustered around Professional Studies.

While during subsequent years the faculty and administration often reconsidered and rewrote the description of the "aims" or "mission" of the college, the basic goals remained remarkably constant. On the other hand, the development of the curriculum and expansion of the college's academic programs were constantly in process during Sister Nona's presidency.

By 1955, along with the existing majors in elementary education and business education, the college offered majors in English, history, and art education. The North Central Association, among its recommendations during the first accreditation process, had suggested expanding the limited program of liberal arts majors. In April 1958, the president announced to the college community that the faculty had decided to add majors in art and biology, and to offer a Bachelor of Arts degree as well as the Bachelor of Science degree. In the following academic year, students could prepare to teach on the secondary level, with majors in English, history, art, and biology, as well as business education. When this new proposal was presented to the officials of the Wisconsin Department of Public Instruction, their response was "more power to you—go ahead."[16]

Through the fifties and sixties, the college catalogs reflect the steady growth in majors in the arts and sciences. In 1955-56 five majors were offered—education (with concentrations in kindergarten, primary, elementary); business education (secondary); and art education, English, and history as second majors (the 1959-60 catalog was the first to indicate that the college no longer required a major in education for graduation). In 1961-62, students could obtain a Bachelor of Arts degree in art, biology, English, history, mathematics, social science, and elementary education; and a Bachelor of Science in art, biology, business education, elementary education, and medical technology. By 1968 majors were offered in art, biology, business, business education, elementary education, English, French, history, mathematics, medical technology, performing arts, social science, sociology, Spanish, and theology. The distinction between the B.A. and the B.S. remained constant—each college catalog describes the additional amount of foreign language required for the B.A. degree.

In the fall of 1958, in the face of a growing demand for medical technologists and at the request of Dr. E. A. Brucker of St. Mary's Hospital in Madison, a faculty committee was set up to develop a curriculum that would lead to a Bachelor of Science degree in Medical Technology. The committee, after studying programs across the nation, proposed a curriculum for Edgewood College that would include three years of study at Edgewood combined with a fourth year internship in a medical technology hospital program. The faculty and the trustees approved the new degree program, and it was inaugurated in September 1959. Over subsequent years, several hospitals collaborated with medical technology internships—St. Mary's and Madison General [later, Meriter] locally, and Holy Cross Hospital in Chicago.

Another health-care related program was developed in 1959 by Sister Jane Frances with the St. Mary's Hospital Nursing School administration. In this collaborative program, nursing students from St. Mary's and, later, students from Methodist Hospital Nursing School took thirty-two credits of liberal arts courses during a year of study at Edgewood in conjunction with their nursing program. This program was continued until 1970, when both nursing schools decided to go to two-year R.N. programs, which meant the end of the collaborative venture.

The Dean Welcomes Seminarians
Sister Barbara (Melchior) Beyenka, academic dean, welcomes some of the first seminarians: Tim Shaw, Paul Digman, and Jeff Lanphear.

In collaboration with the diocese of Madison, a joint institutional program was first explored in March 1965 by Sister Nona and Msgr. George Wirz, rector of Holy Name Seminary. This program—to provide college-level education for the Madison diocese seminarians—began with a pilot project under which twelve seminarians studied at Edgewood College during the spring of 1967. The program was expanded the following fall, when sixty-five seminarians became full-time students at the college. Seminarians chose various majors and courses of study, and they participated actively in a variety of college organizations.

The *aggiornamento* that Vatican Council II ushered into Catholic life during the sixties brought a correspondingly fresh vitality to religious studies and programs on the Edgewood campus. A new development in the theology department included the addition of a Chair of Ecumenical Studies made possible through a Danforth Foundation grant in 1966. The first person appointed to the chair was Lutheran Pastor Lowell Mays. During the 1960s Sister Marie Stephen Reges was an active participant in the Hebrew and Semitic Studies seminars and programs directed by Professor Menaltem Mansoor at the University of Wisconsin, forging new links with the Jewish communities of Madison. She also brought to campus the beloved Rabbi Manfred Swarsensky, of neighboring Temple Beth El, who was later appointed as the first professor in the Chair of Jewish Studies established at the college. Sister Marie Stephen also developed a collaborative program with the faculty of Holy Name seminary to prepare men and women of the diocese for catechetical ministries. In March of 1966, the administration of Edgewood College approved the program, offering a sequence of nine religious studies courses offered one night a week and during the summer. This was the forerunner of the college's Education for Parish Service program, designed to provide a sound academic preparation for lay men and women serving in various ministries of the diocese.

Many lectures and special seminars expanded the horizons of students, staff, faculty, and guests during the sixties. Public symposia focused on subjects such as Dante and Teilhard de Chardin. In 1965, the symposium on Dante brought to the campus Professor Enrico De Negri, renowned scholar from the University of California-Berkeley, as principal lecturer, and other Dante specialists from various universities. In 1966, many Madisonians attended the lectures on Teilhard de Chardin, given by George Barbour of the University of Cincinnati, who had been with Teilhard in China; Joseph Sittler, University of Chicago Divinity School; and John T. Robinson and Van R. Potter of the University of Wisconsin. The 1966

Ecumenical and Academic Collaboration
Sister Marie Stephen Reges, shown here with (l. to r.) Dean Edwin Young and President Fred Harrington of the University of Wisconsin, Mar Athanasius Samuel, Syrian Archbishop of Jerusalem, and Professor Menahem Mansoor, Department of Hebrew and Semitic Studies at the University of Wisconsin—all collaborators in presenting the 1964 biblical archaeological exhibit, "The Book and the Spade."

symposium was organized collaboratively by Sister Louis Russley of Edgewood and Professors John Opitz and Thomas Wegmann of the University of Wisconsin.

The annual Festival of the Arts, a week-long celebration of the arts, brought guest artists and musicians as well as showcasing the talents of students and faculty on campus. These offerings were part of the growing outreach of the college community during the sixties to its neighbors in the Madison area. The Madison Summer Symphony, directed first by Gordon B. Wright and later by David Crosby, found a home at Edgewood in 1960, at the invitation of Sister Lois Nichols of the music department. The orchestra, later called the Wisconsin Chamber Orchestra, offered a series of concerts each summer on the De Ricci Terrace overlooking the lawn where neighbors and friends could come to relax and enjoy the music. Under David Crosby's direction, these summer concerts at Edgewood extended through 1981. After that time the Wisconsin Chamber Orchestra moved its summer series to the grounds of the capitol as "Concerts on the Square."

Changing the Corporate Structure

Since its beginnings in 1927, Edgewood College was part of the St. Clara College Corporation, the corporate body of the Sinsinawa Dominican sisters that

Summer Concerts on the Lawn
The Madison Summer Symphony, later called the Wisconsin Chamber Orchestra, offered summer concerts al fresco from the De Ricci Terrace for over twenty years.

also included the motherhouse and academy at Sinsinawa, and several Congregation-owned high schools. The situation was further complicated at Edgewood by the fact that three separate institutions on campus were being operated under the St. Clara Corporation umbrella.

In March 1954, the administrative officers of the college met with the college lawyer, William McNamara, to discuss formation of an Edgewood College Corporation, separate from the umbrella St. Clara College Corporation. Sister Nona presented the problems involved, explaining that it would be more effective to have Edgewood as a separate organization in order to conduct business with greater facility.

This new incorporation was agreed to by the congregation officials, who were also the officers of St. Clara College Corporation, and the articles of incorporation were drawn up in May 1954. The initial directors or trustees of Edgewood College, Incorporated, were officials of the Congregation (Mother Evelyn Murphy, Sister Benedict Ryan, and Sister Benita Newhouse) and of Edgewood (Sister Nona McGreal and Sister Rose Catherine Leonard). The following year, in May of 1955, the Board of Trustees of St. Clara College transferred the deed to the Edgewood property to Edgewood College, Incorporated. Establishment of the new corporate entity did not entirely separate Edgewood from St. Clara College Corporation, however. Under the Edgewood College Incorporated bylaws, most significant financial, building, and property matters still had to be referred to the officers of the Congregation, in their role as members or directors of the corporation. The evolution of the college's corporate and governance structure would continue through succeeding years.

A step toward establishment of a lay Board of Trustees was taken in the fall of 1957, when Sister Nona established an advisory board, the President's Council. The first members of the President's Council were Carl G. Mayer (chair), William H. Purnell, Mrs. Irving J. Maurer, Frank Byrne, Mrs. Fred Kellogg, Raymond T. McGuire, William McNamara, Joseph Melli, John P. Rocca, Edwin F. Schmitz, John L. Sonderegger, A. Matt Werner, Martin J. Wolman, John Wrage, and Alumnae Association President Jeanne Mikulec. Some of these Council members would become the first lay members of the college Board of Trustees in 1969.

Strengthening Student Enrollment in a Changing World

One might say that the adage, "If you build it, they will come," applies directly to Sister Nona's administration. Her successful drive to develop a college campus and building complex, together with her strengthening of the faculty and the college's academic programs, resulted in dramatically increased growth in student enrollment during the eighteen years of her presidency. In 1949-1950, the year before Sister Nona became president, there were 71 full-time students and a total enrollment of 101. By 1967-68, Sister Nona's last year as president, the total enrollment was 847, with 501 full-time students.[17] By 1950 the cumulative total of all Edgewood College graduates earning bachelor's degrees had been about 200; by 1967 it was 1250.   In other words, 84% of all Edgewood College senior college graduates to 1968 had completed their degrees during Sister Nona's presidency.

These years were times of rapid growth in higher education, as "the number of undergraduate women in Wisconsin colleges and universities doubled between 1954 and 1963 and doubled again by 1975."[18] Minutes of the meetings of the Edgewood College administrators during the fifties and sixties indicate their clear awareness of this growth trend. They worked tirelessly to provide the facilities, the faculty, the staff, and the programs to meet burgeoning educational demands.

A new educational outreach was developed in 1952 with the encouragement of adult women to attend classes and complete degrees. At Edgewood, the first few brave souls were called "Sister Joan's chickadees," because of the registrar's special supportive and advising role with them. Under her careful guidance, their numbers grew, and an early feminist support group—though it was too early to call itself that— formed among the "chickadees," including setting up their own advisory committee in 1962, the year before Betty Friedan's *The Feminist Mystique* energized the U.S. women's movement.

Grace Meyer, a "chickadee" of the early sixties, wrote:

I had no college credits. I was faced with the prospect of being mother, father, and sole support of my four children. After considering every possibility, I decided to go to college. They say, "It's not easy to teach an old dog new tricks," but I have disproved this

Before Co-Education — Campus Dorm Life
From top to bottom: "spinning platters" in the Pine Room of Marshall Hall, with cokes and popcorn; study session in a Regina dorm room (l. to r. Elaine Kubasta, Maureen Haugh, Mary Therese Dolan, Jo Guilbert); freshmen "all dressed up for blind dates lined up by the Social Chairman of Regina Hall" (l. to r. back row: Carol Hoepker, Margaret Courtney, Mary Jo Wilhelm, Rose Wnek, Julie Sawyer, Margaret Dillon, Genevieve Barbian; front row: Sarajane Gille, Bernadette Golla, Gail Ripp).

Edgewood College Archives

fallacy. I will admit it took every ounce of courage I could muster to climb those steps that first day and take a place "near the door" in freshman logic class. But somehow I got through the hour with the feeling that possibly I had been able to follow the teacher as well as most of the bewildered-looking freshmen around me.... I am now about to graduate [1964] and to launch a challenging career of teaching.... As I look ahead, the years do not loom as empty, lonely hurdles to overcome, but as exciting opportunities to help our young people become better individuals and citizens.[19]

Increasing diversity characterized the Edgewood student body during these same years. Even before Sister Nona's arrival as president, a visitator's report made during the 1949-50 process of affiliating Edgewood College with the Catholic University of America noted that "there is no color line at Edgewood," and that "two negresses have been admitted to the September freshman class."[20] A few more African-American students came to the college in the 1950s, and their number increased gradually during the 1960s. In the fall of 1967, thirteen African-Americans and fifteen other "non-white" students were enrolled according to a Federal compliance report, although some students chose not to record their race or ethnicity on official forms.[21]

In the summer of 1964 Edgewood College took a strong stand in supporting its African-American students when the administration was asked by a landlord not to allow "colored students" to live in Aquin House, a rented house near campus where students had been living. College officials refused to comply, and a letter from the college administration was immediately sent to students, explaining the situation and declaring that Edgewood College had

Mary Therese Dolan

decided not to renew the lease for Aquin House. As Americans and Christians we cannot have any part in such an agreement. Consequently, we find that we have forty-four students to whom we have promised housing and who cannot fit in Regina or Marshall.[22]

Julie Sawyer Krier

Struggling at a late July date to find housing for the displaced students, administrators eventually were able to rent an apartment building on Milton Street to house them.

Just as she had encouraged faculty participation in planning and governance, Sister Nona encouraged student involvement in creating a collegial environment. Minutes of the administration meetings during the late fifties record plans to meet with a Faculty-Student Board to discuss such matters as the need to re-consider college policies on alcohol use. In 1959, when the administration was considering an increase in tuition, the administrators "agreed to keep the matter pending until we have met with the officers of the Student Association." A few years later, a Student Request Committee provided a structure for presenting student ideas or recommendations to the administration. The first two requests were "for longer open library hours and for a sidewalk between Regina and Mazzuchelli"—both requests were accepted and acted upon. A "Think Day" was first held on December 7, 1965, so that senior students, the student council, faculty and administrators could meet together to discuss ways of improving the college.

More and more student organizations developed—some flourishing, and some disappearing after a time, with new ones taking their places. The list of student organizations in the college catalogs of the 1950s and 1960s indicates an ebb and flow of student preoccupations during those years: the Young Catholic Students, the Catholic Student Mission Crusade, the Schola Cantorum, the Thespians, Future Teachers of America, the Dominican Third Order, the French Club, the Spanish Club, the International Relations Club, the Young Democrats, the Young Republicans, the Collegiate Council of the United Nations, and others.

Student involvement beyond the campus was encouraged as part of the college's educational mission. A sense of responsibility to the larger human community was inculcated as an ideal in the Edgewood educational environment—an ideal promoted by faculty and staff and led by Sister Nona and Sister Joan whose earlier work in developing a comprehensive curriculum for U.S. Catholic schools, "Guiding Growth in Christian Social Living," had shaped a direction for American Catholic education. The college catalogs during the 1950s had a section entitled "The College in the Community," stating:

The college is for each class a passing society, short-lived… but it can, nevertheless, show students how to be good citizens of their respective communities in two ways. First, it can focus attention upon those aspects of campus life that are fundamental to living together in any group …and, secondly, the college can stress ties with its own local community.

Political organizations flourished on campus, especially during election years, offering opportunities for students to get directly involved in national, state, and local politics. Service opportunities— at St. Martin House on Madison's south side, in area parishes, work with the Red Cross, counseling at children's camps, and other projects—attracted numbers of Edgewood College students, and some students joined the Peace Corps as well as other post-collegiate national service programs after graduation. Mary Fran Limmex of the class of 1964 was the first Edgewood student to join the Peace Corps as a medical technologist, assigned to Afghanistan.

Black Photo

Edgewood College Archives

Two popular student organizations in 1963
Top: The college chorus directed by Sister Chia ta Liana (Milla) Derby.

Below: Advisor Sister Cecilia Carey with the staff of the student yearbook, Torch:
Ann Maxwell, Patricia Thornton, Barbara Botham, Rita McGrath, Nancy Galles,
Sheila Hannon, Cathy Hirschboeck, Virginia Nebel, Sue McCoy, Cathy Brophy,
Janet Sullivan.

Throughout the 1950s, the minutes of the administrators' meetings indicate continuing concern about keeping Edgewood College affordable for low and middle-income students. Student health insurance was first offered to students in January of 1956, and as soon as the student loan program, part of the National Defense Education Act of 1958, was initiated by the federal government, notice was sent to all Edgewood students, informing them of this opportunity. In 1959, the Wisconsin State Scholarship bill provided additional financial support for college students in the state.

Steadily increasing enrollments, coupled with developing financial aid programs and new needs in student services, put severe strains on limited student personnel resources by the late fifties. The dean of the college, the much-loved Sister Jane Frances Weber, had served as dean of both academic and student affairs from 1950 until her death, at the age of fifty-two, in October 1961.   In a message to alumnae, Sister Nona commented on the "hundreds of letters that came in from alumnae telling of her kindness and guidance, her interest in your life's vocation, your present work or growing families."   An alumna, who was present at Sister Jane Frances' funeral Mass in the college chapel, wrote:

Edgewood College Archives

Sister Jane Frances Weber

As the priests left the altar, only their footsteps could be heard on the marble floor as the beautiful St. Joseph's Chapel, filled to overflowing, held the silent memories of young and not so young, of women and men, of religious and laity. Sister Jane Frances, scholar, housemother, Dean, lay peaceful in a gray casket, surrounded by those she loved and who loved her.... Our tears were filled with personal memories of a great woman and a great friend, and words could not convey the loss this life would mean to future students. Sister would have been the last to expect or want tears. If she could have, she would have campused us all, I'm sure![23]

In 1961, the dean's responsibilities were divided. An academic dean, Sister Melchior [Barbara] Beyenka, and a dean of students, Sister Mary Grace Durkin, were appointed to the new positions. Sister Mary Grace served until 1964, when she was granted leave for study at Notre Dame University, and Sister Matthias Michels took her place. Sister Mary Grace's untimely death in 1966 led to an out-pouring of grief similar to that experienced when Sister Jane Frances had died in 1961. Once again, the college and its alumnae felt the shock of premature loss of a beloved dean, and tributes were poured out in the pages of letters and eulogies.   Sister Nona's words at Sister Mary Grace's funeral liturgy in the Edgewood College Chapel spoke eloquently of the college's sense of loss:

Edgewood College Archives

Sister Mary Grace Durkin

She cherished liberty of spirit, yet always supported a common effort. She was wholly personal, yet could love an institution—this institution—in such a way as to make it live and flourish. She could carry its spirit miles beyond the campus to men and women who know of Edgewood College because, in their own words, "Sister Mary Grace loved that place."[24]

When considering student life, the social history of the 1950s and 1960s immediately brings to mind aspects of escapism in American popular culture. Popular TV shows were "Leave It to Beaver," "I Love Lucy," "The Milton Berle Show," and "The

$64,000 Question." The fifties witnessed the rock and roll revolution with Elvis Presley becoming "king" of the pop music scene, while the sixties saw the Beatles sweep the music charts.   In 1955, students everywhere flocked to see James Dean in *Rebel Without A Cause*. A "drop-out" mentality seemed personified by Jack Kerouac and the writings and lifestyles of the Beats.   Sporting events were as popular as ever, with Cassius Clay (later, Muhammad Ali) dominating the boxing world, Jack Nicklaus and Arnold Palmer battling each other, Roger Maris breaking Babe Ruth's home run record, and—in Madison, at least—everyone rejoicing when the Badgers were chosen to represent the Big Ten in the Rose Bowl in 1953 and again in 1963.

Students of those days remembered both fun times and challenging classes:

I remember Saturday night, heading for State Street and a "Bucky burger," dancing at the Villa Maria, pitchers of beer at the Kollege Klub, steak sandwiches at the Brat Haus.... Sister Marie Paula made the biggest impression on my young life. She always made us keep on trying. She was a great teacher, too, and her chem lab was always interesting. She taught us how to make popcorn over a bunsen burner, and she also gave us an education in opera. I can still see her stopping class so that everyone could listen to the finer points of an aria from Boris Godunov.[25]

Another student remembered "sharing food, clothes, advice, help with home-work, and much more," as a Regina Hall resident in the early sixties. She noted that the Social Chairman "lined up blind dates for the mixers and other events" and students would go as a group to the get-togethers either at Edgewood or at the University. "In fact," she added, "I met my future husband at one of these events, and we have been happily married since 1968."[26]

The stereotype of the fifties and early sixties as a tranquil or passive era fails to acknowledge the reality that Edgewood students and faculty of the period, like their counterparts everywhere, lived through difficult and confrontational times.

The Korean War in the early fifties brought home the reality that once again, only a decade after the World War II, young men were being sent to fight and die in a distant part of the world.   College women at Edgewood worried about their brothers and boyfriends, wrote letters, and prayed.   Like their parents, they were troubled when President Truman vetoed the 1950 anti-communist McCarron Act because he thought its enactment would erode the Bill of Rights, and when Congress overrode his veto.   In the early 1950s, Wisconsin's junior senator, Joseph McCarthy, was stirring up emotions and fears by his relentless pursuit of "Commie-sympa-thizers," most notably media figures such as Hollywood directors, writers, and actors. The House Un-American Activities Committee, including a young Republican representative named Richard Nixon, emulated Senator McCarthy in its own "red-baiting" investigations.   Victims of the "hunt" included Paul Robeson, Lillian Hellman, Ring Lardner, Jr., Clifford Odets, Woody Guthrie, and scores of others who were blacklisted.   Senator McCarthy's downfall in 1954 in the course of the *Army vs McCarthy* hearings and his subsequent censure by the U.S. Senate seemed to lessen some of the more virulent paranoia about the Communist threat to America, though strong remnants of anti-communist fears continued through the sixties, and some in Wisconsin maintained fierce loyalty to the senator.

Politics moved front and center in many people's lives during the 1950s, not least on college campuses where groups like the National Student Association rallied young men and women to the cause of civil liberties. Writers, too, stirred American imaginations. Arthur Miller's *The Crucible* offered an ironic parallel between the historical Salem witch hunts and the repressive McCarthyism of the decade. In 1952, Ralph Ellison published *The Invisible Man*, and it quickly became a best-seller, awakening awareness that the "land of the free" still offered segregated facilities, repressive voting regulations, and blatant discrimination against blacks. In the later fifties, James Baldwin's powerful fiction would offer the reading public, particularly on college campuses, more insights into the real world and deep concerns of African-Americans. In the early sixties, after Betty Friedan's *The Feminine Mystique* had become a best-seller, college students and others were awakened to a critical view of the social, economic, and political situation of women in society.

Edgewood College Archives

1960 – Election Fever
Senior Mary Kay Joynt, with a Kennedy campaign poster

Although the French had learned a shocking lesson at the fall of Dien-Bien Phu in the fall of 1954, the United States and its people were not in a learning mood. Probably few if any Edgewood students in 1954 paid much attention to the news of the defeat of crack French paratroopers by a cadre of Vietnamese fighters in a remote corner of the world. Yet only a decade later, this country also began to wade deeply into the mire of a guerrilla war in Southeast Asia and gradually experience the shock and disillusionment earlier felt by the French. The crumbling of European colonial empires during the fifties and sixties—in Africa, in Asia, and around the world— brought the plight and aspirations of so-called "third-world" countries into the consciousness of the American psyche.

Another kind of milestone was reached in the 1960 election of John F. Kennedy as president. The specter of anti-Catholicism that had surfaced in the Al Smith campaign in the twenties seemed diminished. Also, for the first time, television and its coverage of events such as the national conventions and the presidential contenders' debates brought the political process into everyone's living room. In front of TV sets in college lounges or recreation rooms, college students could be "present" at most of the major events of the fifties and sixties, including the somber days following President Kennedy's assassination in 1963.

Disturbing images of police brutality against civil rights marchers during the sixties brought new levels of questioning and reflection to college campuses throughout the nation. Intense faculty-student discussions both in and out of the classrooms took place, as positions were debated and policies critiqued. Action followed reflection, for, in the Dominican tradition, contemplation leads to action. Edgewood College faculty and students, like their counterparts across the nation, joined groups and marched in demonstrations protesting injustice, promoting civil rights, and seeking peace.

A dynamic and new educational experience was underway at Edgewood College as the "real world" pressures of national and global events and politics mounted steadily during the later years of Sister Nona's presidency. When her election to the General Council of the Congregation necessitated her departure from Edgewood in January of 1968, an era was ending, and at Edgewood College, as throughout America, winds of change were swirling in the air. Under President Johnson, programs like Medicare, Head Start, and the Voting Rights Act came into being in the mid-sixties, offering the hope of creating a "Great Society." Yet the Vietnam quagmire was deepening, peace and civil rights protests were intensifying, and the brutal assassinations of Martin Luther King, Jr., and Robert Kennedy were soon to rend the social and political fabric of the late sixties. As a classic Bob Dylan song of the sixties said: "The times, they are a-changing," and few knew where the new changes might take us.

A turbulent decade was symbolized dramatically when the Sacred Heart Academy building, built with great hope after the tragic fire of 1893, was reduced to a heap of rubble by the wrecking ball in November 1969.

Over many decades, it had been home to Dominican Sisters and resident students. Its chapel held memories of countless Masses celebrated, hours of private prayer, and the regular morning and evening chanting of psalms. Its walls had reverberated with treasured melodies of sacred song and organ, of piano and harp. Classes for all Edgewood students had been held in its various nooks and crannies before 1927, and college students still studied there before their own real campus began to take shape in the 1950s.

Its demolition and the dispersal of its contents—both human and physical— reflected the dramatic, often violent upheavals in the nation, the Church, and the world during the late sixties and early seventies. War and anti-war protests, assassinations, riots, conflicts over rights and responsibilities, burning issues of "power," peace, and justice would mark the decade.

CHAPTER SIX

Challenges of a Turbulent Decade

1968-1977

*W*hen Sister Cecilia Carey became president of Edgewood College on February 1, 1968, she took charge of a college that had been developing steadily for nearly two decades and which gave every promise of continuing to grow. During a "Think Day" in 1965, when students, faculty, and administrators gathered to consider the future of the college, one proposal was to consider 1,500 students an "optimal" size for the college.[1] The re-accreditation report of the North Central Association in 1967 noted the strong growth and the many initiatives established during Sister Nona's eighteen-year presidency: "The curriculum has been improved markedly in recent years. The physical plant is excellent. The college's finances are remarkably stable. The general ethos of the institution is excellent."[2] Nevertheless, within her first months as president, Sister Cecilia faced severe and unexpected challenges.

Some of these challenges were rooted in the social unrest generated by the war in Vietnam and the resulting turmoil on college campuses everywhere during the late sixties and early seventies. In addition, within Roman Catholic institutions, the post-Vatican II years had given rise to new stirrings, an increasingly dynamic interest in theology and lay ministry, in ecumenical outreach, and engagement in social justice concerns. At the same time, priests and sisters were leaving their professions in increasing numbers, and many Catholics experienced confusion and anger about liturgical, moral, and social issues. The feminist movement in the U.S. was rapidly gaining momentum and challenging long-held assumptions, while African-Americans were seeking justice and civil rights with increasing militancy.

Sister Cecilia had taught in the English department of Edgewood College during the late 1950s and early 1960s, before going to Cochabamba, Bolivia, where as professor and administrator at la Normal Católica, she prepared Bolivian teachers, while also teaching English at the major seminary of San José. Her Latin American experience had given her a wide perspective on global issues in the social, political, and religious spheres as she and the other Dominican sisters there faced dramatic upheavals in Bolivia. She needed to call on that experience after returning to an Edgewood campus that was vastly different from the one she had left in the summer of 1963.

When Sister Cecilia returned to Edgewood College as president, the campus community was passionately engaged with issues of co-education, anti-war activism, civil rights, the women's movement, more direct involvement of students and faculty in politics both on and off campus, as well as student pressures for greater personal decision-making about their academic studies as well as continuing unhappiness about residence hall regulations. Reform and revolution were on the agendas of many groups during the late sixties and early seventies, and college administrators everywhere were being tested in the process.

Three weeks after Sister Cecilia took office, two important political events occurred on campus in one day. On February 21, 1968, former governor Harold Stassen came to campus to speak about the projected World Conference on Peace and Justice; a rabbi, a minister, and a priest responded in a panel discussion. Earlier that same day, presidential candidate Senator Eugene McCarthy spoke at a campus rally attended by over 500 people, organized by Michael Lybarger of the college history department and by Edgewood's Students for McCarthy.

On March 31, 1968, President Lyndon Johnson announced that he would not run for re-election, and suddenly the spring primaries became even more significant. That spring, many Edgewood students worked hard to support the campaigns of their preferred candidates—some even traveling to distant places to do canvassing before the primaries, as the college student newspaper recorded:

For Edgewood's students campaigning didn't end on April 2nd [Wisconsin's primary election day]. They joined thousands of students from all over the country who swarmed to Indiana and Nebraska to campaign for Senator McCarthy—Liz Berg, Bev Thousand, Bea Voelker, Judy Schmitz, Judy Camp, Jean Becker, Claudia Feldner, Mary McCoy, and Barbara Brost. In Gary, Indiana, canvassers encountered people with interesting racial attitudes, i.e., the white backlash. Whites were often pro-McCarthy simply because they were anti-Kennedy. The fact that McCarthy's position on Civil Rights is just about identical to Kennedy's seemed to make little impression.[3]

Sister Cecilia had barely begun her presidency in the winter of 1968 when news bulletins announced the highest U.S. casualty figures to occur in one week: 543 U.S. troops killed and 2,547 wounded. The My Lai massacre of Vietnamese civilians by U.S. troops occurred in March, although the country would not be aware of that tragedy until a year later. Bad news came day after day during that spring.

On April 4, 1968, Dr. Martin Luther King, Jr., was assassinated in Memphis. The shock waves were felt everywhere, and sporadic riots broke out while National Guard troops with armored vehicles patrolled the streets of some major cities. Classes at Edgewood were suspended for the day of his funeral, April 9. The reactions of Edgewood's African-American students were passionately stated in two articles written for *Signature*, the college magazine:

Was Dr. King's death necessary to bring you to reality? If you have accepted reality, am I still that 'nigger'? Do you know why the black people are burning in Chicago and other cities?.... Your Declaration of Independence states that 'all men are created equal.' Your Constitution guarantees justice and protection. You see, it was written for you. We weren't considered as people.... To some of you I will always remain that 'nigger.' I can forgive, but I will not permit you to forget.[4]

Edgewood College Archives

Student political activism was strong in the months preceding the 1968 presidential election. Senator Eugene McCarthy, one of the Democratic candidates, visited the Edgewood campus for a rally on February 21, 1968, and was warmly welcomed by the 500 who attended, including student Julie Keefe.

Because I'm black, I have so many worries for a person so young. I worry about everything that concerns and affects my people—the blacks of America.... I worry about me. I worry about my being here at Edgewood. I'm in the minority here, so I feel ill at ease at times. To remedy this, I tell myself, 'I'm here, I'm black, and I'm beautiful.'[5]

On May 8, 1968, classes were cancelled for an all-day Teach-In called "Crisis in America." Panels and groups of students and faculty discussed "The Black Student Experience," "The Problem of Poverty," and the Kerner Report, as well as other current issues. The assassination of Robert Kennedy in early June of 1968, while he was campaigning for the Democratic presidential nomination, shocked the nation. The Democratic nominating convention in Chicago that August made headlines when the Chicago police attacked and beat demonstrators outside the convention hotel. A September 1968 issue of the college newspaper reported that "quite a few Edgewoodites" had attended the convention—one Young Democrat reported that she was disappointed with the selection of Hubert Humphrey after all her hard work for the McCarthy campaign, but she was especially impressed with the "poise and coolness" of the young Julian Bond whom she had met.[6] The same issue noted that "Skip" Humphrey had visited the campus to rally support for his father in the fall campaign. Meanwhile, the Young Republicans were rallying to the cause of Richard Nixon, selected by his party as standard-bearer.

During the summer of 1968, three Edgewood College science teachers volunteered to teach in the CHOICE program, which aimed to assist in the education of talented but under-prepared African-American pre-medical college students. The Edgewood teachers taught biology—Sister Jeannette (Elaine) Feldballe— and chemistry—Sister Jean (John Venard) McSweeney at Meharry Medical College in Nashville, Tennessee, while Sister Winfrid Tracy taught chemistry at Albany State College in Albany, Georgia.

In September of 1968, the front page of the student newspaper carried an article about the attendance of two Sinsinawa Sister students from Edgewood— Sister Marie Jordana and Sister Maria Paulita— at the first National Black Sisters Convention in Pittsburgh. The first Black Studies courses were offered at the college in 1968-1969, when Sister Cajetan Spelman taught a course in the history department, "The Negro in American History," and Michael Lybarger taught another history course called "Black History Forum."

The October 1968 issue of the student newspaper covered the boycotting and picketing of A & P grocery stores by those active in "Operation Breadbasket," (seeking just employment opportunities for African-Americans) including Edgewood faculty members Sister Catherine Cordon and Father Richard LaPata, and students Carolyn Becker, Donna McLennan, Jean Becker, Judy Camp, Gwen Daniels, Enrica Morgan, and Sister Ruth Marie. In the same issue, the student editor put in perspective the current campus controversies about student power and academic freedom:

New winds are blowing at Edgewood this year and are causing deeper changes than the falling of crimson and gold leaves on the campus grounds.... This is not at Edgewood College alone; it is a natural product of the enormous changes the world has experienced in the past few years.[7]

ON STUDENT POWER

Today, the big question on college and university campuses world wide is one of "student power." That is, just how much say do students have about how they are going to live their lives on campus? Many methods are being utilized to test how far they can go, unfortunately none seem to have proved too fruitful.

Edgewood college has seen changes in the last few years, but these have been slow to come and have called for much planning by few people. Now is the time for more changes.

When broken down into individual requests many of our questions call for simple, forthright, yes or no answers. Yet when combined, they represent a seemingly insurmountable mass. Along with this there is the realization that something is wrong at Edgewood. And that something is COMMUNICATION; more distinctly UNcommunication at all levels.

Over the years there has been a slow build up of student's complaints that have never reached the faculty and administration, of opinions and views of the administration that have not been related to the students, and a faculty that is left dangling in between--an admittedly vicious circle.

Edgewood College Archives

The October 1, 1968 issue of the student newspaper carried an editorial analysis of "Student Power," written by the editor Lois Bennin.

During 1967 and 1968, students at Edgewood were demanding "more communication," and a public space was established along the hallway on the second floor of De Ricci Hall, a place where any one could post comments, rejoinders, admonitions, poems, art, and cartoons. At times, the graffiti posted on the "I Say, You Say" wall could be heated and demanding, while at other times merely humorous, including satiric spoofs on the college's atmosphere of protest itself. For the first time, in the fall of 1968, faculty meetings were officially open to students, and many attended.

Ironically, just as student demands for self-regulation and participation in college governance were growing, the Student Government Association was "taken over" by students and then dissolved by them. In the words of Sister Matthias Michels, the dean of students:

One big protest of the students was against the Student Association itself, which had been a tightly structured organization with a sort of 'militarized' code of rules and regulations. I thought it a model of 'law and order' but it crashed, and all the stipulations about meetings, nominations, elections, etc. were dumped. The new officers preferred to work in a random mode, taking up an issue as it arose without a plan of action. It was a painful time to be in authority, as the students saw no need for any guidance. Finally one day the student officers simply came to the office of the Dean of Students and flatly told me that 'it was all over.'[8]

Sister Cecilia, in her address to the college community at the President's convocation on September 30, 1969, faced this increasingly chaotic situation directly, stating that among the key areas of her concern that year was the need to "confront the problem of lack of student leadership and its implications for the college if a strong, positive, creative form of student government does not evolve." By the spring of 1970, the students had drawn up a new constitution and wanted it recognized by the administration although there was still a question regarding an "illegally elected president"; however, the administrative officers decided to recognize the president and to approve the new constitution. In April, students demanded that the annual honors convocation be simply referred to as a convocation, "due to the present student reaction to 'academic honors.'"

Shocking events on college campuses convulsed the nation during the spring and summer of 1970. On May 4, during a student protest at Kent State University, Ohio National Guardsmen fired into a crowd, killing four students and wounding nine others. Only ten days later, on the campus of Jackson State University in Mississippi, two young black men were killed by police during a campus protest. Shortly afterwards, the Chancellor of the University of Wisconsin declared a state of emergency, bringing Wisconsin National Guardsmen on campus for the second time that year, and sending students home after canceling final examinations. Then, on August 24, 1970, in the early morning hours, a powerful bomb exploded at Sterling Hall on the University campus, rocking city buildings including those on the Edgewood campus. A graduate student researcher died in that bombing, four others were injured, and Madison had become a war zone.

Anti-war protesters were initially stunned by these events, but the tide of anti-war sentiment grew stronger, especially when the public learned of the deadly "Christmas bombings" of December 1972 in Vietnam that brought widespread international condemnation and forced the Nixon administration to more serious negotiations. A peace accord between the United States and the North Vietnamese resulted in a withdrawal of U.S. troops, although the war continued between the north and south Vietnamese forces until the spring of 1975.

Sister Matthias Michels, professor of art, served as dean of students from 1964 to 1971. Although these were challenging years to work with students, the 1967 college yearbook, *Torch*, was dedicated to her. The students described her as "not only an administrator… but also a friend, confidante, and artist, finding beauty in all things."

Even when the withdrawal of U.S. forces from Vietnam gradually shifted the focus of protests, communication issues remained a sore spot on the Edgewood campus. By the fall of 1971, the Student Senate had asked Sister Cecilia to make some students "members of the administration," to serve as decision makers along with the president, deans, registrar, financial officer, and director of development. The reply was wryly given that "the administration is not empowered to add to the present membership, but further discussion of a solution to better communication will be held."[9]

Conversations and at times confrontations, both official and unofficial, among the administration, faculty, and students, were frequent and often controversial during the early seventies. Sister Cecilia's courage in upholding the traditional academic value of *disputatio,* or open academic exchange and questioning during these difficult times, was appreciated by a long-time member of the philosophy department, Daniel J. Guilfoil, who recalled that there was a great "stir" at one point when homosexuality was being openly discussed on the University campus and at Edgewood:

I invited some folks at the UW to campus to speak to the issues being raised, and so many of our students came that some classes were emptied, much to the distaste of some of our faculty, not only those whose classes were being emptied but some who did not warm to having the subject raised on campus. Sister Cecilia defended my efforts, saying that if we didn't discuss it on campus openly we surely would be discussing it furtively. As I recall, she got some grief over this as well as some cancellation of gifts to the college.[10]

Other issues were also on the minds of students, faculty, and administration during these years. Edgewood College had become *de facto* coeducational under Sister Mary Nona when the agreement between the college and Holy Name Seminary went into effect and seminarians began attending classes at the college. However, pressures were growing to open the doors more widely, and upon the recommendation of the faculty and with the approval of the Board of Trustees, Edgewood College officially became coeducational in January 1970. As Sister Cecilia told the alumnae, the final decision was the result of months of soul-searching, research, and advice, adding: "We have all come to the realization that we can operate more relevantly in today's world as a coeducational college."[11]

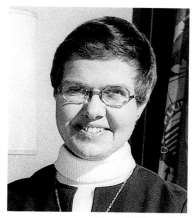

Sister Cecilia Carey, O.P. President of Edgewood College from 1968 to 1977; Ph.D., University of Wisconsin

A sign announcing that Edgewood College was "Now Co-Ed" was put up at the intersection of Woodrow and Monroe Streets, but it was soon stolen. More men joined the seminarians in classes that spring and the following fall, and they began to be elected to student offices—John Kinsman was elected president of the Student Senate for 1970-71, while a married veteran, Lyman "Woody" Woodman, was elected senior class president in 1971.

Below: Seminarians often "hung out" together in Edge-Inn, the student lounge where cokes and cigarettes and conversation offered respite for weary students.

Edgewood College Archives

Edgewood College Archives

Finding the right classroom is always a challenge for new students. Tom Baxter (on the right) seems to be providing directions to his fellow seminarians in a DeRicci hallway.

Edgewood College Archives

Randy Papp and senior class president Lyman "Woody" Woodman survey registration materials at the beginning of a new semester.

Yet even as more men arrived on campus, the feminist movement was also heightening consciousness of women's issues on campus. On September 25, 1971, Bella Abzug, congresswoman from New York and colorful feminist spokeswoman, spoke to Edgewood students, faculty, and guests. With her was another "star attraction," Peter Yarrow of Peter, Paul, and Mary fame. As the college annals record, "It was an exciting evening." In 1971-72, a new anthology of women's poetry, *No More Masks*, was being used in an introductory English literature class, and that spring "A Woman's Place" was begun, offering Edgewood students and staff a series of weekly campus conversations about women's issues and often featuring invited speakers.

With the advent of male students, interest grew in developing an intercollegiate athletic program. The first men's basketball team was a "pick-up" affair, begun in the fall of 1971, and organized by a junior student, John Engelbrecht, who also served as coach. Members of that first year team varied from game to game, at times traveling with only five or six players, but included Randy Papp, Jim Haiar, Mike Connell, Lee Haas, Tim Juvinall, Jahadi El-Akin, Ron Kreul, Dave Frank, Bruce Blakeslee, Kevin Braddock, Jim Wilson, John Ingala, Vance Rayburn, and Kent Lesandrini. The year's high scorers were Lee Haas with 290 points and John Ingala with 206.

Lee Haas recalls that first season:

John, our coach, was an accomplished tennis player, but a bit "challenged" about any knowledge of basketball. However, he threw himself into it, reading books, watching games, and trying to acquire the nuances of the sport. He recruited players, conducted practices, scheduled games, lined up cars for transport, and ordered our first uniforms. The "uniforms" were unique—white mock-turtleneck tops with purple trim (numbers sewn on), and white work-out shorts with horizontal purple stripes on one side (why only one side?).

At the end of the season, John entered us in a tournament, the Tri-State Classic in Iowa, and with six to a car, we made the trip. We won the first night, which gave us the privilege of playing at ten the next morning, but after celebrating our victory that night, we never "woke up" for the morning game and lost, ending up in fourth place.

Most of all, I remember that we all had a lot of fun playing, and our loyal fans enjoyed it! John deserves the credit as the "father" of Edgewood College basketball—which has come a long way during the past thirty years, even reaching NCAA status.[12]

By the end of their first year, the fledgling Eagles had compiled a winning season with seven wins and six defeats, and the administration presented the team with the first college athletic awards at an assembly on May 12, 1972. For their second season, in 1972-73, the Eagles acquired real uniforms that matched (with the restored red and white "Edgewood colors") and a new coach, Phil Pabich, head of the physical education department and student activities director.

Although a women's basketball team had been formed at the college back in 1932, "under the direction of Miss Russell,"[13] it was re-born in 1974-75 as a student, Eileen Dhooghe, got the team started, with the help of faculty members Bill Duddleston and Tom Marinaro. Ed Jakubowski coached the women's basketball team in 1975-76, as it joined the Wisconsin Independent Colleges' Women's Athletic Conference, playing a regular schedule against Mt. Mary, Concordia, Beloit, Alverno, and Cardinal Stritch. During the first year, some of the players were Laura Sturgis, Mary Goonan, Pam Dayton, Mary Torzewski, Nancy Harvey, and Eileen Dhooghe. Eileen Dhooghe McIltrot recalls:

Our uniforms consisted of red athletic shorts and Edgewood College T-shirts, because there was not money for "real" uniforms that first year. We were not in the conference that year, and once we were in the conference during 1975-76, we were off to a slow start—no wins! John Skaar was our coach for the 1976-77 season. In 1977-78, I was able to generate enough interest to start a women's softball team, with Mike Lybarger as our coach. The support of the student body and the faculty/staff for the women athletes was wonderful, right from the beginning. Sister Catherine Moran never missed a home game; she was our best cheerleader![14]

Photos: Eileen Dhooghe McIltrot

Above: Coach Ed Jakubowski with players: 42 Pam Dayton, 44 Nancy Harvey, Kathy Saunders, 33 June Zander, Laura Sturgis, 25 Deb Luven,

Right: Jump ball, with Kathy Saunders at center court, 54 Mary Torzewski, 13 Eileen Dhooghe, 33 June Zander.

The advent of coeducation involved not only new directions in inter-collegiate athletics, but also questions about on-campus housing for men. The college officials studied the situation and decided that Marshall Hall, the smallest dorm on campus, would be the first place to accommodate male students.

Questions of student discipline took on new dimensions in the late sixties and early seventies. In the spring of 1968, women students' requests had been for "open house" visitation, with men allowed in women's rooms—first, just on weekends, with limited hours, but by 1970, residents sought 24-hour visitation rights. Another burning issue of the day, though not a new one, was the right to drink alcohol on campus. At one point, Phil Pabich, student activities director, asked the administration either to have beer sold at mixers or to have higher door admission prices to cover the cost of the beer consumed (the matter was referred to the college lawyer, and the outcome is not recorded).[15] Beer was not the only concern for college administrators—the drug culture during these years involved much more than alcohol. The distinctive smell of marijuana occasionally mingled in dormitory hallways with the less heady scent of tobacco.

Ken Kesey's "Merry Pranksters" were role models for some students on many campuses, including Edgewood's. The Copper Grid (later The Gridiron) on Monroe Street was a local "bar of choice" for many, and one "merry prank" involved removing the large portrait of Sister Jane Frances Weber from the entryway of Weber Hall and transporting it to hang on a wall over the bar in the Copper Grid. The dean of students, Sister Matthias Michels, and the first lay residence director, Sharon Cronkite, soon got wind of the episode, tracked down the traveling portrait, and returned it to the college. The 1971 class yearbook, *Torch*, pictured The Copper Grid as "Edgewood's other institution of higher learning." During these years, this bar and the Brat & Brau on Regent Street regularly featured special nights and prices for Edgewood's students.

The 1971 yearbook, however, also declared the first home-made "Gaslight Night" in the fall of 1970 as "THE social event of the year." It was an all-campus "family" affair, involving students, staff, and faculty in a variety of spoofs, skits, dances, and fun—including a rock and roll dance by the tallest basketball player, Randy Papp, and the shortest administrator, Sister Sarita Engstrom, as well as a stunning tango danced by the chaplain, Father Richard LaPata, and Sister Esther Heffernan (with a rose between her teeth). Old-fashioned "fun" uniting students, faculty, and staff could still be a lively part of the Edgewood scene, and Gaslight Night became an annual tradition during the seventies.

Student activism took positive directions in volunteer services such as "Project Understanding," when, in January 1971, twenty students volunteered for a two week period of work among rural black families in one of the poorest counties of Mississippi. Not unlike the Freedom Riders of an earlier generation of students, Edgewood students rode south in an old bus owned by a seminarian, John Kinsman, and pitched in to do what they could in construction, farm work, tutoring, and community center projects. These volunteer activities in Mississippi continued during subsequent summers, January Winterims, and other vacation periods for several years. Kent Lesandrini, who travelled on that first Mississippi trip, recalls the experience:

Gaslight Night, 1970: Above: Rock & Roll demo by dean of students, Sister Sarita Engstrom, and senior Randy Papp. Left: Tango danced by the chaplain, Father Richard La Pata and Sister Esther Heffernan—unforgettable moments at the annual faculty-staff-student party.

I was skeptical at first because I was reading Eldridge Cleaver at the time and I could just imagine what they would think of a bunch of middle class white kids from the North coming down to "save the South." But John was relentless, so I went. We stayed with black families in some very poor parts of Mississippi and worked in the Head Start Center. The families were really amazing—very warm and welcoming. We were (uncomfortably) like honored guests instead of workers trying to help out for a few weeks. Overall, I think we got more out of this than they did, but I don't think they felt that way.[16]

While the Edgewood ideal of service to others remained alive and well in these turbulent times, students demanded and got the right to nominate the speakers at their commencements. In spite of the verbal fireworks students often launched at college administrators and faculty, it is interesting to note that the first student choices for their own commencement speakers were Sister Cecilia Carey, their college president, and Sydney Harth, an Edgewood English professor.

Some physical changes were dramatically altering the look of the campus and the lives of the Dominican sisters. In the spring of 1969, building inspectors decreed that the old Sacred Heart Academy building, constructed in 1894 after the tragic fire of November 1893, was no longer safe as living quarters for the nearly ninety Dominican sisters who lived there—students, faculty, and staff of the three Edgewood schools. The required extensive renovations were deemed prohibitively costly, and so, in November 1969, the old landmark building was razed, after the sisters had moved out to rented homes or apartments, to Regina Hall, to the high school Tower, to the apartment over the college chapel, and into four mobile homes placed among the oak trees near the gymnasium.

Edgewood College Archives

The college library was located for many years on the ground floor, under St. Joseph Chapel, and was presided over by Sister Jerome Heyman, director of the library for thirty years, from 1953 to 1983, after succeeding Sister Mary Claude Flanner, the first senior college librarian. Helping Sister Jerome here is her student work-study assistant, Kent Lesandrini.

The tearing down of Sacred Heart Academy and the dispersal of its art and artifacts, including stained glass, chapel furniture, elaborate brass door fixtures, and antiques (some given by the Washburn family) sadly marked for many the end of an era, as did the changes evident among the sisters themselves, many of whom had now returned to using baptismal rather than religious names and had changed from the traditional white habit and black veil into contemporary dress.

The question of how to provide on-campus housing arrangements for the Edgewood sisters was answered in 1973 by the prioress of the Sinsinawa Congregation, Sister Marie Amanda Allard, and her council. A no-interest loan from the congregation enabled the sisters at Edgewood to build two pre-fabricated residences on campus near Edgewood Drive: Siena Apartments, housing twenty sisters, and Rosewood House, housing six sisters. Some sisters continued to live in houses bought by the congregation in the vicinity of Edgewood, while others remained in rented houses and apartments. The on-campus housing built for the sisters was designed so that it could be used later for college student housing when the number of sisters serving at the Edgewood schools declined, as it was beginning to do in the seventies. From a peak of thirty-seven Sinsinawa Dominican sisters serving on the faculty and staff of Edgewood College in 1970, the number began to shrink during the seventies, to thirty-three sisters serving in full or part-time positions in 1978.

Many other changes were underway, including a nearly complete turnover of administrative officers. Except for John Butler, the development director who had begun his work under Sister Nona, other officials from Sister Nona's administration resigned in the first two or three years of Sister Cecilia's administration, and a new group joined her in preparing to meet the many challenges of a new decade. Sister Marian Harty replaced Sister Barbara Beyenka as academic dean in January 1970; Sister Sarita Engstrom replaced Sister Matthias Michels as dean of students about the same time, and she in turn was replaced by Sister Jean Richter in January 1972, who was succeeded for one year in 1975 by Dr. Joshua Edwards, who was followed by Sister Anne Marie Doyle in 1976. Sister Joan Smith, who had served since 1946 as registrar, resigned in 1970, and was replaced by Sister Mary Clare Gilligan, who was succeeded by Sister Dolores Grasse in 1974. Sister Margaret Mihm, who had replaced Sister Calasancta as business officer in 1968, was replaced by Albert Rouse in April 1971.

In 1971 two teachers, both well-known and loved in the Madison community as well as at the college, retired— Sister Lois Nichols, who had taught music for twenty years at Edgewood, and Sister Alexius Wagner, who had taught for thirty-four years in the business department, initiating its program of business education.

A significant change in the governance of the college occurred in 1969, when for the first time the college's Board of Trustees included three lay members as well as Dominican Sisters.[17] The first lay members were two men from the former President's Council— Carl Mayer, vice-president of the Oscar Mayer Company, and John L.

Edgewood College Archives

Sister Marian Harty, a member of the mathematics department, succeeded Sister Barbara Beyenka as academic dean, serving from 1970 to 1979.

Edgewood College Archives

Al Rouse followed Sister Calasancta Wright and Sister Margaret Mihm as college business officer in April 1971. Here he shares an idea with Phil Hansen, who became manager of the college food service in June 1971. Both men continued to serve the Edgewood College community with skill and dedication under four college presidents. The community honored their gifts of service by selecting each as a recipient of the annual "Stevie" award, "exemplifying the mission of Edgewood College"—Phil Hansen in 1988 and Al Rouse in 1997.

Sonderegger, President of Rennebohm Drug Stores—and Gerald Settles, President of the Midwest Aluminum Company. On November 10, 1969, the Board met and elected its first lay officers: Carl Mayer, chairman, and John Sonderegger, vice-chairman. In May 1972, the Board unanimously approved the addition of two faculty members with voice and vote;[18] the first faculty members of the Board were Michael Lybarger, history department, and Sister Pauline Lambert, French department. In 1973, the Board added an alumna representative, Barbara Chryst, class of 1961.

From an administrative perspective, perhaps the biggest challenge of Sister Cecilia's presidency was immediately evident in her first year, when Edgewood's enrollment experienced a steep decline to 751 students in September 1968 from a previous high of 847 students in September 1967. Since the college relied heavily on tuition income, this had a devastating effect on that year's operating budget, and it required an unanticipated struggle to find new resources and cut expenses in a time of inflation. The following year saw the decline continue, with a September 1969 enrollment of only 676.[19] The fall of 1970 brought an upswing, with 714 students enrolled, but the following fall of 1971 saw another downturn, this time to 530 students, a drastic decrease of 26%, in part occurring because of the cessation of the nursing program collaboration with St. Mary's Hospital and Methodist Hospital and a continuing decline in the seminary enrollment. The collaborative program with Holy Name seminary was discontinued in 1976.

While the decline in student enrollment during these years was serious, the problem was exacerbated by the economy's spiraling inflation which sent all costs rapidly higher. At times, Sister Cecilia indicated to the trustees that operating costs

Sister Cecilia Carey presents an award to Carl Mayer, first lay chairperson of the college's Board of Trustees. Looking on is John Sonderegger, who succeeded Mayer as chair of the board. Both Mayer and Sonderegger had served on the President's Council, a group of lay advisors, before their election to the Board of Trustees in 1969.

were increasing at a double-digit rate. Because of the earlier increase in student enrollment during the sixties, along with the increasing complexity of administrative services needed, the numbers of faculty and staff had grown steadily. In the peak year of 1967-68, with the highest number of students, there were 42 full-time faculty and 18 part-time faculty.[20] In 1968-69, with a decrease in enrollment of 12%, there was an increase to 43 full-time faculty and 22 part-time faculty. And in the still declining student enrollment year of 1969-70, there were 48 full-time faculty (an addition of five from the preceding year) and 16 part-time faculty (a decrease of six from the preceding year).

Painful as it was, staff cuts were urgently needed at a time when the recession of 1970 was deepening. By 1971-72, when the student enrollment was down to 530, the number of full-time faculty had been reduced to 27. After that year, as the American economy improved, and as student enrollments began to increase again, faculty numbers grew larger—to 33 full-time and 22 part-time faculty in 1974-75. That same year, Sister Cecilia was able to report to the faculty and staff some very good news: the college annalist recorded that "she spoke with confidence—the enrollment was 'holding up' and the budget was balanced for the first time in several years."[21] Still, the annual reports of the college business officer during this period give evidence of a precarious balancing act, moving only gradually from annual deficits into modestly balanced budgets.

The efforts needed to bring the college budget into balance meant that building projects in this period had to be put on hold. One such project to fall victim to the financial crunch was an on-campus planetarium project, initiated in 1965, with efforts by Sister Louis Russley of the geo-science department to obtain a National Science Foundation grant for astronomical equipment. The NSF turned down the first grant request in l967, but another request was made during the spring of 1968, during Sister Cecilia's first weeks in office. In May 1968, the NSF awarded a grant of $21,000 to purchase planetarium equipment, and an issue of *Edgewise* announced the news, predicting that "the entire structure will cost around $80,000. and will be located between the Indian mound and the oak tree."[22]

During the following spring, the Oscar Mayer Foundation awarded a grant of $30,000 for the building. Subsequently a grant of $15,000 was obtained from the Frank J. Lewis Foundation. The Board of Trustees gave approval for initial construction plans, and in the fall of 1970 a contract was signed with Spitz Laboratories for purchase of astronomical equipment, totaling $39,461.

By 1970-71, however, the United States was heading into a severe recession at the same time that the college was experiencing declining enrollments. The Board of Trustees declared a temporary moratorium on building, and the planetarium project was put on hold. During 1971-72, the National Science Foundation requested reports on the use of the equipment grant, while Spitz Laboratories sought responses regarding the date for shipment of the contracted equipment. Sister Cecilia and the trustees faced a dilemma—some monies for the project were in hand, though not enough to fully fund the project, while at the same time the college was attempting to turn around the deficits that were occurring in the annual budgets.

Finally, on May 16, 1972, the Board gave its decision to Sister Cecilia—to cancel the planetarium project and to seek cancellation of pending contracts—both painful prospects. Her first task was to deal with the Spitz Laboratories contract. On June 19, 1972, she wrote to A. B. Collins, the president of Spitz, saying, "This letter must serve as notification of our intent not to purchase the Spitz planetarium equipment." Collins' reply indicated that the college would owe $19,000 as a penalty for canceling the contract. Negotiations continued, and on January 23, 1973, Sister Cecilia wrote to A.B. Collins offering $5,000 as a cancellation fee. In a letter of April 3, 1973, A.B. Collins wrote to Sister Cecilia with wry resignation, saying that after careful consideration, he would accept the $5,000 fee if it were accompanied by, "from time to time, a short prayer for our well being."[23] No doubt breathing a sigh of relief, Sister Cecilia responded with gratitude and the promise of prayers "as a binding part of a contract," as well as the check.[24]

Another relatively happy outcome occurred when the Oscar Mayer Foundation allowed re-allocation of its grant of $30,000, with $15,000 going to the new Human Issues program, and $15,000 to the president's discretionary fund. However, $21,000 from the NSF grant had to be refunded to the government in October 1974, and near the conclusion of Sister Cecilia's term, the $15,000 Frank J. Lewis Foundation grant was also refunded by the College.

Even without a building project on the horizon, the financial situation that faced Sister Cecilia and the trustees during the seventies was truly grim. In the fall of 1971 the enrollment had plummeted to 530 students, with a full-time enrollment of only 345. Sister Cecilia and the trustees had to explore new ways of increasing enrollment and raising money. In 1971 one such effort was the decision to hire a public relations firm based in Milwaukee—Communiqué— to research public perceptions of Edgewood College, and to suggest strategies to improve the college's image and attract new students. While there had been advertising for the college in the past as well as regular development of public relations materials,[25] Communiqué's market research indicated that the public image of the college was fuzzy and overshadowed in the Madison community by the image of the high school, better known to the local community due to its longer existence (and loyal alumni), its strong educational programs, and its consistently successful sports teams.

The Board saw the need to respond dramatically to the dismal outlook described in the Communiqué report after its initial attitude survey conducted in the fall of 1971:

The college market in general is shrinking, but the market segment from which Edgewood has traditionally attracted students is shrinking even faster. A small Catholic college perceived to be in the traditional mold offers marginal appeal at best by today's standards. Add to this Edgewood's perceived high price tag; its narrow curricula, emphasis on education degrees, an insufficient promotional budget, an obscure identity, and intense competition, we can begin to see why Edgewood's enrollment is declining.... If anything is lacking from Edgewood's promotional effort it is persuasion. Edgewood is simply too modest in selling itself to prospective students.[26]

While the Edgewood trustees were hesitant about the significant financial investment required for the various phases proposed in the Communiqué project, they agreed with the conclusions of the survey report that aggressive marketing was needed to turn around the perceptions of the college in the region and to increase enrollment. Sister Cecilia, in her 1970-71 report to the trustees clearly stated the problem:

We stand at the present moment in a position shared by most private institutions, one of precarious balance. While our academic program has received not only approval, but actual commendation, we are not so successful in marketing its excellence.[27]

The college's contract with Communiqué was extended to the next phase of the public relations campaign. An advertising blitz was proposed for the fall of 1972, complete with slogans such as "Go to Where It's Going On," and a theme of "We Don't Just Study It, We Do It," the use of bumper stickers and the creation of radio and TV spots.

Faculty reaction to these slogans and to the new marketing efforts, was largely negative, as one might imagine, and tensions about the continuation of the program continued. Internally Sister Cecilia was facing attitudes similar to those described by Jill Ker Conway, president of Smith College, when she initiated a public relations and marketing campaign:

Beneath this [faculty] complacency was a taboo on marketing Smith.... Marketing was seen as a commercial activity which polluted the purity of the academic's role, and anyone who advocated it was dismissed as a crass proponent of the corporate mentality ready to reduce education to a commodity. That was why more good administrative careers had been ruined by college-image studies than by failing football teams. But we had to undertake one.[28]

Difficult though it was at times, the Board of Trustees led the way in raising the money to continue the increased communication and public relations efforts in the various phases of the Communiqué project. At the same time, three full-time admissions counselors were hired and in their first year they visited many high schools. Whether Communiqué's image-building or the stepped-up recruitment efforts were causes, the enrollments began to increase—from the low of 329 full-time students in the fall of 1971 to a high of 421 full-time students in the fall of 1976, at the beginning of Sister Cecilia's last year as president.

Whatever its perceived "image," the Edgewood campus was actually a very lively place in the seventies. For example, during 1972, Senator Eugene McCarthy was once again on campus in March, reading his poetry and discussing political issues of the day. This was the first spring that 18-year olds were eligible to vote, and the April primaries evoked much excitement on college campuses as many students prepared to vote for the first time. A number of students boycotted classes on April 14, 1972, protesting the continuing war in south-east Asia; and during the second week of May, faculty and students participated in a Fast for Peace, as "an act of sympathy with the suffering of the war victims of Indo-China."[29] That spring the college celebrated the publication of two books by its faculty members: Sister Esther

Heffernan's *Making It in Prison: The Square, the Cool, and the Life*, which was to become a classic study of women in prison, and Sister Barbara Beyenka's scholarly translation of St. Ambrose's *De Noe et Arca*, published by the Catholic University of America Press as part of its Patristic Studies series.

In January of 1975, a symposium on "Money, Power, and the Human Spirit" brought renowned scholars to campus: Rev. Raymond Pannikar, theologian at U.C.—Santa Barbara; David Steindl-Rast, OSB, Sister Mary José Hobday, and Dr. Joseph Sittler of the University of Chicago Divinity School, among others. During the spring of 1976, a series of forums considered aspects of the general theme "Native Americans: Test Case for Democracy in a Diverse Society." Sponsored by a grant from the Wisconsin Humanities Committee, the forums climaxed with a day-long symposium in April.

In spite of the continuing financial struggles of the college to maintain a balanced budget and to increase enrollment, new curricular ventures were under way on campus from the beginning of Sister Cecilia's term as president. In the spring of 1968 a major in theology was approved by the faculty and the Board of Trustees. During 1968-69, a wide-ranging curricular study was initiated, directed by the "Committee on Revaluation," which included the president and five faculty members. The self-study necessary for implementation of wide-ranging curricular reforms was given impetus in April 1969 by a Title III grant of $93,000 from the U.S. Office of Education's program for developing institutions. This grant enabled the college to engage Dean (Emeritus) Mark Ingraham of the University of Wisconsin as consultant, and give released time during 1969-70 to three faculty members who had served on the Revaluation Committee—Sisters Clemente Davlin, Jeannette Feldballe, and Esther Heffernan— to continue an extensive curriculum study and to make recommendations that would provide a thoroughly revamped degree program for Edgewood students. In the spring of 1970, the faculty adopted their recommendations, and the new curriculum went into effect in the fall of 1970.

Among its new requirements were a 4-1-4 course plan (four courses in the fall and four courses in the spring semesters, with a Winterim period in January when a student could take one course), freshman seminars for all incoming students, inter-disciplinary courses for sophomore-juniors, and senior seminars as capstone courses for upperclassmen.

The concept of the freshman seminar was described as being "designed to explore the relevancy of liberal arts subjects to each other and to a possible career, to set up an advising system, and most of all to permit each student to increase his knowledge of himself." The seminar instructors were drawn from various academic departments.

Sister Esther Heffernan, who was one of the early seminar instructors, recalled:

Like many creative projects with a variety of goals not entirely agreed upon by those involved, the freshman seminars led a controversial life. While most faculty agreed in principle that they were a great idea, in reality the participating faculty went their own ways in shaping the seminars while the students began to question whether they were "real" courses with understandable objectives. After repeated calls for review, a pendulum swing in curricular revision led to their replacement by structured disciplinary skill courses. [30]

Photo: Mary Paynter, O.P.

Sister Esther Heffernan, teacher of sociology and criminal justice at Edgewood College since 1956.

Photo: H. N. Hone
Edgewood College Archives

Mark Ingraham, former Dean of the College of Letters and Science at the University of Wisconsin and consultant for curriculum and planning at Edgewood College. His wise and gracious assistance facilitated development of a collaborative program between the University and Edgewood College. Grateful students and faculty selected him in 1972 as the first recipient of an Edgewood honorary degree.

While the senior seminar program, intended to provide an integrative liberal arts study as a degree capstone, and the intermediate inter-disciplinary courses did not last long beyond their first experimental years, the concepts behind them took new form in the fall of 1974 when the Human Issues program was initiated with a grant from the Arthur Vining Davis Foundation. John Kane, the first director of the program, called it "a distinct departure... an attempt to move beyond the special disciplines in order to confront broader questions.... On a campus like Edgewood this sort of program can only be approached in an inter-disciplinary way."[31] The rationale of the program stated that it "grew out of the urgent need to address ourselves to some of the larger human issues which people must face today in this highly specialized and technological world.... One is confronted with two fundamental questions whose encounter can help one face the future with hope: what does it mean to be human? and what kinds of human relations do we want in order to be fully human?"[32]

The 1970 curriculum revision had also reduced the general degree requirements from a minimum of 55 credits to a minimum of 32 credits, and gave greater flexibility in choice of courses to satisfy these general requirements. Ironically, perhaps, the reduction of required degree courses hit the philosophy and religious studies departments particularly hard at precisely the same time that the incoming student population was rapidly shifting from graduates of private (mostly Catholic) high schools to graduates of public high schools.[33]

Each department worked out its own changes in major and minor requirements—with many variations during the next few years, ranging from increased variety in offerings (such as field courses in the geo-sciences: "South Florida Landscape," "Wild Rice Areas of Wisconsin and Minnesota") or development of new concentrations within a major (such as Accounting and Small Business Management in the business department, or a teaching minor in religious studies), or new majors such as psychology, child life, economics, political science, and criminal justice.

Curricular reform was given on-going status in 1970 by the establishment of a standing faculty committee, the Educational Development Committee. Its responsibilities were to serve as a locus for continuous academic planning, to evaluate and develop the college curriculum, and to make recommendations to faculty and administration regarding curricular changes.

An important dimension was added in 1970 with a formal collaborative agreement between the University of Wisconsin and Edgewood College established through the efforts of Dean Mark Ingraham. Students at either institution could enroll in courses not offered in their home institution. This enabled University students to take, for example, religious studies courses at Edgewood, and Edgewood students to take advanced courses not offered at their college. Reciprocal library privileges gave Edgewood students and faculty easy access to the rich resources of the world-class UW libraries.

In 1970, a comprehensive report was prepared under the direction of Dr. Joseph Schmiedicke for the application for re-accreditation by NCATE, the national program assessing college teacher education programs. On June 9, 1971, the college received word that its teacher education program had been approved with "unqualified accreditation for ten years."[34]

The college expanded its outreach to the Madison-area community by establishing an Office of Continuing Education in 1970, with the former dean Sister Barbara Beyenka as its first director. During the first year, 108 students were enrolled in the non-credit courses; by the fourth year 582 were enrolled; in the sixth year 881 took continuing education courses. In 1976, Claryce Dierschke joined as assistant to the director, and the following fall Sister Virginia Pfluger succeeded Sister Barbara as director.[35]

New educational directions continued throughout the seventies, with the revival of the Associate of Arts degree program in 1974, and the North Central Association's approval of the granting of graduate credit for advanced courses in 1976. The latter was the first step toward establishing a graduate degree program at Edgewood College.

Through all these new developments, student involvement was assured, with student members serving on the Educational Development Committee, the Faculty-Student-Administration Board, Student Life, Resident Affairs, Teacher Education Committee, Development and Public Relations Committee, among others.

In 1973-74, the college celebrated the 700th anniversary of the death of St. Thomas Aquinas, medieval Dominican theologian. The year-long "Aquinas Commemoration"—a series of lectures and panel discussions—was organized by the philosophy department under the direction of Sister Catherine Cordon. New initiatives in Catholic theology and in ecumenical outreach were evident in the various courses, lectures, and discussions sponsored by the religious studies and philosophy departments.

Sister Marie Stephen Reges' close ties to the Madison and University Jewish communities gave impetus to the establishment of a course "Jewish Life and Thought," team-taught by Sister Marie Stephen and Rabbi Michael Remson in the fall of 1974. During the spring of 1975, Edgewood and the University of Wisconsin jointly sponsored a Biblical Archaeology Exhibit at the UW Center. In 1976, Rabbi Manfred Swarsensky accepted the Chair of Jewish Life and Thought in the Religious Studies Department. Rabbi Swarsensky had been honored by being awarded the college's second honorary degree in 1973 for his untiring work in promoting ecumenical dialogue. His first course, offered during the fall of 1976 and limited to thirty students, filled instantly and 150 more who wanted to enroll had to be turned down.[36]

The population of the college had markedly changed during the early seventies. In 1970, the percentage of Wisconsin students entering the college was only 47%, while the number of Illinois students was 35%. State tuition grant programs were shifting the ratio, since many could no longer afford to travel out of state and lose their state scholarships. By 1975 over 60% of incoming freshmen were from Wisconsin and only 25% from Illinois, and the proportion of in-state students would continue to grow, as did the numbers of graduates from public high schools.[37]

During the spring and fall of 1975, faculty seminars studied the role of the faculty and re-examined the goals and purposes of the college, and a five-year planning process was set in motion that would be part of the preparation for

Photo: J. D. Patrick   Edgewood College Archives

Rabbi Manfred Swarsensky receives the doctoral hood from his friend and colleague, Sister Marie Stephen Reges, on the occasion of his receiving the second honorary degree ever awarded by Edgewood College in May 1973.

"I am humbly grateful that a religion-oriented college with which I feel a deep spiritual affinity is bestowing this honorary degree upon me."

Rabbi Manfred Swarsensky

North Central Association re-accreditation. In the fall of 1976, the college began preparations for its fiftieth anniversary with a symposium on educational issues, featuring Bishop William McManus, chairman of the U.S. Bishops' Committee on Education, and the Bishop of Madison, Cletus F. O'Donnell, president of the National Catholic Education Association. Faculty members at the symposium began an intensive study of the five-year planning projections in the light of the college's commitment to offer a liberal education within a Christian community of learners.

That same fall the campus ministry program was reorganized, and for the first time a priest-sister team replaced the single chaplain of the past.[38] The new ministry team was formed by Father David W. Woeste, former director of the Madison diocesan religious education center and secretary to the late Bishop William P. O'Connor, and Sister Clare Wagner, former provincial councilor and experienced teacher/administrator in several Dominican high schools, including Edgewood High School.

Late in Sister Cecilia's term as president, and during one year between the summer of 1975 and the spring of 1976, two events occurred which marked the end of an era at Edgewood College: the retirement of Sister Mary Rosary Corrigan and the death of Sister Joan Smith.

Sister Mary Rosary had spent 34 years on the Edgewood campus, teaching Campus School kindergarteners for eleven years, and then serving as head of the education department and director of teacher education in the senior college. In 1973 she became the first director of the college's Early Childhood Education Center.

Edgewood College Archives

Sister Mary Rosary Corrigan directed the education department at the college for many years, beginning in 1941. She retired in 1975, after founding the Edgewood Nursery School and beginning an Early Childhood Education program.

Her personality and wisdom, as well as her educational expertise, were remembered fondly by hundreds of alumnae who themselves became teachers under her guidance.

Rae Carol Rocca, a graduate of the class of 1961 and herself an outstanding teacher in the Madison public schools system, recalled:

Sister Mary Rosary was a gem! My memories of are very vivid. She was energetic and positive, and what she taught me, I have tried to instill in my student teachers: always make positive statements (not negative ones), never let a child leave angry or sad at the end of the day, be firm but fair, and make learning fun! Her legacy lives on all these years in that those she taught are still teaching her values and insights to new young teachers today.[39]

Another former student, Mary Mickle Pezdirtz, remembered:

How special were the days of student teaching with that wonderful educator, Sister Mary Rosary! She ran the kindergarten as a true "garden of children." She treated each child carefully, as one would a plant, nurturing it and guiding it and feeding it spiritually. I was majoring in K-Primary, and I wanted to be just like Sister Mary Rosary.

In recognition of her outstanding work, the Wisconsin Department of Public Instruction honored Sister Mary Rosary during her final year at Edgewood with its Distinguished Service Award, and she was also named "Outstanding Educator of America," a title all her former students agreed with.

A few months later, in April 1976, the Edgewood College community and hundreds of alumnae were saddened to learn of the death of the much-loved Sister Joan Smith, registrar of the college from 1946 to 1969. Her pioneer work with adult women, known as "Sister Joan's chickadees," encouraged many to return to college or

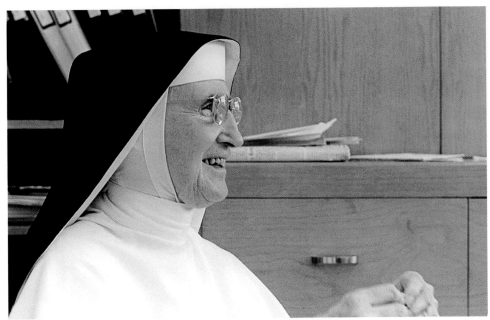

Edgewood College Archives

Sister Joan Smith, registrar at the college from 1946 to 1969, served as special counselor and friend to generations of Edgewood College students, especially to the student sisters and to the adult women whom she encouraged to continue their education.

to begin their degree work. She, with Sister De Ricci Fitzgerald, had been instrumental during the 1930s and 1940s in developing Edgewood into a senior college[40] and planning its teacher education curriculum. In 1934, while studying for her master's degree at Teachers College, Columbia University, she was already writing to Sister De Ricci about new trends in education: balancing the teaching of subject-matter with concern for students' real-life needs and the development of values, the need for teachers of elementary students to have a larger, richer cultural background, a concern for developing initiative and decision-making in the child.[41]

During the 1940s, while she and Sister Nona were working in Washington, D.C., on the *Guiding Growth in Christian Social Living* curriculum for the U.S. Bishops' Commission on American Citizenship, Sister Joan frequently wrote to Sister De Ricci, inquiring about the progress of the new baccalaureate degree program at Edgewood College, and promising daily prayers for its success. She was well aware of the needs of the college, writing in 1945, the year before her appointment as registrar:

We hear rumors about a possible building program at Edgewood. This gives joy to my heart because it is a venture that we will have to make, I feel sure. We need a place where our teachers can be trained systematically, and a place where our principals can come together to exchange ideas and get inspiration. I hope that you will provide for a real auditorium with a good stage, where groups can come for lectures, concerts, plays, etc.[42]

During her twenty-three years as registrar of Edgewood College, Sister Joan was instrumental in preparing for the college's accreditation by the North Central Association and the National Council for Accreditation of Teacher Education. She continued to publish articles in educational journals and served on the Board of the National Catholic Education Association. Sister Joan's death on April 22, 1976, marked another end of an era—even as Sister Cecilia was preparing to enter what would be the final year of her presidency.

During 1977, Sister Cecilia was elected by the sisters of her congregation to its highest post of leadership, becoming Prioress of the Congregation of the Sinsinawa Dominican Sisters. In assuming this new position during the summer of 1977, she resigned as president of Edgewood College, having led the college through a turbulent decade.

Difficult as those years had been, she could look back at significant accomplishments. Student enrollment, which had dipped to a low of 530 in 1971, had climbed to 730 in 1975-76. From 1968 through 1973, the college faced annual operating deficits, but during the last several years of Sister Cecilia's presidency the college removed all capital debt and achieved several years of budgets in the black.[43] Although student tuition between 1970 and 1977 had increased 100% (from $1,100 to $2,200 per year), student financial aid had increased 175%—from $198,000 to $542,000. A stable economic position had been achieved, a new curriculum was in place, and new programs were flourishing.

The farewells to Sister Cecilia included high praise from the college's trustees who knew well that she had been "a bridge over troubled waters" during a most difficult period of Edgewood College's history. The faculty's appreciation of her wit and humor was evident in the popular song parodies sung to her during the farewell champagne brunch held in her honor in Phil's Diner on May 15, 1977. One former

Sister Cecilia Carey reviews the special logo created for the golden jubilee of the college in 1977. She could reflect on a turbulent decade past and rejoice in beginning a jubilee time of festivities during her final year at Edgewood.

faculty member, Sister Clemente Davlin, who had been a colleague of Sister Cecilia in Edgewood's English department during the late fifties and early sixties, recently reflected on Sister Cecilia's inaugural speech, seeing in it the qualities that would mark her decade as president:

I think the fact that I have kept a copy of her speech all these years and have unearthed it each time I've worked on anything related to the mission of Catholic higher education means that I thought it a uniquely valuable statement of that mission.

Reading it now brings back to me in a deeply emotional way the pain of that time, though I had almost forgotten that. Her statement of the problems of that moment are forthright and vivid, as are her statements of possible responses.... She calls for "anguished scrutiny" by which she means, I think, self-scrutiny, and a search for "not a definition, but a living means of reconciliation." She calls the college "not to state but to demonstrate... an open-ended search, directed to exploring today's anguished needs and the kind of value scales whose application can be the only solution for effecting reconciliation in an alienated society...."

This is a president who values what her predecessor handed on to her but who is accepting the office with full awareness that she is in a new, troubled moment with problems that cannot be faced with old or easy answers. Obviously she loves students in spite of feeling their antipathy, even hostility and misunderstanding.... Finally, she is herself, her style marked by clarity and wit.[44]

Indeed, the students would miss her keenly, since she had consistently listened to them, acted on their behalf, and always taken them seriously. One student of that era, Anne Kirschner of the 1973 class, reflected later on her own experiences during the early years of Sister Cecilia's presidency:

Academically, I am very satisfied with the education I received at Edgewood. I especially recall the interest and attention given not only by my faculty advisor but by every instructor in my department.... In the four years I was there the college underwent many changes. I credit Edgewood with the courage to make those changes... and I feel it to be one of the crucial elements that saved Edgewood from being buried in the graveyard of many small private colleges. I honestly feel that my Edgewood years gave me the most valuable experiences of my life. At a time when confusion and self-doubt seemed to be the order of the day Edgewood provided me the support and direction I needed.[45]

When Sister Cecilia was interviewed shortly after becoming president, she spoke of having selected the poetry of modernist Marianne Moore as the subject of her Ph.D. dissertation because of her deep interest in Moore's "analysis of the pressures and tensions in the contemporary world, and her concern for human integrity in that world."[46] Little did she know how that perception foreshadowed her own situation when she, too, would be called on during the years of her presidency of Edgewood College to act creatively and decisively in the midst of tremendous "pressures and tensions," while sustaining a deep "concern for human integrity." Probably no president of Edgewood College would ever again be called to serve during such a maelstrom period in American history and in the history of higher education. Surely no one would do it with more integrity, grace, and wit.

CHAPTER SEVEN

Transition Years

1977-1987

*A*fter a turbulent decade, Edgewood College—like the rest of the nation—seemed ready for a period of stability and steady growth. Sister Alice O'Rourke became the college's eighth president in August 1977, a few months after another new president had assumed office in Washington, D.C.

The inauguration of Jimmy Carter in 1977 seemed to augur well for a fresh and hopeful national renewal. People were beginning to look beyond the turmoil of the Vietnam years and the Watergate scandal. In 1976 the country had joyfully celebrated its 200th birthday with a glorious parade of tall ships in New York harbor. However, unexpected pressures on President Carter quickly developed. Having won election as a Washington outsider, he soon faced difficult struggles with Congress, rapidly upward spiraling inflation, and new hot spots in foreign affairs. He succeeded in bringing Israel and Egypt to a peaceful resolution with the Camp David accords in September 1978, but crises in Iran and Iraq led to another round of rising oil prices in 1979-80, with the price of oil doubling between 1978 and 1981. The Middle East had suddenly become America's new battleground, a fact made devastatingly clear in 1979 with the fall of the Shah and the rise of Ayatollah Khomeni in Iran, together with the ascent to power of Saddam Hussein in Iraq, followed by Iraq's invasion of Iran. The pace of conflict in the Middle East quickened dramatically with the taking of American hostages on November 4, 1979, when militants seized the U.S. embassy in Teheran. An abortive attempt to rescue them failed, dooming

Joseph Jackson – Edgewood College Archives

New Directions Changed the Face of the Campus Between 1977 and 1987. Challenged by changing educational and demographic trends, the college placed more resources into developing programs for adult students during these transition years at both undergraduate and graduate levels. By 1980, the new Weekend Degree and four-year nursing programs were up and running, and preliminary consideration of graduate course offerings was under way.

Registration time for the 1980 fall term brought Cindy Martinelli (with daughter Cori) to consult with Judy Wilber of the financial aid office. Waiting in line are Melissa Klein and Bridget Serig.

Jimmy Carter's quest for a second term in office.   In November 1980, Ronald Reagan won the presidency, soundly defeating Carter.

The complex economic and social pressures of the Carter-Reagan years were reflected in a transitional decade at Edgewood College, 1977 – 1987, during the terms of two college presidents, Sister Alice O'Rourke and Sister Mary Ewens. Challenging new directions in higher education, including a declining enrollment of traditional-age college students and an increased emphasis on providing degree programs for working adults, as well as dramatic cost increases due to inflation —all had profound effects that contributed to dramatic changes at Edgewood College during these transition years.

1977 – 1983 :   Sister Alice O'Rourke

Sister Alice O'Rourke came to Edgewood with broad experience in higher education, having received her Ph.D. in American diplomatic history from the University of California – Berkeley. She had served as professor and chair of the history department at Rosary College in Illinois and as dean of students there, as well as history professor and elected chairperson of the Academic Council at Saginaw Valley College in Michigan.   Closer to home, she had been a member of the Edgewood College Board of Trustees from 1967 to 1973, while serving on the General Council of the Sinsinawa congregation of sisters.

In the fall of 1977, as Sister Alice O'Rourke entered the presidency of Edgewood College, a new opportunity for stability and growth seemed within reach. A reporter for *The Wisconsin State Journal*, interviewing the new president in September 1977, wrote confidently:

Sister Alice O'Rourke is assuming the reins of the four-year liberal arts institution at what looks like an opportune time. The college is in the black for the third time in the past four years; it is holding its own in enrolment; the dormitories are full; and there doesn't seem to be a need for a large building program.[1]

Similarly, after an interview with Sister Alice O'Rourke during her first month in office as the president of Edgewood College, Phil Haslanger of *The Capital Times* described the new president and the positive prospects for the college's next decade:

Sister Alice O'Rourke sat at the end of the conference table in her spartan office and talked in her quiet, deliberate way about education at Edgewood College. A historian by training, a Sinsinawa Dominican sister by vocation… she has taken over the leadership position at the college in a year when it is celebrating its 50th anniversary and at a time when it is trying to consolidate some of the dramatic changes of the past decade into a mean-ingful program for the future. 'One of the reasons I was willing to assume the position at Edgewood was that I was satisfied with its philosophy,' Sister Alice said, describing that philosophy as 'intellectual competence within the context of Christian values and service.'

Her comments do not suggest any dramatic changes in the offing for the college, but rather some fine tuning of the existing directions.[2]

The sense of stability and "fine tuning" seemed appropriate in the fall of 1977 as the college celebrated its fiftieth anniversary with a wide range of festivities—

Edgewood College Archives

**Sister Alice O'Rourke, O.P.
President of Edgewood College
from 1977 – 1983; Ph.D.,
University of California-Berkeley**

lectures, a "Fiesta of Ideas," concerts, and a Golden Jubilee Benefit Ball. The Oscar Rennebohm Foundation presented a check for $50,000 to Sister Alice in September, the largest single gift ever received by the college, one earmarked for student scholarships. Over 500 guests attended the Golden Jubilee Benefit Ball in September, and just as many enjoyed the gala concert in December presented by various music groups: the Wisconsin Chamber Orchestra conducted by David Crosby, the Baroque Chorus of Madison, the Festival Choir, the Edgewood Community Choir and Brass Ensemble, and the Edgewood College Choir.

Edgewood College Archives

Ruth Mary Fox in the library of her Regina apartment

One sadness marred the fall jubilee festivities—the death of Ruth Mary Fox, who had lived on the Edgewood campus since 1963 as professor-in-residence after her retirement from a long career as scholar and teacher at the University of Wisconsin-Milwaukee. A graduate of St. Clara College at Sinsinawa, she remained close to the Sinsinawa Dominican sisters throughout her lifetime. When she made her retirement home at Edgewood in 1963, she taught creative writing to college students and continued her own writing career while becoming a revered campus figure. She had written to Sister Nona in 1960, saying that she planned "to write the last chapter of my life" at Edgewood. The last words of that chapter were uttered at the memorial Mass in her honor, celebrated on October 15, 1977, in the Edgewood College Chapel. The college library received a bequest of 3,000 books from her library, many related to Dante, her chief intellectual interest, and the subject of her book *Dante Lights the Way*.

During Sister Alice O'Rourke's first weeks at Edgewood in the fall of 1977, the college faced a budget shortfall due to a dip in student enrollment. For three of the preceding four years, budgets had edged into the black as student enrollment gradually increased, reaching 424 full-time students during Sister Cecilia's last year as president.[3] However, as Sister Alice reviewed actual enrollment statistics for the fall semester of 1977, she could see that a deficit inevitably loomed, because the registrar's figures listed only 385 full-time students, even though the over-all head count remained about the same as during the preceding year. She moved quickly to trim costs wherever possible, and the deficit of $3,345 during Sister Alice's first year was not significant. However, the following year, 1978-79, saw a further decline in enrollment, down to 330 full-time and 149 part-time students, resulting in a budget deficit of $169,143, the worst in the college's history.[4] Sister Alice O'Rourke, a scholar of diplomatic history, would need all her skills of diplomacy and leadership as well as her long experience in higher education to negotiate the unexpectedly rough waters of a new period in Edgewood College's history.

What had happened and what needed to be done? When one looks back at the late seventies, several factors explain the dramatically deteriorating situation for Edgewood College and for many other small private colleges.

First, inflation in the U.S. reached 11% in 1977 and was to climb even higher in the next few years, to 12.5% in 1978 and to 13.3% in 1979, quickly pushing all college costs beyond budget projections, while income—from tuition and gifts—lagged behind. With fixed expenses for salaries, benefits, and inflation-driven costs of maintenance, repairs, and supplies, the gap between income and expenses suddenly loomed large for the college. Borrowing to meet obligations meant incurring interest rates approaching 20%, adding to the tight financial squeeze.

A second reality – the college's lack of significant endowment funds and its history of relatively low annual gift income—meant that the college was almost entirely dependent on tuition income for achieving a balanced budget. Even a small shift in enrollment could seriously affect the college budget.

A third factor, related to the second, was that the need to increase enrollment came at a time when the traditional college-age student population was no longer growing and there was a decreasing demand for elementary and secondary teachers—an area of professional preparation long dominant among the educational programs at Edgewood College.

Finally, at Edgewood College, contributed services of the Dominican sisters among faculty, administrators, and staff accounted for about 35% of all income (apart from tuition and fees) as listed in the annual budgets during the late seventies.[5] As the number of sisters declined and lay employees took their places, salary and benefit costs rose significantly while the contributed services figure diminished.

D. Patrick – Edgewood College Archives

E. Philip Farley, chairperson of the Board of Trustees, congratulates Sister Alice O'Rourke at her inauguration as the eighth president of Edgewood College. Sister Marian Harty, academic dean, joins the assembly in applauding Sister Alice.

How could these challenges be met?

Obviously little could be done about the upward inflationary spiral afflicting the American economy, so cutting expenditures, coupled with creative efforts at fund-raising and developing new programs to attract and retain students, became Sister Alice's goals during her presidency.

She herself took the lead in the arduous task of cost-cutting. After a Board of Trustees meeting on February 23, 1978, when board members insisted that expenses be cut, Sister Alice decided on the following day to eliminate her own formal inauguration as president, an event which had been scheduled for April 1978. She wrote to E. Philip Farley, chairperson of the board, "As one of the first objects of cost-cutting, I recommend the cancellation of the inauguration.... plans have not proceeded so far as to create any serious inconvenience for anyone by a cancellation." This personal effort to lead the way in the painful process of trimming costs was typical of Sister Alice's approach—she would not ask others to do anything she would not do herself. As she said to John Butler, development director, "Judging among the so-called targets for cost-cutting, the elimination of the inauguration is one of the least painful prospects." The Board did not accept her proposal, however, and the formal inauguration of Sister Alice O'Rourke as the eighth president of Edgewood College took place on April 21, 1978, with Madison's Bishop Cletus O'Donnell and Bishop Edward O'Rourke of Peoria, Sister Alice's brother, among the many guests.

In August 1978 the North Central Association of Colleges and Schools notified the president that Edgewood College had been reaccredited, and in the same year the National Council for the Accreditation of Teacher Education issued its reaccreditation of the college, with the NCATE evaluators stating that "all standards have been met, with many showing exceptional strength." Similarly, the solid foundation of the college's educational mission was evident, and the NCA evaluation team noted a number of strengths—the well-qualified and dedicated faculty, the administrative structure, the initiation of a five-year plan, the management of financial affairs and a debt-free situation, the academic programs—"especially education," and the "practical commitment to educate the particular students who choose Edgewood, whatever their abilities and backgrounds."

Nevertheless, the report of the NCA evaluation team also indicated some areas of concern: student retention ("41% of entering freshmen in 1968 had graduated in 1972; only 28% of entering freshmen graduated in 1975"), development (endowment was "practically negligible" and gifts from alumni, parents, and board members "seem especially low"), co-education (a policy that "seems more an accident than a policy carefully examined for its full ramifications"), faculty compensation, the proportion of part-time to full-time faculty, library facilities ("a low, even subterranean, profile, with catacomb-like" approaches), the lack of an auditorium and an adequate athletic facility.

It was clear that changes were needed, changes that necessitated stepped-up fund-raising and new directions in program development as well as recruitment and retention efforts. One of the most significant fund-raising programs during the late seventies was the decision by the three Edgewood schools to collaborate in a joint effort leading up to the campus centennial year 1981, the hundredth anniversary of Governor Cadwallader Washburn's gift of his Edgewood villa and property to the Dominican sisters. This campaign—Edgewood Century II—was announced in the fall of 1979, with Patrick Luby, vice-president of Oscar Mayer and Co., as general chair, and Bishop Cletus O'Donnell, Bishop A. C. Schumacher of the Southern Wisconsin District of the American Lutheran Church, and Rabbi Manfred Swarsensky as honorary co-chairs. The boards and administrators of the three institutions hoped to raise $1,000,000 by 1981, the time of the Edgewood centennial year, with the resulting funds divided among the three schools for capital improvements or endowments.

The college's share of the funds received from the Century II campaign was earmarked for a new building that would provide long-needed space for student recreation and activities, and offices for staff. With the offsetting campaign expenses, however, the funds raised did not meet the needed outlay for construction, and loans

Students cheer as Sister Alice breaks ground for the new activities center, while Pat Buckley, student senate officer, and trustee James Fiore enjoy watching the president "move the earth."

had to be undertaken.[6] On May 3, 1981, ground was broken for the first new building on campus since the completion of Weber Hall in 1965.   This addition to De Ricci Hall contained a large student lounge and recreation area with tables, sofas, a computer classroom, a snack bar, and rooms where student groups could meet and work, as well as offices for the growing student services staff. It was designed with an eye to the future—the building supports were prepared for the erection of a second story which could house the much-needed new library. The space freed areas in other parts of De Ricci hall for the addition of two classrooms and faculty offices as well.

The construction of the new student activities center in 1981- 82 was a time of rejoicing, yet in November, that joy was dampened by the news of Rabbi Manfred Swarsensky's death. The beloved teacher had taught his class, Jewish Life and Thought, at Edgewood until a week before his death, and all at Edgewood as well as the citizens of Madison were shocked and saddened by the loss of a great and good teacher, a valued friend, a humble man of God.

As plans for the Century II campaign and the new student center were underway, the college engaged in new program and recruitment ventures and experienced some changes in administrative personnel. Sister Barbara Hubeny succeeded Sister Ann Marie Conway as admissions director in August 1978, and Sister Jean McSweeney succeeded Sister Marian Harty as academic dean in the summer of 1979. Sister Jean stated in her first dean's report that "September 1979 saw the introduction of three academic features which have had a significant influence." These were the beginning of a baccalaureate program in nursing, a Weekend Degree program for business majors, and the introduction of the "Communication Skills" component of the new general education requirements.

The new nursing program, costly in its initial years, gradually grew in strength. The college received $146,800 from the U.S. Department of Health and Human Services to implement the first year of the project. Nursing classes were able to use the facilities of Madison General Hospital's McConnell Hall, which had formerly housed the hospital's own nursing program. The first program director in 1979 was Linda Simunek, followed by Phyllis McGrath in 1980. In 1981-82, Julie Hover was appointed chairperson, and she led the steady growth and development of the Edgewood nursing major until her retirement in 1995.

The most immediately successful venture was the Weekend Degree program which responded to educational needs in the Madison community and to a developing trend in higher education of focusing on working adults who needed to combine studies for a degree with their continuing work life. From its inception, the

The activities center was enjoyed by students who could get a snack, watch TV, play ping-pong, or just relax in the evening or between classes. Shared study as well as conversations made the new center a favorite place, and Jim Smith and Teresa Keller found a quiet moment or two to prepare for class.

Weekend Degree program, under the direction of Sister Helen Dailey, began to turn around Edgewood's declining enrollment. In 1978-79, the college had experienced its lowest enrollment figures since 1959-60, with only 479 students. But during the following year, 1979-80, with the new programs in place, an enrollment upswing began with a fall enrollment of 667, including 365 full-time students and 302 part-time students, a significant increase.

The first graduate of the Weekend Degree program was Barry Fewson, who received his bachelor's degree in December of 1980. Fewson credited the encouragement he received from the Edgewood staff, as well as the support offered by his wife and two children and his employer, Madison General (Meriter) Hospital, with facilitating his achievement. Fewson's experience was replicated in the lives of many of his peers who found that the new Weekend Degree program at Edgewood College met their expectations. Madison corporations became aware of the college and appreciative of what it offered their employees, many paying the tuition in whole or in part for employees who were enrolled.

The Weekend Degree program, planned initially by Sister Virginia Pfluger, director of continuing education, was carefully designed to combine intellectual rigor with personal support and scheduling convenient for working adults. The curriculum was identical to that required of other students, taught by the same faculty, but delivered in an alternate weekend time frame. Classes were held on Friday nights and through the day on Saturdays and Sundays, staffed during these times as well as during the week by Sister Helen Dailey, director, by assistant director Sister Jean Richter, and by Debra Wiese, administrative assistant. The directors were authorized to expedite functions usually carried out during the week by various administrative offices. Face-to-face advising, weekend noon hour socials, and a Weekend Degree newsletter about students' achievements, joys and sorrows—all

Edgewood College Archives

Sister Helen Dailey, director, encourages a prospective student to consider the Weekend Degree program, which responded to the needs of working adults in the Madison area.

contributed to developing a closely knit and supportive community setting for students in the program. As early as June of 1950, Sister Joan Smith had seen the possibility for Edgewood College to "take on characteristics… that will serve the adult public as well as the youth of the region."[7] Thirty years later, her dream was fully realized in the college's Weekend Degree program.

In 1980-81, for the first time in four years, the college budget ended in the black with a surplus of $28,675, while 214 freshmen and 120 transfer students boosted the total enrollment to 728, including 458 full-time students. The trend continued during the following year, with another positive year-end budget total. During the "turn-around year" in 1980, Sister Alice projected not only a sense of hope for the future but also her clear conviction about collegial solidarity, stating:

I am pleased to report that during 1979-80 the college experienced an enrollment increase and anticipates a similar increase for 1980-81. We attribute the improvement to a variety of factors: popularity of new programs, such as the Nursing and the Child Life majors, and the Weekend Degree Program for Business majors; the strengthening of traditional programs; expanded services to students in the areas of academic advising and personal and career counseling (which have helped to account for a higher rate of retention); energetic efforts of the admissions and public relations offices; wide publicity for the college, the high school and the grade school resulting from the Edgewood Century II campaign; continuing effectiveness of the faculty in giving instruction to an increasingly diverse student body and in serving civic, religious, professional, and cultural groups on and off campus; devoted efforts of members of the administrative, clerical and maintenance staffs in supporting the total educational mission of Edgewood College.[8]

It was typical of Sister Alice to credit the maintenance and secretarial staffs in the same breath as the college administrators and faculty. Each and every member of the Edgewood community was, in her eyes, important in carrying out the college's educational mission.

In 1979, computer literacy was being considered as an important new element in the general education program, and a concentration in computer science was being planned in the mathematics department. That same year, the National Science Foundation granted Edgewood College $61,000 to strengthen undergraduate science education, and a federal Title III grant was used to fund a program aimed at strengthening student retention, under the direction of the dean of students, Sister Anne Marie Doyle, who was succeeded as dean in 1981 by Ann Zanzig. John Butler, who had served as development and public relations director for fifteen years, retired in the spring of 1981, and Claire Geesaman, who had been the president's administrative assistant, became the college's development director.

While editors and columnists of the student newspaper often lamented campus apathy during this period, lively events did take place on campus. Pax Christi sponsored a debate on the SALT II talks and the arms race in December of 1979, and during the following spring counseling sessions were held regarding draft registration. "Hunger Banquets," with proceeds to Oxfam or Bread for the World,

Some Staff Members of the 1970s and 1980s

Sister Alice O'Rourke credited the entire staff as crucial "in supporting the total educational mission of Edgewood College."

Edgewood College Archives

1 Sister Dolores Grasse	5 Donna Fuelleman	9 Wilma Sanks	13 Jane Wilhelm
2 Claryce Dierschke	6 Mary Ley	10 Debra Wiese	14 Ken Dickman
3 Phil Hansen	7 Sister Pat Leahy	11 Sister Virginia Ripp	15 Daisy Schara
4 Kit Hildebrand	8 Evelyn Jennings	12 Julie Fisk	

were student-sponsored events. A boycott of Nestlé products because of the company's promotion of infant formula in third world countries was supported by many students, faculty, and staff. The Human Issues department sponsored a series of discussions called the Peace and Non-Violence Forum during 1981– 82.

Halloween costume parties and dances sponsored by the student senate remained perennial successes, as were other seasonal events such as Octoberfest in Vilas Park, Christmas tree decorating, Mardi Gras parties, Spring Fest in April, and May Day with music and student-faculty softball games, as well as on-going music, art, and drama productions. Before Christmas in 1979, the college annalist noted that two successful medieval banquets on campus included not only performances by Edgewood choirs and the Madison Consort of Early Music, but also a disputation by the campus Scrooge Society on the topic "It is More Blessed to Receive than to Give," directed by faculty member Fred Kauffeld, founder of the Scrooge Society and Magistrate of the Disputation.

In the fall of 1982, a new program began—"Education for Parish Service"—coordinated by Sister Marie Stephen Reges of the religious studies department and endorsed by Bishop Cletus O'Donnell and Bishop George Wirz. This program provided a two-year cycle of study in theology, scripture, church history, and spirituality, and was planned to meet the needs of the increasing number of lay ministers in the parishes of the diocese. The program, which Sister Marie Stephen had been told had to have at least fifteen students enrolled in order to begin, actually enrolled fifty-one men and women of the Madison diocese for its first term in 1982.[9]

Meanwhile, the Weekend Degree program continued to grow steadily. The rapid shift in proportion of traditional-age students to adult learners between 1977

Edgewood College Archives

Edgewood College Archives

Above: The 1980 Mardi Gras liturgy in chapel was preceded by a distribution of colorful balloons.

Left: The winners of the annual Halloween costume contest sponsored by the student senate: "Kiss" in 1981.

and 1982, as well as an increase in the number of part-time students, had far-ranging implications for the college, as did the change from the traditional choice of education-related majors to other fields such as business, nursing, and social science.   By 1982-83, during Sister Alice's final year as president, 63% of the student body was over the age of 23, 72% were from Dane County, and the proportion of part-time to full-time students was 344 to 448.   During the spring semester the percentage of weekend degree students reached 31% of the total student enrollment.   By then, the two majors with the largest populations were business and nursing, while the elementary education major had fallen to third place, tied with social science.

A faculty member recalled that the new program directions initiated during Sister Alice's presidency were not always supported, at least initially:

During Sister Alice's tenure, the many changes she initiated caused some friction. I watched when some faculty directed anger toward her as she explained her initiatives, but she never lost her composure. There was a vocal contingent who felt that offering business programs "contaminated" the liberal arts tradition of the college, and some faculty fought the Weekend Degree Program, believing it would dilute "academic rigor." She would nod sympathetically and listen, but not be deterred.[10]

In retrospect, the new initiatives, particularly the Weekend Degree program, "saved" the college by quickly and dramatically increasing enrollment, thereby moving the college toward a more stable financial situation in the early 1980s. At the same time, however, the shift in the growing proportion of part-time and older students dramatically changed the demographics of the student body and the campus climate. The full-time traditional age male enrollment dropped, with one consequence being the withdrawal of the men's basketball team from intercollegiate conference membership in the spring semester of 1981-82, due to a lack of recruits for the team.[11] This was a dramatic change from the 1977-78 basketball season when the Edgewood College Eagles, under Coach Barry Bilkey, had won the championship of the Wisconsin Conference of Independent Colleges, and an outstanding Eagles team member and nursing major, Keith French, had been named "most valuable" conference player, eventually going on to the NBA draft.

In November 1980, Sally Christensen, the women's basketball coach, made history when she was named college athletic director, probably the first woman athletic

Edgewood College Archives

Coach Barry Bilkey presents the 1977-78 WCIC basketball championship trophy to Sister Alice, as team members Jeff Kaul, Keith French, and Tom McGuire look on.

Edgewood College Archives

Another outreach program was begun in the fall of 1982—a series of discussions about "women's voices" in literature with the women inmates at the Dane County jail led by Sister Ann McCullough of the English department. This program, initially funded by a Wisconsin Humanities Insight Grant, was continued for thirteen years by Sister Ann, who is pictured here with one of the deputies.

"Using literature with women in jail often introduced them to different views and broader horizons than they had known. I think to some degree that effort was successful. I know for sure that I learned more from those women than they could ever have learned from me."

Sister Ann McCullough

director among Wisconsin's coeducational colleges. A sports columnist in *Screed*, the student newspaper, said of her at the end of the 1980-81 school year:

I think that there would never be anyone who could possibly replace Tom Marinaro—boy, were we wrong. When Sally Christensen stepped on the stage in the role of Athletic Director, a lot of people decided to sit back and watch. Others offered a helping hand. What Sally did in her first seven months at Edgewood was to take a shaky department and place it on firm ground. In the past year, Sally shines bright as one of the highs.[12]

In October 1982, as Sister Alice's sixth year as president was beginning, she announced that she would not seek reappointment, stating that she had entered the office of president intending to remain only one term. Although these had been difficult years, the faculty, staff, and students deeply appreciated her leadership—largely because she had fostered a strong bond of community at Edgewood. Lucy Keane, editor of the student newspaper, after learning of Sister Alice's decision, reflected student reaction:

Sister Alice is a gentle soft-spoken woman with a smile that overwhelms those who contact her. Sister Alice has a genuine interest in even the smallest concern of the Edgewood community.... She could always be found at socials, student-faculty games, or just walking around the campus.... Her rapport with students has continually been supportive and receptive.[13]

One business department faculty member, Elaine Beaubien, who was hired by Sister Alice in 1980, remembers the distinctive quality of her leadership:

The formula for leadership is to help people successfully achieve their goals. A leader finds out what the team needs, gives them opportunity for personal and professional development and doesn't ever take people for granted. Sister Alice O'Rourke was the president of Edgewood College when I joined the faculty in 1980. She was the best manager and the best leader I have ever worked with.

She was everywhere at the college—in hallway and classrooms, in offices or the cafeteria, at parties, at all campus events. Alice was accessible, but more importantly, she was visible. She was just there, sharing our experiences. There were tears in her eyes when she had to announce at a faculty meeting that she couldn't give us a salary increase the following year. We were awash in red ink, but we were clearly in it together.

She was a diehard Cubs fan, and she loved everything about baseball. The students, staff, and faculty loved having their president playing softball with them in the annual spring game. She never lost her dignity by showing her humanity.... But there were also times when she would just sit on the bench (as I always did) and cheer us on. Alice was like that, she never needed to be a star.

During her six years here, Alice held our college together during a time of incredible stress and change, and she set the stage for later decades of growth. Alice's legacy is not so much what she did herself, but what she enabled us to do and become because of her vision.[14]

On May 5, 1983, a special reception was held in the activities center honoring Sister Alice. Faculty, staff, and trustees joined in warmly affectionate "good-byes" at the crowded event, concluded by a rousing chorus of "May the Good Lord Bless and Keep You Till We Meet Again." Members of the college community concurred in the decision to award Sister Alice an honorary doctorate at commencement, and not only was the degree given but a baseball autographed by her beloved Chicago Cubs was also presented to Sister Alice, a lifelong fan. In her inaugural address, Sister Alice O'Rourke had outlined some of the challenges that she saw facing the college at the beginning of her term as president—"to make our actions reflect our ideals.... to preserve the opportunity for free inquiry.... to maintain a strong liberal arts curriculum while providing opportunities for career preparation.... to expand students' sense of responsibility for service [and to do this] through contact with persons on and off campus whose lives reflect a commitment to deep spiritual values."[15] Hers was an unwavering commitment to meeting those challenges as she sought to strengthen the college's life and mission during her six year term as president.

Sister Mary Ewens   1983 – 1987

Sister Mary Ewens became the ninth president of Edgewood College on July 1, 1983, coming from her position as dean of the Rosary College Graduate School of Fine Arts at Villa Schifanoia, in Florence, Italy. Sister Mary Ewens had received a Ph.D. in American Studies from the University of Minnesota and had been a professor and department chairperson of American Studies at Rosary College, before going to Italy. She knew the Edgewood campus and Madison scene well, having been a boarding student at Edgewood High School in the early fifties, before the college campus developed by Sister Nona McGreal had been built.

As Sister Alice O'Rourke was nearing the end of her term and Sister Mary Ewens about to arrive, the editor of the college publication *Edgewood College Today* spoke of the challenges that lay ahead:

The present, to say nothing of the future, is perilous to all of higher education, public and private, small colleges and large universities. All have been as adversely affected by inflation as any sector of society. All are currently feeling the crunch of the recession economy. Independent colleges feel the impact of government reductions in student aid. Tax-supported institutions are asked to trim their budgets, while independent institutions <u>must</u> do so. Further, due to demographic realities, colleges can no longer rely on automatically increasing enrollments.[16]

As had happened in the past, a new president at Edgewood College was to face difficult situations and the need to find new ways of meeting the challenges. Sister Mary Ewens saw her own role clearly, stating:

Every college president takes up the position at a particular stage in the college's development, and the job is shaped by the needs of the college at that time. Sister Nona

Edgewood College Archives

Sister Mary Ewens, O.P.
President of Edgewood College
from 1983 – 1987; Ph.D.,
University of Minnesota

faced the task of literally building Edgewood College. Sister Cecilia brought a gift for organization, and Sister Alice's term saw new developments in curriculum and the building of the Student Activities Center. It has become clear to me that my role will be to put the college on a sound financial basis so that its educational mission may continue.[17]

This assessment and the setting of directions for her term became clearer to the new president during her first year in office. During that first year the fact of declining full-time student enrollment created the need to cut expenditures and increase revenues. While an enrollment dip had been predicted, the actual figures for the first semester of 1983-84 were discouraging. Although the head count was about the same as in the preceding fall, the number of full-time students and resident students had fallen, while the number of Weekend Degree students had risen to 36% of the student body. Years of inflation and other circumstances had more than doubled the college's annual total expenses in the six years between 1977, when Sister Alice O'Rourke became president, and 1983, when Sister Mary Ewens began her term of office.

During Sister Mary Ewens' first months, the college faced a possible deficit of $100,000 for that fiscal year, and cost-cutting was in order, including a freeze on faculty salaries. Fortunately, the college ended that year in the black, with an accumulated surplus of $25,000, mainly the result of receiving a $370,000 bequest from the Sage estate and from the faculty salary freeze.[18]

The formal inauguration of Sister Mary Ewens was held on November 12, 1983, with Bishop George Wirz giving the invocation, and Patrick Luby, chairperson of the Board of Trustees, presenting the new president to the assembly and investing her with a replica of the Edgewood College seal, cast by Sister Ruella Bouchonville of the art department. Sister Mary's brother, James Ewens, S.J., Bishop Wirz, and Rev. Stephen Gilmour, campus ministry, concelebrated a Eucharist in the college chapel before the inauguration ceremony.

Sister Mary Ewens was very active during her first year in office, initiating many new directions despite a deteriorating eye condition that seriously affected her sight. During the fall semester the president asked faculty and staff to form a "College Advancement Team" to help recruit students, and during the second semester a group was formed to advise the Board of Trustees regarding an overall college marketing strategy. She encouraged the office secretaries to form a staff association to facilitate communication of concerns. Sister Mary appointed the academic dean, Sister Jean McSweeney, chairperson of the faculty meetings, and Sister Janice Costello, college librarian, succeeding Sister Jerome Heyman who had retired after serving thirty years in that position. During the following summer, Sister Janice directed the move of the library reference and current periodical collection to the Regina dining hall, with the Regina lounge becoming the new dining area. What had been Ruth Mary Fox's apartment, connected to Regina, also became library space. This move, Sister Mary Ewens' first remodeling project, brought the main desk, reference and reading areas of the library out of the "subterranean" setting described in the last North Central Association report and into the bright light of the attractive large-windowed Regina space. Library circulation doubled within the following three years.

Edgewood College Archives

The library reading room with the main reference collection was moved to the bright and open space of the first floor of Regina Hall in 1983.

As the 1983-84 academic year began, the Oscar Rennebohm Foundation, through the efforts of John Sonderegger, foundation secretary and long-time trustee of the college, made a grant of $50,000 to the college, and the board of trustees initiated a three-year plan to further raise donations. In the spring of 1984 the board funded a marketing study by Cresenell, Munsell, Tultz, and Zirbel, Inc. The study, similar to the survey done some years earlier by Communiqué, revealed Edgewood College's perceived strengths (location, small size, quality academic programs) and weaknesses—its image in the community and its cost as a private institution. A new tree logo was designed to grace college stationery and publications, while new "school colors"—green and white—were chosen to represent the college more effectively to its publics.

Edgewood College Religious Studies Dept.

Religious studies department members laid careful plans for a graduate program in the years before its approval by the board of trustees and the North Central Association: Sister Marie Stephen Reges, Father Benjamin Russell, Sister Mary Margaret Pazdan, and Sister Loretta Dornisch, chairperson.

A green and white logo, featuring a tree, appeared on college publications in the mid-1980s.

Confirmation of national accreditation of Edgewood's baccalaureate program in nursing by the National League of Nursing came in December 1983, while other plans were well underway for developing master's degree programs in business, education, and religious studies.   This new graduate program direction responded to needs that had been voiced for some time by students, especially by those in the Weekend Degree program, and proposals were being carefully developed during the early eighties by the faculty graduate committee and the three departments involved.

Despite many successful innovations, financial deficits still loomed for the college. Sister Mary set up a planning committee to formulate a five-year budgeting plan, while the faculty council reviewed and revised the by-laws for the Academic Assembly. The creation of a college faculty budget and planning committee was an important innovation during Sister Mary's first year in office, and the five members—Bill Duddleston, Sister Marian Harty, Sister Esther Heffernan, Charlotte Meyer, and Joseph Schmiedicke—joined administrators Sister Mary Ewens, Sister Jean McSweeney, Ann Zanzig, Al Rouse, and Clare Geesaman, meeting frequently during the fall of 1983 and into 1984 to discuss ways and means of dealing with projected deficits, even considering a "worst-case scenario" for retrenchment, which included the possibility of keeping five majors—business, computer information systems, nursing, psychology, and education.[19] However, a compromise was worked out within the budget and planning committee to re-organize and prune some academic departments in order to retain liberal arts majors.

Drastic cost-cutting was proposed, and the college community learned in the spring of 1984 that the proposed college budget for 1984-85 eliminated funding for the position of Human Issues director, the athletic director and inter-collegiate athletics, five of the eleven student services positions, some aspects of the music department program, and all theater courses and student productions. As had happened under preceding administrations, some of the decisions were contested by faculty and students alike. Lucy Keane, editor of the student newspaper, wrote of the confusion and stress experienced in the entire college community as details of the budget were being worked out that spring:

Clearly, the process of developing a budget [for 1984-85] that will be approved by the board of trustees is a painful one. By attending the Academic Assembly meetings last week, I was more than a little aware of the tensions in the air. The stress was apparent in the face of Sister Mary Ewens, president, who spent thirty-five minutes introducing the budget proposals, leaving no time for questions or discussion....   She compared the budget cuts at Edgewood to "pruning a tree." The tension was equally apparent at the second meeting of the Academic Assembly, this time in the face of Sister Jean McSweeney, who explained that the fact that the board had not made any final decisions at that time gave people the feeling of "spinning our wheels."[20]

The upset felt by students at the proposed academic program cuts was intensified by their experience at an open "Town Hall" meeting held on March 29, 1984, in the activities center. A front page article in the student newspaper described the meeting between the college's budget and planning committee and students, saying that "with the single exception of Bill Duddleston, the committee seemed to be almost nonchalant about the axing.... The liberal arts tradition of Edgewood is to be sacrificed in a meek attempt to stem financial realities that should have been dealt with months and in some cases years ago."[21]

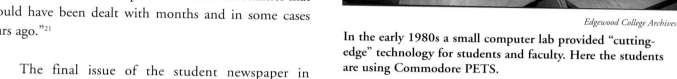

Edgewood College Archives

In the early 1980s a small computer lab provided "cutting-edge" technology for students and faculty. Here the students are using Commodore PETS.

The final issue of the student newspaper in May 1984 carried more hopeful words, with Lucy Keane, the graduating editor, saying, "Edgewood has weathered its past favorably, and Edgewood will continue to do so for a very long time. I'm grateful for the knowledge and experiences that I received here. Thank you!"[22] The front page article in this same issue was written by Sister Marie Stephen Reges, who, in her usual warm and reassuring manner, reminded readers that the college had been through hard times before but had always risen to new and better days:

From the articles in the last issue of Screed *one might be led to believe that the enrollment of undergrads during weekdays will plummet to the depths and its [Edgewood's] light go out. But those who feel this way disregard the historical fact of the resilience of their college in facing similar low tides in the past.*[23]

The "low tides' of these days and the conflicts evoked by them, as members of the community disagreed among themselves how best to weather the storm, indeed recalled earlier difficult moments in the college's history, times of tension and financial crises— times of severe stress faced by earlier generations of students, faculty, and administrators. The college had weathered those storms in the past and would do so again, promised Sister Marie Stephen.

The following year—1984-85—was marked by more changes and innovations, as a new campus day care center was set up in the lower level of Weber Hall under Sisters Deborah Beck and Mary Helen Schmitz, Tom Kotulak succeeded Sister Barbara Hubeny as admissions director, Michael Engh, S.J., became college chaplain, Kathleen Green Woit was named as development and public relations director with Evelyn Jennings as her assistant, Mary Parrinello Ley became alumni director, and Sister Patricia Leahy succeeded Sister Carmela Pierick as director of the continuing education program. The position of director of the Human Issues office, held by Sister Miriam Brown, was terminated. Early in the second semester, Judith Martin replaced Sister Dolores Grasse as registrar, and Sister Dolores replaced Kathy DeYoung as information management coordinator

A change in college administrative structure for 1984-85 significantly enlarged the academic dean's responsibility for leadership and for coordinating the planning, programming, personnel, and budgeting in all academic areas. With the

Edgewood College Archives

Sister Jean McSweeney, O.P., directed the academic program of the college under several titles: academic dean (1979-84), academic vice-president (1984-85), provost (1985-87).

new responsibilities came a new title for Sister Jean McSweeney: vice-president for academic affairs. This change was closely related to a redefined role for the college president, a role focused more on external relations and fund-raising than on internal affairs, a direction approved by the board of trustees which realized that the continuing deficit problem needed special attention.

With the elimination of an athletic director and coaches for the fall of 1984, faculty and staff moved to assist the students in maintaining a sports program—Bill Duddleston volunteered as the women's volleyball coach, Mike Lybarger served as the softball team's coach, Joan Schilling helped students form a running group, Tom Loden coached the men's basketball team, and Steve Brown coached the women's basketball team.[24] The student newspaper reported that, with the support of a petition signed by students, faculty, and staff, the board of trustees at its September meeting had decided to fund the continuation of athletic programs, adding a modest budget item of $3,545 for that purpose. The article concluded: "The student body here at Edgewood College CAN and DOES make things happen."

Similarly, with the removal of a program director for the Human Issues program, faculty members, serving as the Human Issues Education Committee, took on the responsibility for overseeing this keystone academic requirement: Cynthia Rolling, Sister Catherine Cordon and Sister Marie Stephen Reges, with Sister Jean Richter continuing as Human Issues coordinator for the Weekend Degree students.

The tradition of student involvement in community service took a new direction during 1984-85, as DRASTICS (the adult students' association) initiated a program of feeding the hungry at Luke House on Madison's east side every second Sunday of the month. Members of the Edgewood community—students, faculty, staff—joined forces to provide food, cook, serve, and welcome persons who come to Luke House for Sunday evening dinner. The idea for regular Edgewood involvement with the food program was sparked by Lori Bernhagen and Merri Tiedt of DRASTICS.

Student groups created a lively campus atmosphere on occasions such as the traditional Christmas party, the spring festival, or May Day when the whole campus resounded with music, games, and a strong sense of community among faculty, staff, and students. In the college dorms, students' choices of music albums by U2, AC/DC, Duran Duran, Michael Jackson, Bruce Springsteen, and Twisted Sister topped the lists, while groups gathered around TV sets to faithfully watch *Dallas* and *Dynasty* among others. Movies like *ET* and *The Breakfast Club*, or the *Star Wars* and *Indiana Jones* series, drew large audiences to Madison's movie houses, and college students frequented films starring Robert Redford, Burt Reynolds, Clint Eastwood, Jane Fonda or Meryl Streep.

On the national scene, the campaign of Walter Mondale and Geraldine Ferraro in 1984 had cheered Democrats, who were hopeful of reclaiming the presidency, and women, who finally saw one of their own on a national presidential ticket—but their hopes were dashed when the popular Ronald Reagan captured the votes needed for his second term of office. His administration would eventually

Springtime brought outdoor activities—from sitting in the sun on Regina Terrace after lunch, to May Day games and music on De Ricci Terrace, while two faculty members—Fred Kauffeld and Bill Duddleston—once donned temporary face tattoos in honor of the "rites of spring."

come under congressional fire when it was revealed that during these years, the U.S. government was clandestinely assisting the rebels (the "contras") in Nicaragua and selling arms to Iran. But a key operator in those controversial secret deals—Lt. Col. Oliver North—did not become a national figure until 1986-87 when the covert operations were exposed and when nationally televised congressional hearings projected his testimony into every household. In the international arena, Mikhail Gorbachev's assumption of leadership of the Soviet Union was to lead within a few years to the dramatic collapse of what President Reagan had called "the evil empire" and change the course of the long drawn-out "cold war."

Reflecting the optimism of the women's movement that had brought Geraldine Ferraro to the national Democratic ticket, faculty members formalized a new interdisciplinary academic program in January 1985, when the Women's Studies minor was approved. Committee members involved in planning this interdisciplinary program included Charlotte Meyer, Andrea Byrum, Cynthia Rolling, Colleen Cantlon, Jim Lorman, Tess Welch, Sister Esther Heffernan, Sister Jean McSweeney, Sister Loretta Dornisch, Julie Hover, and students Suzanne Maas and Nancy Bennett. The first course offered and cross-listed with departmental offerings was "Readings in Women's Issues," (Women's Studies 480 / Social Science 480), taught by Sister Esther Heffernan to nine students during the January 1986 Winterim term.

The North Central Association visitation team arrived on campus in January 1985 to examine the plans for the proposed new graduate degree programs. Their report indicated the need to add faculty in some key areas as well as the sense that financial and program planning was not yet fully developed for the three graduate programs. The hiring of a director of graduate programs was imperative. Still, the report concluded with the statement, "We believe that the basic ingredients for respectable master's programs exist." In response to this, John Fiss was appointed by the president to begin his duties as graduate director on June 1, 1985. After much discussion, it was decided that only the business department would begin to offer a master's degree program in the fall of 1985, with education and religious studies beginning in January 1986. The fiscal year ended on June 30th with a deficit of $19,741.

News of the deaths of Father Stephen Gilmour, chaplain for three years, of Sister Mariam Yaeger, long-time faculty member in the education and psychology departments, and of Lewis Siberz, architect of many of the college buildings, saddened the campus during the academic year 1984-85. Benjamin Russell, O.P., of the religious studies department, a faculty member who had headed the committee preparing for graduate program accreditation and who had been the commencement speaker in May 1985, left the college during the summer of 1985 to take up his new appointment as vice-president and academic dean of the Aquinas Institute in St. Louis, while Kathleen Woit resigned as director of development and public relations to become assistant chancellor at the University of Wisconsin-Whitewater.

More changes were underway in the fall of 1985, as the college administrative structure was revised again, with the appointment of Sister Jean McSweeney as provost, "the internal chief officer" of the college, for a two year term, while the president became "the chief external officer, relating to the outside community."[25] The office of vice-president of academic affairs was, for the time being, assumed by two faculty members—Sister Marian Harty as acting academic dean and Cynthia Rolling as associate academic dean— while a search for a

Edgewood College Archives

Benjamin Russell, O.P., commencement speaker, and Sister Mary Ewens, president, applaud Sister Marie Stephen Reges who was surprised at the May 1985 graduation ceremony by being named professor emerita – the first such honor awarded at Edgewood College.

new chief academic officer was set in motion. A new development and public relations director joined the administrative staff—Nancy Chase McMahon. One consequence of administrative re-structuring was an additional cost of $40,000 projected in that year's budget, at the same time as deep program and course cuts were occurring—a situation that distressed many faculty and students.

That fall, faculty members were further upset by the realization that, according to the newly revised trustees' bylaws, faculty representatives on the board of trustees —Alan Talarczyk and Cynthia Rolling, at that time—would have voice but not vote, a significant change from the original policy. After further consideration of the matter, voting privileges were returned to the faculty representatives at the board meeting of November 7, 1985, with the comment by trustee Jack Walker that the removal of their voting privileges had been "an error"; at the same time, the board voted to give the college president voting privileges. Concerns of the faculty led to a request to the board bylaws committee to establish some form of faculty representation on board committees so that better communication could be achieved.

Gifts significantly brightened the 1985-86 year: Viola Hopkins left a large bequest to the college library, and Quad/Graphics Printing Company contributed a gift-in-kind of 50,000 copies of a handsome color brochure for the college's use. Sister Mary Ewens announced that Jerry Hiegel, former chair of the board of trustees had raised $100,000 in gifts and pledges for the new MBA program, while the Bishop Cletus O'Donnell Scholarship Fund provided $15,000 for assisting students of the Madison diocese to participate in Edgewood's religious studies graduate program.[26] However, the best news of the fall term was the announcement of a challenge grant from the Oscar Rennebohm Foundation for $500,000 to help build endowment—a critical need of the college. This was the largest gift ever received by Edgewood College, and was motivated, as John Sonderegger said, by "a strong public perception that Edgewood College is a vital asset to the greater Madison area community, providing a valuable service that uniquely meets the vocational, social, and religious needs of various age groups."[27]

The full-time student undergraduate enrollment in the fall of 1985 fell to 374, continuing a discouraging trend seen each year since 1980 when 458 full-time undergraduates were enrolled. Beginning in 1981, as the Weekend Degree program grew, the proportion of part-time to full-time students steadily increased, until the number of part-time undergraduates exceeded full-time enrollment (443 part-time to 374 full-time) in the fall of 1984. Because of the full-time undergraduate student enrollment decline, Marshall Hall was not used as a residence hall during 1985-86, with a few male residents being housed in one wing of Regina Hall.   By the fall of 1985 73% of the students enrolled at Edgewood College were over the age of 23—a dramatic change that had been steadily occurring since 1978 when the percentage was 38%.

Many college students in Madison, including undergraduates at Edgewood, were unhappy as the new semester began in 1985 because of the changes mandated by a new Wisconsin law that raised the legal drinking age from 19 to 21, an age requirement last experienced in 1972.   Edgewood College, like other Wisconsin

Fall Enrollment—1977–1986

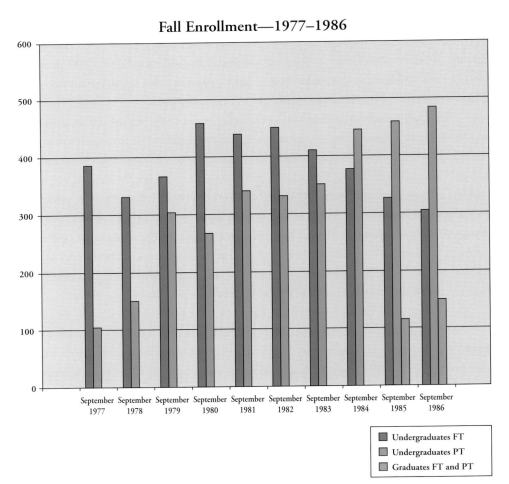

Edgewood College Institutional Research

institutions, had to change its on-campus alcohol policies for 1985-86, while residence halls staff had to worry more about clandestine campus drinking, since area bars were now off-limits for most traditional-age underclassmen. Still, in 1986, comedy ruled on U.S. television, and college students were enjoying the most popular evening series—*The Cosby Show* and *Cheers*. Music albums by Madonna and Prince were among the favorites, with U2, Bruce Springsteen, and Michael Jackson still high on the charts.

The United States and the world were shaken in early 1986 by two catastrophes. In January 1986, during what seemed just another scheduled space flight, the Challenger space shuttle exploded shortly after takeoff—while horrified audiences watched on TV, including thousands of school children excited by the presence on that mission of a teacher, Christa McAuliffe. The world had grown accustomed to routine space launches and perhaps, in taking them for granted, had forgotten the inherent risks and dangers. The Challenger disaster changed that complacency—no one who viewed the tragedy would ever forget it. On the international scene in April 1986, the volcanic-like explosion at the Chernobyl nuclear power station in Russia shocked the world, serving as a wake-up call regarding the potential hazards of the nuclear power industry. Its cloud of radioactive particles quickly spread through northern Europe, into Asia, and throughout the northern hemisphere, while the long term effects of the Chernobyl nuclear accident would linger for years to come.

The steady decline in inflation rates during the eighties was a boon, although with a gradually declining enrollment of full-time undergraduates and increased hiring of lay staff (coupled with a decreasing number of Dominican sisters), the college still faced a difficult struggle to meet annual expenses. At the end of 1985-86, the deficit was $61,690. However, by June 30, 1986, the college endowment fund had a significantly increased balance of $767,000 (principally due to the Oscar Rennebohm Foundation gift), while the scholarship trust fund had a balance of $329,000, with the college investments placed as 50% in common stock, 45% in bonds, and 5% in short-term investments.

At the May 1986 trustee meeting, Sister Mary Ewens gave a mid-term report, marking the halfway point in her six year term as president. She indicated several key accomplishments of the past three years: accreditation of new master's programs and of the nursing major, a re-written college mission statement, change of organizational structure and creation of the provost position, a detailed marketing study, an identification—with a planning consultant—of forty critical issues and formation of task forces to address those issues, the Rennebohm challenge grant for endowment, the expansion of the corporate base of college support, the cultivation of foundations and new sources of funds, the move of the college library into new space, the hiring of a new college athletic director, and her own involvement in various areas of public service. She also highlighted her plans for the future, including stepped-up student recruitment, development of scholarship funds, additional work on planned giving and research on foundations.

During the summer of 1986, formal approval of the master's degree programs in business, education, and religious studies was announced by the North Central Association, and in July certificates were awarded to those who had completed the first two full years of the Education for Parish Service program. These programs, together with the continuing success of the Weekend Degree offerings, enlarged the commitment of the college and its resources to serving the adult community of the Madison area and the diocese, an educational direction greatly stepped up during this transitional decade under two presidents.

The fall semester of 1986-87 opened at Edgewood with the presence of a new academic dean on campus, Judith Wimmer; an associate dean, Cynthia Rolling; a new admissions director, Sister Angela Donovan; and a new athletic director, Steven Larson, who had begun his work with recruitment during the preceding April. A new women's volleyball coach, Sharon Faliede and a new assistant basketball coach, Mike Fisher, had also been added to the athletic department. The Edgewood basketball teams were returning to conference play, after a four year hiatus. An election by the Sinsinawa Dominican sisters resulted in changes among the Edgewood corporate members as Sister Kaye Ashe replaced Sister Cecilia Carey as prioress of the congregation. Among the many changes of the year, administrative offices were moved,

Edgewood College Archives

Steve Larson, athletic director and basketball coach, arrived at Edgewood College in the spring of 1986 and set about recruitment of students and rejuvenation of the college's athletic programs.

with Sister Mary Ewens relocating to a remodeled area of the activities center, and the academic dean moving to what had been the president's office in De Ricci hall.

Preparations for the North Central Association re-accreditation process began in the fall of 1986, with the president's appointment of a self-study steering committee: Sister Jean McSweeney, Judy Wimmer, Joseph Schmiedicke, Sister Esther Heffernan, Julie Hover, and Sister Ann McCullough as chairperson. This group worked through the 1986-87 year preparing the comprehensive self-study with the assistance of all offices and departments of the college.

During the early fall of 1986, the search for a new provost began, since Sister Jean McSweeney had announced her decision not to continue in that office after the completion of her term. The college faced an unanticipated projected deficit of $79,000 for the first semester of the new year, due primarily to the decline in the number of full-time students—only 304 full-time undergraduate students were enrolled, the lowest number since the fall of 1959. To alleviate the situation, in November the board of trustees recommended borrowing on a short term basis to meet the cash flow needs of the first semester, requesting the Trinity High School Corporation to change the college debt payment plan from a five-year to a ten-year plan, and achieving reductions of $100,000 in the current expenditures budget.[28] At the same meeting the faculty representatives on the board presented another recommendation drawn up as a cost-cutting strategy by the chairpersons of the academic departments—the elimination of the provost position and a reconsideration of the role of the president. This recommendation reflected a college-wide concern that increasing administrative costs were not being offset by a significant increase in fundraising and development.[29] The board members agreed to give all the recommendations to the executive committee "for consideration of appropriate action of the board of trustees as soon as possible and that nothing be done about the provost position until the executive committee reports back to the board."[30]

Edgewood College Archives

The terms of four Sinsinawa Dominican college presidents spanned nearly forty years of the college's history—from 1950 to 1987—Sister Mary Nona McGreal, Sister Cecilia Carey, Sister Alice O'Rourke, and Sister Mary Ewens.

At its next meeting, on November 25, 1986, the board of trustees accepted with regret the resignation of Sister Mary Ewens as Edgewood College president, effective June 1, 1987. Sister Mary cited "personal reasons and a desire to return to research and teaching" as her reasons for resigning. The search for a provost was terminated and a new search for a president began. The board decided, with the concurrence of the Dominican sisters, not to limit the pool of candidates to Sinsinawa Dominicans. As the college annalist noted, "The year would end with offices being vacated by the president, the provost, and the directors of admissions and development. It was a year to remember."

A transitional decade at Edgewood College was closing in 1986-87, and Edgewood College was about to enter a new era. Dramatic changes had occurred during the decade, and, as had happened so often in the past, a new beginning would be heralded by the inauguration of a new president.

CHAPTER EIGHT

A New Era

*T*he academic year 1987-88 began with a new president as the leader of Edgewood College. For the first time, the college's president was not a Sinsinawa Dominican sister.[1] Nevertheless, James Ebben, who was to lead the college into a new decade and a new century, was deeply rooted in Dominican educational tradition. He had been educated by the Racine (WI) Dominicans and had worked with the Adrian (MI) Dominicans at Siena Heights College since 1976, where he was vice-president for planning before being chosen as the tenth president of Edgewood College. His sense of Edgewood's history and tradition was evident in his inaugural address:

Edgewood College is built on almost 800 years of Dominican tradition.... There is no end to the building of a strong college. Every president from Sister Grace James in 1927 to now has confronted the challenges of moving this college forward in time. Today is no different. As I accept the presidency of Edgewood College, we again confront the critical challenge, the key challenge of providing a high quality Dominican education.[2]

The challenges Jim Ebben faced in assuming the presidency were indeed critical. Some of the immediate crises confronting him as he prepared to "move the college forward" were the same as those faced by his predecessors as they had entered the office of president—financial deficits, sagging enrollment, staff turnover, the need for new facilities, and uncertainty about future directions. A new administrative team would have to be brought together during that fall semester, since only

A President, A Plan, A New Era
James A. Ebben was inaugurated as college president in 1987, and a plan was developed that involved establishing close relationships with the other Edgewood schools, the neighbors, and the Madison community. The results were soon evident in a newly enlarged gymnasium, a library, a residence hall, a science center, a humanities building, and a beautified campus. As the student population steadily grew, faculty, staff, and programs were added, and the college experienced new life and liveliness in every area.

Pictured here, clockwise from top, are the Henry J. Predolin Humanities Center, the Diamond Jubilee rose garden with the college logo, the Sonderegger Science Center, and the Oscar Rennebohm Library.

three administrators remained—Al Rouse, business officer since 1971; Judith Martin, registrar since 1985; and Judith Wimmer, who had been academic dean for one year. The president needed to rely on the expertise of other relative newcomers in the fall of 1987—such as Douglas Hutchings, development director; Roby Blust, admissions director; Sister Jane Boland, dean of students; and Sister Sarah Naughton, the new chairperson of the board of trustees. More administrative changes would occur within the next two years. In 1988 Ellen Fehring became registrar and Sister Maureen McDonnell was appointed director of campus ministry; Richard Mackie assumed the position of development director in 1989. Existing strengths provided a secure base for the future: a well-qualified and dedicated faculty and staff and a committed board of trustees.

But new beginnings are not without trials by fire. The full-time undergraduate enrollment, which had been steadily declining since 1980, took an upswing in the fall of 1987 with 39 more full-time students than in the fall of 1986, but the ratio of full-time undergraduates was still precariously low relative to the number of part-time students—341 to 507. When Al Rouse met with the new president to review the financial situation of the college, he presented a bleak picture:

I had to tell him that the cumulative debt was $303,000 at the end of the 1986-87 fiscal year, about $50,000 more than had been anticipated. As I recall, his reaction was one of deep concern, but he didn't waste any time—he simply went right to work to turn the situation around. He immediately led the budget and planning committee to develop a five-year plan that would set Edgewood College on a new course.[3]

James A. Ebben, President of Edgewood College 1987-
Ph.D., Michigan State University

Jim Ebben had also to face a personal trial by fire—emergency heart bypass surgery—in March 1988, just as the North Central Association evaluation team was beginning its re-accreditation visit to the campus. As Ebben recalls: "I spent the morning visiting with the team and went directly to the hospital after our meeting."[4] Fortunately, the surgery went well, as did the North Central Association visit; the president was soon able to return to his office in good health, and the accreditation of the college was successfully renewed.

Once again, out of fiery experience Edgewood College would rise like a phoenix and a new era begin. At his inauguration on November 6, 1987, President Ebben's address clearly stated the prospect of a new era when he laid out the main elements of his plan: "continuing to develop a committed, competent faculty, building the facilities we need to support our educational mission, and offering programs that prepare our students for service in society."[5] He promised further that Edgewood College would remain "true to our past," sending forth "men and women who are broadly educated in the arts, sciences, and humanities... people who have strong Christian values."

In order to accomplish these goals, the new president realized that dramatic efforts were needed—the college must immediately increase its number of full-time students, faculty and staff salaries must be raised, new facilities must be built, and a major fund-raising campaign undertaken.

The president's vision of the college's needs was supported by the report made by the North Central Association's evaluation team. The report stated that the "new president has been in office for only eight months and is having a positive impact at all levels of the college. He has articulated an enabling vision that is shared throughout the academic community."[6] However, among the areas of concern outlined in the report were the low full-time student enrollment, inadequate faculty compensation, a history of weak fund-raising results, the lack of consistent curricular review, and the need for new facilities—especially a library and gymnasium. The report pointed out that "the college has had to depend heavily on tuition, the contributed services of the Sinsinawa Sisters, and other non-gift income for its major revenues." The work of the president and the new development director was praised, and the report asserted that "the development effort appears poised for success." The report also commended the plans and strategies of the new admissions director and his staff, indicating that improved admissions efforts were being seen "as a college-wide goal," but urging greater emphasis on "overall planning." The report concluded by noting the college's basic strengths and granting it a ten-year renewal of accreditation, with an interim financial review scheduled for 1990.

In the early fall of 1987, Ebben convened the college's budget and planning committee to set about intensive planning efforts aimed at setting five-year goals and devising strategies to achieve them.[7] By the end of October, the committee had developed clear directions. Plans for the immediate future included assessment of the academic programs and the quality of student life, a study of trends and the creation of five-year projections, development of a plan to improve salaries and benefits for all employees, gymnasium renovation as a necessary support for efforts at student recruitment and fund-raising, coupled with the longer range aim of building a library and fine arts building within ten years.[8]

Buildings and Campus

Almost immediately, President Ebben set about the much-needed building program. Only the 1981 student activities center had been added to the original campus complex developed in the 1950s and early 1960s. The existing gymnasium was inadequate for intercollegiate play since its basketball floor was ten feet short of the minimum requirement; the library, though improved in 1983-84, needed much more space; and faculty offices as well as classrooms and labs were sorely needed. During Ebben's first year in office, renovation of the gymnasium began, enlarging it to regulation court length and adding bleachers, offices, and bathrooms. Renamed the Todd Wehr Edgedome, after the donor of a gift earmarked for its renovation, the gymnasium was ready for use in the fall of 1988—the first in a series of new facilities built on the campus. Athletic director and coach Steve Larson had begun rebuilding the moribund athletic program when he arrived in April 1986. At the same time, a new science facility was being considered and initial planning for a library and a fine arts building was underway. As in the past, there were critics of the choice of the gymnasium as a first building project, but that choice was tied to a larger plan that included stepped-up recruitment of full-time students. The solid financial footing provided by an improved enrollment base together with new fund-raising efforts set other building plans in motion. The 1988 gymnasium renovation was just the beginning of the realization of a new master plan—akin to the one Sister Nona McGreal had laid out in the early 1950s.

The phrase—"master plan"—evokes the long and complex story of how Edgewood College during the 1990s worked out a partnership with neighborhood associations, the local aldermen, the city zoning board, and the other Edgewood schools to achieve a collaborative agreement that all could live with. Thus began a new era in Edgewood's neighborhood and community relations during the 1990s as the college building program developed.

The first new building after the completion of the gymnasium renovation met the long-standing need for more adequate library facilities. With a grant from the Oscar Rennebohm Foundation, library construction west of Weber Hall began in 1990—providing 40,000 square feet of space with a beautiful windowed reading and reference area looking out over the campus to Lake Wingra. Other facilities were book stacks, offices, the Bernardine Clapp Archives, a computer laboratory, and classrooms.[9]

The increasingly successful recruitment efforts created a need for more student housing. For the first time since the completion of Weber Hall in the mid-1960s, planning was begun for a new residence hall. It was initially intended to be located near Marshall Hall on the upper campus, a plan that led indirectly to the formation of an Edgewood Campus Master Plan. When the plan was made public, neighbors in the residences near Edgewood Avenue, fearing an onslaught of noise, increased car traffic, and boisterous student activities, revitalized the Vilas Neighborhood Association in 1992 to counter the plan. Their concerns led to the construction of the new residence in a different place, near Edgewood Drive behind Weber Hall and the Regina Chapel. Marie Stephen Reges Hall was dedicated in the fall of 1994, with Sister "Stevie" herself blessing the hall while proclaiming, "May all who will dwell here live in peace and joy!"

Construction of the new residence hall, however, required Edgewood to negotiate with the city of Madison on new access to the Edgewood Park and Pleasure Drive along Lake Wingra. The ensuing discussions raised questions about the status of the 1905 agreement on the Drive, the extent of future building on the campus, the use of the drive by parents dropping off and picking up their children from the Edgewood Campus School, and the increasing number of cars using the streets adjoining Edgewood's property. A second association, the Dudgeon-Monroe Neighborhood Association, joined with the Vilas Neighborhood Association to voice their concerns. Their representatives on

The beauty of the Oscar Rennebohm Library is enhanced by the magnificent view of the woods and Lake Wingra from the reading and study areas.

the City Council and the City Planning Commission required the development of a ten-year master plan for the entire campus before a conditional use permit could be obtained for additional expansion by any of the three Edgewood institutions, with consideration given to the impact that expansion would have on traffic and parking, neighborhood property values, and environmental land use. With funding available for a science building to be shared by all three schools and planning in the works for a humanities and fine arts buildings for the growing college as well as potential expansion plans for the campus and high schools, the three institutions set to work to develop a ten-year Edgewood Master Plan for the entire campus. With high hopes, Edgewood submitted an initial master plan in March 1996 dealing with many of the concerns and requesting a conditional use permit for the construction of the new science building. In the face of organized opposition by the neighbors the permit was denied.

In an effort to bring all the parties together, an Edgewood Neighborhood Working Group was formed in the summer of 1996 with representatives from the two neighborhood associations and the three Edgewood institutions, assisted by consultants and the on-going participation of the two aldermen. After a process described by the two aldermen in the letter to the neighbors as the culmination of "thirteen months of detailed discussions and much hard work by all concerned,"[10] and the signing of a "Memorandum of Understanding of Unresolved Issues" in April 1997, the neighborhood associations pledged to support a new conditional use permit. On May 19, 1997, the City Planning Commission approved a much modified conditional use permit that included not only the science building but also a parking structure, a new main entrance to campus with a drop off and parking for the Campus School, reconstructed athletic fields for Edgewood High School, and restricted entry to the college campus from Woodrow Street.

In response to these successful efforts, the president of the Dudgeon-Monroe Neighborhood Association wrote that "another result was the development of a good relationship between Edgewood and the neighbors, including a firm foundation for the continuation of that positive relationship."[11] Sister Esther Heffernan, a member of the Edgewood Neighborhood Working Group, says:

This "firm foundation" led to the forming of an Edgewood/Neighborhood Liaison Committee that has continued to meet regularly to ensure that as far as possible there will not be "unresolved issues" in the future. Now as you enter the campus down the tree-lined Edgewood College Drive you see one symbol of that progress—the beauty of sprays of water from a fountain shaped by negotiations over storm water management!"

With the Campus Master Plan approved, construction of the new science facility could proceed. Three and a half years earlier, on October 13, 1993, the presidents of the three Edgewood schools—Sister Nancy Rae Reisdorf (Campus School), Tom Shipley (High School), and Jim Ebben (College)—with Bishop William Bullock, Leona Sonderegger, William Young, and the faculty, staff and students of the three schools gathered outside the library to witness the announcement of a lead gift of $3,000,000 from the Sonderegger family and the Oscar Rennebohm Foundation that enabled the plan for the state-of-the-art building. William Young, trustee and member of the Rennebohm Foundation board, described the unique collaborative

Sister Marie Stephen Reges lived with and counseled generations of resident students over the years, and so it was fitting that the newest residence hall on campus be named in her honor. She came to Edgewood in 1959, teaching in the mathematics and theology departments and serving as a housemother in Regina in those early years.

dimension of the science center: "It will be jointly planned by the Edgewood Campus School, Edgewood High School, and Edgewood College to accommodate the needs and provide educational opportunities for elementary, secondary, and higher education science." A committee of science faculty from the three schools set about intensive planning for the equipment and space use needs for the academic programs that the new facility would house. The actual ground-breaking occurred on June 6, 1997, a few weeks after the approval of the Edgewood Master Plan.

The Sonderegger Science Center and the adjoining parking ramp were constructed in 1997-99, and the $10,000,000 facility became the nation's first to offer kindergarten through college science education. At the dedication of the Center on May 15, 1999, Sally Ride, physics professor, former astronaut and the first U.S. woman in space, was the principal speaker stating, "My involvement in the space program would have been impossible without the kind of science education your center will offer."[12] Leona Sonderegger said, "The family wants to do this in memory of John [Sonderegger] for all the years he worked with the Dominican Sisters at Edgewood College, as a member of the President's Council and as one of the first three lay members of the college board of trustees." Carl G. Mayer, another former member of the President's Council and the first lay chairperson of the trustees, was honored on April 29, 2000, by the dedication of "Helix" by Patrick Zentz, a kinetic sculpture placed at the entrance to the science center.

Two months after the Sonderegger Science Center was dedicated, ground was broken for the Henry J. Predolin Humanities Center, funded by a major gift from Henry Predolin in memory of his son. The building was designed to house classrooms, a computer lab, a student café and commons area, and offices for the president, the Center for Diversity, the dean of students, student activities director. Faculty offices for several humanities departments, the Human Issues Program center, and the Study Abroad center are housed there. Two major meeting facilities are the Don and Marilyn Anderson auditorium and the Sister Mary Nona McGreal faculty commons. The new main entrance drive leading directly to the foyer of the Predolin Center is, as Jim Ebben says, "the heart and the 'front door' of our college."

Derek Walcott, Nobel Laureate in literature, read from his most recent poetry at the dedication of the Center on September 29, 2000.

With new buildings on campus, various remodeling projects could be begun. In Regina Hall, the Nicolet Instruments computer labs, classrooms, offices, and music practice rooms were built in the space vacated by the library move. In 1994-95, most of the basement of the new library, originally intended for storage and stack space, was converted into offices for the business, nursing, and communication arts departments. Later, the lower level of the Sonderegger Science Center was developed to house new nursing labs and classrooms as well as an all-college fitness center.

The Sonderegger Science Center offers science education to students from kindergarten through college in a state-of-the-art facility.

It required Solomonic wisdom and a newly created space committee to address all the conflicting requests for renovated space, because it was clear that even with the new buildings completed, classroom and office space was still at a premium, with steadily increasing numbers of students, faculty, and staff.

Along with building and renovation projects, the 1990s saw new efforts at increased preservation and enhancement of the natural beauty of the campus itself. The key figure in this was Tim Andrews, who joined the staff as coordinator of landscape and grounds on February 1, 1997. He describes his first days on campus:

The melting snow revealed piles of leaves everywhere, weedy compacted turf in sad shape, and much construction residue. The trees were of prime concern to me as a certified arborist. They provide the backbone of our landscape and are, after all, our namesake. Shortly after I arrived, I asked Sister Mo [Maureen McDonnell] what she thought my most important responsibility was. She answered, "To encourage the entire Edgewood community to be involved and care about their grounds." Environmental issues are central today, and my most rewarding experiences have been the introduction of members of the Edgewood community to the natural environment that surrounds them.[13]

Beginning in the spring of 2000, Jim Lorman, biology professor, worked with Edgewood students to create a rain garden between the science center and the campus school. By 2002 three more rain gardens had been created on campus. Just as the fountain and retention pond added beauty to the campus while fulfilling a practical environmental need, so do the campus rain gardens, while educating the students who worked on them and serving as models for our neighbors in the Lake Wingra Watershed area. Jim Lorman coordinates the on-going Edgewood Wingra Watershed project, extending students' classroom learning by engaging in environmental issues, working with others to identify and solve problems, and collaborating with groups such as the Friends of Lake Wingra to promote understanding and good management of the Wingra Watershed.

Yevgeny Yevtushenko, renowned Russian poet of the post-Stalin era, gave lively poetry readings to rapt audiences while at Edgewood College March 19 and 20, 2001.

The most significant and revered elements of the Edgewood campus are the sixteen Native American effigy and burial mounds built by generations of people of the Late Woodland era cultures hundreds of years ago. From early days, Dominican sisters and their students had been aware of the magnificent bird or eagle effigy mound on the southwest side of the campus. Another exciting discovery occurred during the fall of 2001, as Tim Andrews explains:

When plans were being drawn for a studio arts building near Rosewood,, concern was expressed that the building footprint might affect a missing bear effigy mound. I asked Leslie Eisenberg from the burial sites preservation division of the Wisconsin Historical Society to examine the site with me, and she brought an old map showing the mounds along what is now Edgewood Park and Pleasure Drive—and the missing Bear. Much had changed during the past 100 years. The lake level had been raised by damming Wingra Creek. The Park and Pleasure Drive had been moved northward. But the mounds were still the same distance from each other as they always had been since they were built by generations of native people who carried lakeshore soil in baskets to the mound site when they were here gathering rice in the fall. I realized that our Bear had to be clear of the building footprint by nearly 100 feet.

One day while frosty winter winds were blowing the last leaves from the trees along the drive, I was driving my truck along the west end of the drive, and suddenly our Bear revealed itself to me. The 80 foot effigy mound, with the head missing (just as in the old map) was right there, close to the Drive on the lake side, and for 100 years none of the walkers, joggers, bicyclists, or motorists had suspected that this great silent Bear was lying there, perfectly still, just a few feet away.[14]

The mounds on campus remain a vital part of Edgewood's long history, reminding each member of the community of the sacredness of the place and witnessing to the lives of the native peoples who lived here hundreds of years ago.

Student Life

As had happened during Sister Nona McGreal's presidency, one could say of Jim Ebben's years as president—"If you build it, they will come." During the fall of 1987, before the North Central Association visit, the college had an enrollment of only 341 full-time undergraduates. The college's goal for fall 1988 full-time under-graduate enrollment was 375—an aim exceeded by the actual enrollment of 392 that next fall. In 1992, the number of full-time undergraduates (707) exceeded the number of part-time undergraduates (611) for the first time since 1983.

Student recruitment was developed during the 1990s under successive admis-sions directors Roby Blust, Kevin Kucera, and Scott Flanagan. In 1995, a retention committee began extensive study of the situation under the direction of the dean of students—Maggie Balistreri-Clarke, who had succeeded Sister Jane Boland in that office in August 1994. Intensified efforts raised the retention rate for freshmen contin-uing to sophomore status: from 62% in 1994 to 75% in 2001, when the full-time undergraduate enrollment had grown to 1217.[15] The steady growth not only provided financial stability during these years, but also increased the number of resident students on campus and re-invigorated student organizations, activities, and athletic teams.

As in the past, student interests fluctuate and organizations spring up and disappear. By the college's Diamond Jubilee year, more than thirty new or renewed

Student Enrollments—1986–2001

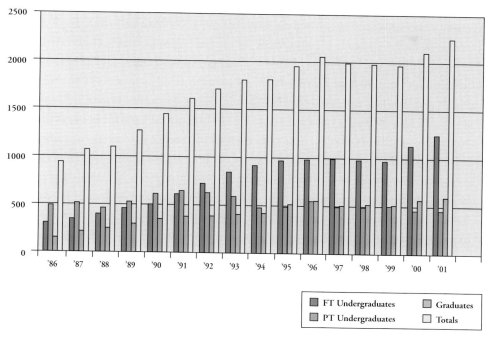

Edgewood College Institutional Research

student organizations offered opportunities for student co-curricular activities. Some long-established ones continue, like the student newspaper, the Student Government Association, Amnesty International, the International Club, and the Student Education Association. Meanwhile newer groups like Friends Like Us (an education and advocacy group for lesbian, gay, bisexual and transgender individuals and their allies), E-CATS (Edgewood College Art Therapy Students), and Habitat for Humanity offer new opportunities for student participation. The Office of Student Activities, under the direction of Beth John since 2000, aims "to get students involved," according to its mission statement.

Sister Maureen McDonnell has served as director of campus ministry since 1988, collaborating with Father Louis Morrone OP, 1992-95, with Stephen Bullock since 1995, and with others through the years to provide opportunities for students to share and develop their faith, plan and participate in campus liturgies and prayer services, and join in social activities and service projects. Leading students to participate in prayer, study, and action related to justice and peace (such as participation in the annual vigils at the U.S. School of the Americas), Sister "Mo" has been a quietly dynamic spiritual force on campus exemplifying the Dominican motto, "Contemplate and share with others the fruits of your contemplation."

Service projects, started by earlier generations of students, remain vital—such as helping in the Luke House meal program or volunteering service during the academic year, Winterim, or spring break. The traditional Edgewood outreach of service for the larger community, described in the Christian Social Living educational philosophy developed by Sister Mary Nona McGreal and Sister Joan Smith, was renewed in the 1990s as the Human Issues program developed a "public or community face, through the Center for Democracy in Action and the engagement of Community Scholars," according to Judy Adrian, coordinator of the Center and the Human Issues Program.   The initial group of Community Scholars included Anthony Brown, Neil Heinen, Nancy Johnson, Carol Lobes, and Andrea Potter. Director Larry Engel describes the Center's mission: "to facilitate citizenship development and opportunities for participation in public life and service.... The Center consciously locates itself at the interface of the academy and public life and draws its faculty from both sectors."   Similarly, education majors extend their community service to Cabrini Green in Chicago under the direction of Tom Holub and assist in the pre-college program under Courtney Moffatt, while other students provide tutoring, computer instruction, and other needed service in housing projects, schools, and community centers from Madison to Appalachia, New Orleans, Mississippi, Native American reservations, and elsewhere.

One graduate of the late 1990s, David Dison, joined the Teach for America program after graduation.   His first assignment was in Greenville, Mississippi, in the fall of 2001, and he wrote to his former Edgewood advisor describing his work and his reactions:

It's been a tough but amazing experience here. I've had the opportunity not only to teach special education students in one of the two public high schools here but also to coach football, basketball, and tennis. Although my students can be a handful at times, I love all of them and I know that they are giving and being all that they can. Many of our school districts are under federal desegregation orders, but little has changed—the two public high schools here are 95% black, while the four private high schools are 95% white.

My experience at Edgewood—though I was no honor student—taught me that service is the most fulfilling part of one's life. I know that some of my colleagues here did not have the same opportunity as I did to go to a college that was tightly-knit and personal. What I'm trying to say is—thanks for putting up with all of my ups and downs as a student, and I think you would be proud of the teacher that I'm trying to become.[16]

Student activism has remained alive and well at Edgewood College through the years. As campus life began to take on added vitality early in Jim Ebben's presidency, the specter of nuclear war and Middle East conflict darkened the mood of the country. Political issues again engaged students in campus debates and public rallies. In September 1987, nineteen students, faculty, and staff participated in the Wisconsin Nuclear Weapons Freeze Campaign. They held a prayer service in the college chapel before going to Turner Hall for a marathon dance fund-raiser, and Edgewood's was the largest group participating in the Madison program.[17] A chapter of Pax Christi was begun again on campus that October, and the student programming board presented programs on the Iran/Contra affair.

In August 1990, the Iraqi army invaded Kuwait, and in January 1991, air strikes launched the Gulf War. U.N. land troops quickly swept the invaders from Kuwait in Operation Desert Storm. Alumna Natasha Kassulke recalls the Edgewood campus culture of those days:

What I remember was the activism. Students were interested in politics again, and it showed in our cultural choices. The Gulf War and the war in Somalia got our atten-

tion and turned us on to songs about peace and about heroes. Amnesty International was active on campus and sponsored not only letter-writing campaigns but also concerts by local rock groups such as the Gomers. In 1992, TV brought us images of the Los Angeles riot after four white policemen were acquitted of beating Rodney King.[18]

The mood of Edgewood College students, faculty, and staff in the 1990s and into the new century was not so far removed from the social activism of the late 1960s and 1970s as people sometimes imagined.

The 1990s brought additional athletic teams, with men's teams competing in basketball, baseball, cross-country, golf, tennis, and soccer.   Opportunities for women increased, too, and women's teams were organized in basketball, cross-country, golf, soccer, tennis, softball, and volleyball. One sign of how far the athletic department had come since Steve Larson arrived in the spring of 1986 was the college's move back into intercollegiate association competition in 1987, then into the Lake Michigan Conference in 1990, and into the NCAA – Division III in 1994. The men's and women's teams have won many conference championships and honors. For example, during 2000-01, the women's soccer and baseball teams were in the NCAA-III tournament as were the men's soccer and basketball teams, after winning Lake Michigan Conference championships. That same year Steve Larson and Stu Schaefer were named LMC coaches of the year (the fifth time the honor had been given to Larson), and Rob Sergenian of the soccer team was given player of the year conference honors.

Coach Alexander's 2001 men's soccer team members are seen below in action against Loras College. From left to right are Mark Losby, a Loras player, goalkeeper Justin Meyer, and defender Jon Rouse.

The 2001 women's soccer team won their ninth consecutive Lake Michigan Conference championship, earning a third straight NCAA III national tournament appearance under the guidance of Coach Tim Alexander. Above, from left to right, Brianna Kilgore, Michelle Jensen, Kayla Sparks, Bridget Joachim, and Rosakay Carillo wait for resumption of play against the Loras College women. Alexander is the only soccer coach to win Lake Michigan Conference Coach of the Year honors in the same year in both men's and women's soccer, and he did so three times in the 1990s.

Popular culture continued to evolve in the 1990s. Like other generations of collegians, Edgewood students welcomed every aspect. Natasha Kassulke remembers:

E-mail became the letter writing of our generation. Technology changed our language and suddenly we were all "connected." SPAM was Internet lingo—not something we ate out of a can. Some people gambled on line and bought concert tickets online. Shopping was at the click of a mouse. With the invention of MP3 and writable CDs, music was everywhere. Nine Inch Nails brought techno to the forefront and Marilyn Manson was out to upset everyone.

Designer fashions were in Vogue and in vogue. Tommy Hilfiger, DKNY, and others rose to the top of the laundry basket. Boys' jeans got bigger and baggier. Tattoos and body piercing burgeoned. Some of us watched the World Wrestling Federation, in-line skated, learned to box because of Tae-bo, and collected beanie babies. We watched "Friends" and made some, too. We laughed, We cried. We danced.[19]

Films like *Jurassic Park, Mrs. Doubtfire, Forrest Gump*, and *The Lion King* topped the lists in the early 1990s, and in 1997 Titanic became the blockbuster that surpassed even the phenomenal success of the earlier *Star Wars* films. On the popular music scene, the late 1980s sounds of Milli Vanilli and Mötley Crüe gave way in the early 1990s to Seattle "grunge" music, and bands like Nirvana, Pearl Jam, and Soundgarden ruled the charts. Punk and ska along with rap mingled with new rock trends, while teen-oriented pop groups jostled for dominance—Britney Spears, the Spice Girls, Backstreet Boys, and 'N Sync.

The demographics of the student body changed in various ways over the years. Although Wisconsin students always formed a strong majority in the student body, the proportion of students from other states was relatively high in earlier years—e.g., in 1963, 34% of the student population at Edgewood College came from outside Wisconsin.[20]   However, by 1988, the registrar reported that of 1054 students at Edgewood, only 32 were from other states (and half of these were from Illinois).[21] This shift was due in large part to the rise of state scholarship programs and a focus on in-state recruiting. A decline in Sinsinawa Dominican sisters' presence in high schools throughout the United States was another factor in this shift, since during the 1950s and 1960s, out-of-state students had often been recruited from high schools by the sisters teaching there.

The proportion of Roman Catholics among the students also declined. In the fall of 1958, the registrar reported that 88% of the students were Roman Catholics; by 1988 the percentage of Catholics was 43%, and by the fall of 2001, the proportion of students describing themselves as Roman Catholic had fallen to 38%. However, in contrast to the 1950s, in recent years increasing numbers of students choose not to indicate any religious affiliation on questionnaires, so the actual number is difficult to know.

Similarly, in recent years many students elect to not indicate their ethnic or racial status, so that data regarding actual minority enrollment is difficult to ascertain. In the fall of 1987, the registrar reported that 29 students of the 848 undergraduates had described themselves as belonging to one or another minority group, while about 300 students did not indicate any ethnic or racial self-description.[22] In spite of efforts such as the creation of a Multi-Cultural Committee in 1993, diversity

The Regina Theatre stage offers a rich variety of dramatic offerings. Pictured here are scenes from a tragedy—Jean Racine's Phèdre, and from a comedy—Oscar Wilde's The Importance of Being Earnest. Appearing in the former were Cara Devine and Kelly Kiorpes. The 1890s comedy cast included (l. to r.) Sarah Luedtke, Liz Angle, Tony Sales, Selena Warsaw-Lane, Morey Burnard, Kelly Kiorpes.

among the student body, faculty, and staff remained relatively small, and during the 1990s minority students averaged between 3% and 4% of the student body.

Clearly, efforts were needed to encourage and support diversity within the college community. Affirmative action statements had been included in the college's catalogs since the 1960s, with the most recent statement approved by the College Assembly in 1997. A diversity statement approved by the College Assembly in March 1997 clearly affirmed the inclusiveness of the community: "Edgewood College welcomes to its learning community women and men of diverse backgrounds, religious affiliations, ethnic and racial identifications, and sexual orientation." Nonetheless, the North Central Association's evaluators stated in the 1998 report,

College community diversity, while slightly improved from ten years ago, remains minimal. The college must develop and implement new strategic initiatives to attract and retain diverse faculty, staff, and students.[23]

Aside from various general scholarships and grants, the AHANA scholarship fund to assist students who are African-American, Hispanic, Asian-American, or Native American was established by Dan and Ann Neviaser. In 2002-03, between $150,000 to $200,000 of the Neviaser AHANA scholarship was awarded to incoming students. Also, the State of Wisconsin provides funds to Edgewood College for grants to minority students beyond the freshman level, and a grass-roots effort by faculty and staff in 2000 established the Martin de Porres scholarship. Scott Flanagan, admissions director, describes some positive results of the college's efforts to increase diversity between 1997 and 2001:

Students of color (AHANA) have increased from 60 to 97 in that period, a 61.7% increase, while overall head count had a 7% increase. In two of the past three years, approximately 7% of the freshman class has been AHANA students, while during the

1990s that figure was approximately 4% each year.   Specific outreach efforts are being made in the local area through pre-college programs, building relationships with Minority Services Coordinators in the Madison schools, and working with specific schools in Milwaukee and Chicago as well.[24]

Another action flowing from the college's concern about diversity was the establishment of the Center for Ethnic Diversity in the mid-1990s. The Center's mission, with the collaboration of faculty, staff, and students, is to promote multi-cultural education through college-wide programming and by making resources available to the college community. The first director was Debra Barrera-Pontillo. Pearl Leonard-Rock became director in 2000, and two years later she renamed the center as the Center for Diversity, stating, "I believe that this name change better reflects the richness of diversity and is inclusive of everything that represents culture—language, race, ethnicity, and other qualities."[25]

Financial Stability

Although the first year of Jim Ebben's presidency began with the challenging fact of a large deficit and a relatively small upswing in student enrollment, the year ended in the black, with a positive balance of $106,714[26]—a harbinger of the financial stability that was being established. Each fiscal year since 1987 to the present has ended in the black, providing a secure platform for growth based mainly on steadily increasing full-time student enrollment. At the same time, the efforts of development directors and their staffs were significant during this period of building and expansion—Doug Hutchings was followed in 1989 by Rick Mackie, and in 1998 John Uselman was named director. Fund-raising efforts by the president, the trustees, the development directors and their staffs bore fruit, with primary focus during the 1990s on building projects. The value of the college plant and property assets rose from $7,239,610 estimated in July 1990 to $31,874,389 in July 2001.[27]

The need to increase endowment as another key to financial stability had been recognized by the Oscar Rennebohm Foundation when its challenge gift of $500,000 for endowment purposes was made to the college in 1985. The endowment funds stood at $1,109,220 in 1988, during Jim Ebben's first year in office. At the time of the North Central Association visit ten years later, the endowment had risen modestly to approximately $3,000,000, and the NCA 1998 report stated that "endowment remains as a kind of Achilles heel for Edgewood. The current level obviously does not represent much of a safety net. Enrollment and tuition with it would not have to suffer much of a perturbation before potentially serious financial realities would arise."[28] By the summer of 2001, the market value of the endowment funds had increased to $4,755,410. John Uselman, director of development, says,

With the steadily rising costs of education and the number of students in financial need, one can see the importance of scholarship endowment funds. Gifts are important for the donors, too, allowing them to make a statement about what they value, because their gifts enable more students to share the values of the educational mission of Edgewood College.[29]

Global Awareness

A significant educational development of the 1980s and 1990s was increased global awareness. The college had a long history of extending the learning experiences of its faculty and students beyond the immediate campus environs and familiar culture. Faculty members had always shared the richness of their own study and travel experiences with students. For example, the first president of the college and head of the French department, Sister Grace James, had lived and studied in the 1920s in Switzerland. Over the years many other faculty members had studied abroad or had come to Edgewood from various countries and cultures, like Sister Amanda Courtaux in the 1930s (from France) and Mary Pothen in the 1950s (from India).

Students, faculty, and staff enjoy the annual International Food Day, featuring both tasty foods prepared by students from many nations and a musical feast in many languages.

Sister Catherine Moran was the first Edgewood professor appointed Fulbright lecturer, teaching at a university in Argentina in 1965. In 1986-87, Sister Joan Leonard, of the religious studies department, received a similar appointment to teach in Portugal, and Charlotte Meyer, of the English department, to teach in Croatia for the 1988-89 academic year. The following year, Sister Winifred Morgan, also from the English department, was selected as a Fulbright lecturer in Salamanca and Valladolid, Spain, and Steven Davis, of the social sciences department, was appointed to teach at Masaryk University in the Czech Republic in 1999.

The study of languages and world cultures had long been encouraged at Edgewood College. The junior college curriculum offered German, French, Latin, and Greek to students. In the senior college, French and Spanish remained consistently in the curriculum, and with the initiation of the collaborative program at the University of Wisconsin in the 1970s, a wider range of language offerings became available for Edgewood students. From 1989 through 1992, Ichiro Noro taught Japanese language courses at Edgewood. In November 1990, the Sister Catherine Moran Language Laboratory was dedicated, replacing the older lab facility and offering state-of-the art equipment and satellite download programs to facilitate student language and cultural learning.

Edgewood College students choosing to enroll in study-abroad programs selected mainly European experiences, offered either by Edgewood or by other colleges and universities. Professors Andrea Byrum, Ian Davies, and Frank Casale, among others, regularly arranged study abroad experiences for students. Vernon Sell of the music department took college groups to other countries during the 1980s and 1990s, and he was instrumental in bringing many European concert groups to the Edgewood campus.[30] Groups of students also participated in short-term experiences abroad during Winterim, spring break, or summer in programs such as the January trips to Cuba (2000 and 2001) or the spring 2002 Social Democracy (Human Issues) class visit to the Borodyanka (Ukraine) Community Center near the site of the Chernobyl reactor explosion.

During the 1940s and 1950s, the college welcomed students from various countries, beginning in 1948 with two students from China, one from Colombia, and one from Peru. The number of international students fluctuated but gradually increased during the 1950s and 1960s. In the mid-1960s Sister Nona McGreal established a Committee on Foreign Students to assist the advisor of international students. Sister Catherine Cordon served as advisor from 1965 into the early 1980s, followed by Andrea Byrum, Sister Mary Ann Schintz, Laurie Bickart, Meg Skinner, Helen Jameson, and Larry Laffrey. During the late 1960s, students from Jordan, China, Iran, Costa Rica, Germany, Guatemala, Ghana, Denmark, Hong Kong, Mexico, Bolivia, Trinidad, Ireland, Nigeria, Taiwan, Cuba, Israel, Ethiopia, Kenya, and Malaysia were listed among the growing ranks of international students at Edgewood. In the fall of 1987-88, 21 international students representing 14 countries were attending Edgewood College, and in 1992, 53 students from 25 countries were enrolled. The number of international students peaked in 1997, when 116 from 30 countries were on campus, forming 6.25% of the total student enrollment that fall. In January 2002, 83 students from 26 countries were on the Edgewood campus.[31]

The students who came from abroad to study at Edgewood during the 1990s increasingly represented Pacific Rim nations, although Edgewood's educational interest in this area had long been developing. Following two years of Chinese language study under the NDEA Title VI Foreign Language Fellowship program, Sister Mary Ann Schintz of the history department spent 1969-70 in Hong Kong and Taiwan as a Fulbright-Hays Research Scholar. In 1971 Sister Mary Ann began teaching courses in the history and culture of Japan, China, Korea, and Vietnam. In 1979-80, Edgewood College received grant funding from the "Citizen Education for Cultural Understanding" program offered through the U.S. Office of Health, Education, and Welfare. Co-directed by Sister Nancy Rae Reisdorf and Sister Mary Ann Schintz, the grant program included a three-week summer workshop in global education for 65 teachers from the Madison area.[32] In the mid-1980s, the president, Sister Mary Ewens, established a faculty task force on international education, chaired by Sister Mary Ann Schintz.

The realization of the importance of Pacific Rim nations in global education was heightened during Jim Ebben's first year as president when the college received a grant from the Oscar Rennebohm Foundation to fund an exploratory visit to Japan, Thailand, South Korea, Singapore, Hong Kong, Taiwan and Malaysia. President Ebben traveled with trustees William Young and Sister Sarah Naughton on that first trip. In 1994, Sister Ann McCullough went with William Young to renew and extend the exploration of educational links for Edgewood in these countries. These initiatives were followed by Jim and Marilyn Ebben's trips with trustees William Young and Sister Sarah Naughton on Pacific Rim journeys in 2000, 2001, and 2002, meeting with Thailand's Princess Sirindhorn and visiting colleges, universities, and government agencies. Subsequently, teachers from Thai institutions began annual visits to the Edgewood schools. In 2001 Judith Wimmer, academic dean, joined the group at Vajiravudh College in Bangkok, Thailand. In 2002, Sister Maggie Hopkins also traveled on the Asian trip, and a larger all-campus group (Louise Stracener and Frances Rowe from the college, Dennis McKinley, president of the high school, and Fran Vizek from the campus school) joined the others on the Vajiravudh College

Sister Catherine Cordon, philosophy professor and long-time advisor of international students, meets Tamayo Ichikawa in front of the Oscar Rennebohm library.

campus. Dr. Chai Anan Samudavanija, director of Vajiravudh College, was awarded an honorary doctorate at Edgewood College's May 2002 commencement.

In 2001, an Oscar Rennebohm Foundation grant established the William H. Young Center for International Outreach on the college campus, with Sister Sarah Naughton as director.   Sister Sarah explains its purpose:

The Foundation funded the Center "to promote cultural and educational exchanges between the Edgewood schools and selected private and public institutions of southeast and east Asian countries, particularly but not restricted to Thailand and South Korea." The Foundation grant of $500,000 will be distributed over five years. During the first year, we assisted the people from the three Edgewood schools who traveled to Vajiravudh College in January. The Center also coordinated the April visit of Vajiravudh teachers to our Edgewood campus. Future plans include continuing exploration of sites in South Korea and elsewhere, the development of an international advisory board, and additional funding development for international outreach programs.[33]

Accreditation

In 1976 the college had requested and been approved by the North Central Association to offer graduate level courses, though not graduate degrees. In 1985 the college began offering three master's degree programs—in business, education, and religious studies—which were granted North Central Association accreditation. In succeeding years, plans for additional master's degree programs were made in the fields of nursing administration and marriage and family therapy, programs approved by the North Central Association in 1994. In 1996 Edgewood College received unconditional approval for the development of new programs at the master's level. This encouraging affirmation was a tribute to the pioneering efforts, plans, and successes of the three departments that had initiated graduate programs in 1985, as well as the nursing and psychology faculty who had developed the newer master's programs. In 1999 the Commission on Collegiate Nursing Education also accredited the nursing programs which had long been recognized by the National League of Nursing.

The North Central Association ten-year accreditation visit was due in 1998, so President Ebben appointed a self-study steering committee, headed by Sister Ann McCullough (who had also chaired the NCA self-study ten years earlier) to begin work in March 1996.[34] As part of the self-study process, the entire college community was engaged during 1996-97 in a reconsideration of the college's mission and vision statements. The president's task force directing the study and revision of the mission and vision statements was headed by Jim Burgess, chairperson of the board of trustees.   After much study and discussion by the entire college community, the new mission statement was approved by the College Assembly in October 1996, and the vision statements in February 1997.

The renewed college mission statement declares:

Sponsored by the Sinsinawa Dominicans, Edgewood College is a community of learners that affirms both its Catholic heritage and its respect for other religious traditions. The liberal arts are the foundation of all our curricular offerings in the humanities, arts, sciences, and professional programs. Committed to excellence in teaching and learning, we seek to develop intellect, spirit, imagination, and heart. We welcome women and men who reflect the rich diversity of the world's cultures and perspectives. We foster open,

Sister Maureen McDonnell, campus ministry director, shares a joyful moment with Sister Joan Leonard of the religious studies department.

caring, thoughtful engagement with one another and an enduring commitment to service, all in an educational community that seeks truth, compassion, justice, and partnership.

The traditions of the college are simply and directly reflected in its mission statement. Its Dominican and Catholic characteristics are affirmed, while its statement of respect for other religious traditions goes back to a principle consistently articulated by Father Samuel Mazzuchelli and by the Sinsinawa sisters who, in 1871, had opened St. Regina Academy, the "grandmother" of the schools at Edgewood.

The North Central Association's evaluators, after their March 1998 visit to the campus, lauded the many advances made since the visitation ten years earlier, stating that the college "has largely addressed the concerns expressed in the 1988 North Central team report."[35] The evaluators further noted that "the college community is characterized by a strong and widely shared sense of mission and common purpose," that "executive leadership is strong, consistent, and persistent in advancing the mission and general well-being of the college," that "faculty are increasingly well credentialed, clearly committed to the college mission, and selfless in their dedication," and that staff "are well-informed, dedicated to the mission, and very competent."

Some areas were seen by the evaluators as "challenges": developing and implementing new strategic initiatives to effectively guide decision-making in the light of the college's mission and vision statements; devising effective ways to attract and retain diverse faculty, staff, and students; addressing retention issues, particularly regarding freshmen; enhancing the endowment to provide stronger financial security; examining the perception of excessive reliance on part-time faculty; collecting, analyzing, and using assessment of the academic programs.[36]

The final result of the 1998 report of the evaluators was approval of the college's North Central Association accreditation for another ten year period. Also, in 1998, the National Council for the Accreditation of Teacher Education programs (NCATE) evaluation team visited Edgewood after an extensive self-study of the education department had been completed, and the college was again reaccredited, with a follow-up visit scheduled for the fall of 2002.

New Programs

Two programs targeting the needs of specific groups of students were developed about the same time during the late 1980s. Two faculty members—Sister Winifred Morgan and Jewell Fitzgerald—worked with the Associate Academic Dean, Cynthia Rolling, on a plan to resuscitate the college's Honors Program. At the same time, plans were under way for creating a learning center to assist students who needed help with study skills or other academic assistance. Fran Leap, of the religious studies department, was named Assistant Academic Dean in 1989 and continued developing the two new programs. Kathy Levin was the first director of the Learning Resource Center, followed by Kathie Moran, who also began a support program for students with learning disabilities. Later, the Challenge Program for students academically at-risk was initiated in 1995. The Honors Program and the Challenge Program are under the direction of the Associate Academic Dean, Carol Cohen, who succeeded Fran Leap in 1991.

Two new degree programs were added in the tradition of educational service to the adult community initiated by Sister Joan Smith in the 1950s and given strong impetus by the Weekend Degree Program in the 1970s and 1980s. The first, at the graduate level, was the response of the education department to requests from graduates and from district superintendents for the initiation of the first doctoral level program at Edgewood—the Doctor of Education degree, an innovative doctoral program designed to prepare administrative leaders at the superintendent level. The North Central Association evaluators, in their report after a focused visit in June 2001, found "Edgewood College poised to address a new level of academic responsibility in higher education."[37] The evaluation report further stated that the "team members did not note areas that require special attention immediately or in the near future." The report pointed to evident strengths: "the excitement and willingness to embark on the development of the Doctor of Education degree as consistent with the College mission and with the academic integrity of current practices...[and the fact that] Edgewood College has a long history of demonstrated responsibility and integrity in the development and implementation of undergraduate and master's level degree programs in education." This accreditation and recognition climaxed a long and proud tradition in the college's history—preparing excellent teachers and administrators for the nation's schools. Edgewood College had presented the first bachelor of science in education degrees to graduates in 1942. Sixty years later, for the spring semester of 2002, the college welcomed the first cohort of students to the new doctoral program.

Joseph Schmiedicke and Sam Barosko, of the education department, discuss their plans for the Doctor of Education degree, begun with a first cohort of students in the spring semester of 2002. The North Central Association accreditation of this degree marked another milestone, being the first at the doctoral level offered by Edgewood College.

Secondly, the college's newest undergraduate degree program—the Bachelor of Business Administration degree—admitted its first students for classes beginning in the fall of 2002. The college had begun offering a few accelerated courses in 1998, as a steady decrease in enrollment in the Weekend Degree program during the 1990s became evident. The BBA degree program is designed to provide all courses required for the degree in a format of four-credit courses in a six-term cycle, with two seven-week terms in each of the fall, spring, and summer sessions.

Ongoing developments in existing programs have renewed the academic life of the college. During the 1990s, the music and art departments grew in enrollments and added new programs—instrumental groups were formed for the first time, and choral groups expanded, while art therapy and graphic design programs enlarged student opportunities in art. In May 1999 the college received a three-year grant from the Teagle Foundation to "reform math and science education for future teachers."[38] The Teagle Project at Edgewood includes the education, natural science, mathematics and computer science faculty working collaboratively across disciplines with each other and with K-12 teachers and education students. Other departments have built collaborative offerings in inter-disciplinary and cross-listed courses or in academic minors such as English/communication arts, environmental studies, and women's studies.

Computers continue to affect college life in many ways. The first computers were introduced to the campus in the 1970s, and computer use grew tremendously during the 1990s, paralleling the pace of Moore's Law.[39]   Sister Marian Harty, of the mathematics and computer science department and former academic dean, recalls:

The computer lab off the student activity center was equipped by an NSF grant that provided funds beginning in the 1979-80 academic year.   The lab had four kinds of computers—and employers of the early graduates noted that having learned on a variety of computers made the graduates more adaptable and flexible in business situations.   These computers were Commodore PETS running on cassette tapes, Apples and TRS80s with 5½ inch floppy drives, and Teraks using eight-inch floppies which were primarily used for teaching the Pascal programming language.   The faculty of the mathematics and computer science department bought, set up, maintained, and supervised the use of the computers, since there were no staff persons to do this.[40]

In the early 1980s development of the major in Computer Information Systems was assisted by a National Science Foundation grant.   Computers began to appear in many areas—administrative, staff, and faculty offices, the library, student computer labs and dorm rooms, and in "smart classrooms" equipped with the latest technology, as students, faculty, and staff learned new meanings for old words—virus, worm, hacker, gopher, web and spam, among others.

Obviously, a support staff was needed to assist with the mushrooming demands. An Office of Computer Services with Ron Krebecek as its first director was begun in 1990, the year before Tim Berners-Lee of CERN posted the computer code of the World Wide Web.   Subsequent directors were Tom Guckenberg and Walter Wentz. The need to keep up with the rapid pace of advancement in computer technology and use of the internet led the college to invest in a fiber-optic backbone laid throughout the campus and to provide office computers for faculty and staff, e-mail, smart cards, on-line registration, an intranet, and a college Web site. The first courses using Web-based materials were created by faculty members in 1994-95 and dozens have followed.[41] A distance learning room was furnished in the Sonderegger Science Center, and the first course offered via video to students in other

Julie Dunbar, chairperson of the music department, conducted the Edgewood College Wind Ensemble in a concert at the Sinsinawa Motherhouse Chapel in 2001.   The instrumental and choral groups perform on tour as well as at the college.

Joseph Testa conducts the campus choral groups.   Here he rehearses with the Edgewood College Chamber Singers.   Back row, l to r: Kevin Janisch, Craig Erlandson, Michelle Pestlin, Brian Breezer, Joseph Pleuss, Angela Cook, Elise Kessler.   Front row, l to r: Mindy Boehnen, Rebecca Wares, Devin Ray, Jill Anderson, Aris Gialamas, Liza Wondra, Kris Gasch, Brianna Donovan.   Dr. Testa is at the piano.

Wisconsin Foundation for Independent Colleges was French language and literature, taught by Sayeeda Mamoon in the fall and spring semesters of 2000-2001. Beginning that same year, Edgewood students could "attend" courses being offered from other WFIC institutions through the technology of the Sonderegger distance learning room.

The college librarians, under directors Claudia Rohr (1987-1991) and Mary Jane Scherdin, integrated the use of computer technology into library services to provide an on-line library catalog and to enable access to databases and off-campus resources. The library got its first computer in 1985 and used it to access cooperative cataloging files, including the Network Library System from the University of Wisconsin by the fall of 1987. By 2002, the library had 40 computers for staff and patron use, and 25 more in the library computer laboratory for class instruction. From the library Web page, created in 1994-95, Edgewood students and faculty can access 35 high quality databases as well as the Edgewood library catalog and, via Web links, other libraries and resources. The reference librarians continue to work closely with faculty and students, offering instruction in research in both print and electronic sources.

Faculty and Staff

One of the top priorities set by the new president and the planning committee in 1987 was the improvement of faculty and staff salaries and benefits. Immediate goals were to reach the 50th percentile of salaries at the nation's church-related institutions within five years, improve TIAA benefits, and add disability and group life insurance.[42] This plan also included the aim of bringing the Dominican sisters' stipends up to lay-equivalent salaries and beginning to provide them benefits, a goal achieved in the mid-1990s. Another goal was to continue to increase the percentage of faculty members with doctoral or other terminal degrees. Progress was evident: the percentage of full-time faculty with such degrees in 1987 was 63%, while by 2001 it had risen to 77%.

The number of faculty and staff grew steadily to keep pace with both increasing enrollment, new programs and new services, growing from 44 full-time and 33 part-time teachers in 1986 to 85 full-time and 126 part-time faculty in 2001.

The college established new ways of honoring the contributions of staff and faculty. In the spring of 1987, the college created an award for professor emerita Sister Marie Stephen Reges to honor her qualities "exemplifying the mission of Edgewood College," and she became the first recipient of the annual "Stevie" award. Subsequent recipients were Phil Hansen, Bill Duddleston, Sister Patricia Leahy, Debra Wiese, Joseph Schmiedicke, Claryce Dierschke, Donna Fuelleman, Vernon Sell, Nancy Nelson, Al Rouse, Mary Tejeda, JoAnn Granquist, Sister Maureen McDonnell, Steven Post, and Bernie Rivers. In 1991, the Wisconsin Power and Light Company (later named Alliant Energy) established the annual James R. Underkofler Excellence in Undergraduate

Art department professors David Smith and Melanie Herzog meet in the De Ricci Gallery and compare notes during the opening of the exhibit by fellow department member Bob Tarrell.

Teaching Award at selected private colleges in Wisconsin, including Edgewood College. The first Edgewood recipient of this award—selected by a committee of students, alumni, faculty, and trustees—was Barbara Beetem (English), followed in subsequent years by Jewell Fitzgerald (communication arts), Alan Talarczyk (business), Charlotte Meyer (English), James Lorman (natural science), Elaine Estervig-Beaubien (business), Sister Mary Paynter (English), Cynthia Rolling (social sciences), Robert Tarrell (art), John Leonard (religious studies), Colleen Gullickson (nursing), and Vincent Kavalowski (philosophy).   In the spring of 2002, the Edgewood College Business Association surprised Elaine Estervig-Beaubien by presenting her with the first annual Elaine Estervig-Beaubien Award for excellence in business teaching, establishing a new faculty recognition tradition.

The number of Sinsinawa Dominican sisters on the faculty and staff began to decline in the 1970s. Still, in 1986-87, the year before Jim Ebben became president, nearly one-third of the full-time faculty were Dominican sisters (14 sisters and 30 lay men and women), while 32 lay persons and one sister taught part-time. That same year, 13 sisters and 72 lay persons served as full or part-time staff members. By the fall of 2001, the proportion of lay people had markedly increased: 81 lay men and women were full-time faculty with four sisters, while 124 lay persons and two sisters taught part-time.   Among the staff members in 2001, seven sisters and 168 lay persons served in full or part-time positions. As the college moves further into the 21st century, the number of Sinsinawa Dominican sisters among the faculty and staff will continue to decline. However, Dominican sponsorship of the college continues to be strengthened by the presence of sisters among the trustees, by the college's relationship to the sisters who are its corporation members, and by newer institutions such as the office of Dominican Mission, directed by Sister Maggie Hopkins since its inception as the office of Church Relations in 1991, and the Dominican Catholic Identity Committee, established in 1995 and made a standing committee of the College Assembly in 2000. Each spring the college sends members of the faculty and staff to participate in the Dominican Colleges' Summer Seminar at Fanjeaux in southern France, the area where St. Dominic began his original preaching and teaching mission.   The vitality of the Sinsinawa spirit, moreover, is strengthened by traditional celebrations such as Founder's Day and the annual St. Catherine of Siena lecture. The college sponsors visits to the sisters' motherhouse at Sinsinawa for meetings, tours of the exhibits, archives, and historic buildings, and samples of delicious meals and home-baked goods.

More importantly, today's staff and faculty members and alumni treasure the memories of people like Sinsinawa sisters Jeannette Feldballe, Marie Stephen Reges, Catherine Cordon, Catherine Moran, and Joan Leonard, as well as Claryce Dierschke and Laurie Ellen Neustadt—with whom they worked as colleagues and peers and friends, whom they laughed with at parties, struggled and mourned with in difficult times.[43] The faculty and staff of today and tomorrow and the college's alumni are the inheritors of their vital spirit and Dominican values.

Laurie Ellen Neustadt inspired her art therapy students, her colleagues, and the entire Edgewood community by her deeply caring commitment, as well as by her artistry and spirituality. Her memory continues to inspire.

Epilogue

As the college community moves from celebrating its Diamond Jubilee toward its centennial milestone, it is clear that many chapters of the Edgewood College story remain to be created. Our past is a rich tapestry of interwoven stories of people and events, of joys and sorrows, of cycles of growth and decline, and only a few of these stories are recorded in this book. What is yet to come will be shaped by new stories and by the dynamic ideas, values, and struggles of the people who are now a part of the Edgewood community and who will join it during the years that lie ahead. The generations past and present welcome the generations yet to come. May they, too, experience the fire, the light, the energy, the faith, and the wonder of the phoenix story which is at the heart of the still-unfolding story of Edgewood College.

Notes

1 — TRIAL BY FIRE

[1] The first four sisters, known later as "the four cornerstones," had been received into the Third Order of St. Dominic by Father Samuel Mazzuchelli, O.P. at Sinsinawa in 1847. These women began their teaching ministry almost immediately. As more young women entered the community, they were sent first to teach in schools near Sinsinawa and then to establish schools in more distant places. Some of these were only open for a few years, such as St. Rose of Lima Academy in Galena, built by Father Samuel in 1859 and maintained until it closed in 1865. Others have survived to the present day such as Bethlehem Academy, founded in Faribault, Minnesota, in 1865. The sisters taught in parish and public schools and in private academies, the first of which, St. Clara Academy, was opened in Benton, Wisconsin, in 1853, and later transferred to the Mound, Sinsinawa, Wisconsin, in 1867.

[2] Marquette, Clare L. *The Business Activities of C. C. Washburn.* Ph.D. dissertation. 1940. Microfilm #8474 in the Memorial Library of the University of Wisconsin. 409 - 410. Albert, the first Kelsey child, was born in St. Louis in 1870. The Kelseys' second child died in 1872, a third was born at Edgewood in 1873, and Mrs. Kelsey was pregnant with a fourth child in 1874 when Washburn nearly threw them out of his home. In 1874, Washburn was deeply troubled by his own political struggles and the bitter loss of an appointment by his party to senatorial candidacy. The Kelseys moved from Madison to the Philadelphia area, establishing a home in Chestnut Hill. Washburn seems never to have favored A. Warren Kelsey, Jeannette's husband. He made his other son-in-law, Charles Payson, Fanny's husband, one of his three estate executors, and Charles served as president of the La Crosse Lumber Company after Washburn's death. See a detailed account of the family conflict in Karel Bicha, *C. C. Washburn and the Upper Mississippi Valley.* New York: Garland, 1995. 190-201.

[3] O'Connor, Sister Mary Paschala. *Five Decades.* Sinsinawa: Sinsinawa Press, 1954. 256: "The ex-Governor's reason for deeding

away his beautiful home was his change in plans after he had failed to win a second term of office…. In 1879 he offered Edgewood to the City of Madison as a park site, but because of its remoteness from the city it was not accepted. Offering it then to the State as a home for dependent boys, he met a second rejection."

Edgar, William. *The Medal of Gold.* Minneapolis: Bellman, 1925. 116 – 117: "He [Washburn] had owned a very beautiful place situated on one of the lakes near Madison. After offering it to the State of Wisconsin, to be used as a girls' industrial school and finding that the Legislature, for some technical reason, had been unable to accept the gift, he had presented it to a Catholic sisterhood which had been very successful in the conduct of several girls' schools in the vicinity. This organization gratefully accepted and he had transferred it, to be used as an educational institution, the value being approximately $50,000.

"C.C. Washburn." *Memoirs of La Crosse County,* 58. "He offered his beautiful summer home in Wingra Park to the City of Madison for an orphanage, and upon the city declining the generous offer, presented it to the Catholic church [*sic*] for a girls school."

A tradition among the Dominican Sisters suggests that Governor Washburn also offered the property to the University of Wisconsin—a reasonable possibility, since he had given the Washburn Observatory to the University three years earlier, in 1878. However, when the sisters wrote to Jeannette Washburn Kelsey asking if she knew of this, she replied that she had never heard that from her father. On the other hand, a grand-niece, Dr. Annette Washburn, told the sisters that she had heard that as a traditional story in the family (see letter from Dr. Washburn to Sister Paschala O'Connor in the Sinsinawa Dominican Archives).

In exploring the history of the sisters' acquisition of Edgewood, Sister Paschala O'Connor found that a "Mr. Bartlett," a Protestant whose children attended St. Regina Academy, "was instrumental in getting the Governor, Mr. Washburn, to attend with him a public examination of the children under Sister Alexius Duffy, who was the Superior. Out of this came the donation of the Governor to the community of his country home which he called Edgewood Villa." Sister Serena says that both Sister Thomas Aquinas O'Neill and Sister Vincent Ferrer Bradford had told her this in their reminiscences about "the old days in Madison." See the letter from Sister M. Serena to Sister Paschala, dated April 5, 1950, in the Sinsinawa Dominican Archives.

4   St. Clara Convent Annals, quoted by O'Connor, 229. The Trustees of the Corporation of St. Clara Female Academy, meeting in special session on May 1, 1881, unanimously voted to accept Governor Washburn's offer "of his beautiful Villa of Edgewood." See the *Book of Trustees* (1847 – 1927) at the Dominican Archives, Sinsinawa, Wisconsin.

The deed transferring the property from C.C. Washburn to St. Clara Female Academy [the corporate name for the Sinsinawa Dominican Sisters at that time], is dated 26 May 1881, signed in New York, and witnessed by Washburn's son-in-law Charles Payson and George Woodman, the son of his former partner Cyrus Woodman. The Deed describes the property as "a gift...to be used and occupied and given and granted upon the express condition that they shall be used and occupied as a school." See copy of this deed in the Edgewood College Archives.

5   See *History of Dane County, Wisconsin.* Chicago: Western Historical Co., 1880, 514.

It is intriguing to note that Rev. Samuel Mazzuchelli, O.P., founder of the Sinsinawa Dominican Sisters, had once planned to acquire property on the Madison isthmus. In a letter written to Bishop Rosati of St. Louis in 1837 Father Samuel wrote: "There is a good promise of a lot in the town of Madison, the capital of the territory. The deeds will shortly be made." Quoted in O'Connor, 170 –71.

No record remains of his actually having done this, however. Possibly the country's depression in the Panic of 1837 put such plans on hold. However, it would seem that Father Mazzuchelli's interest in obtaining land for building a church in the Four Lakes area was planted by James Duane Doty. The two men had spent eight days together in "difficult travel" on horseback from Green Bay to Prairie du Chien, and they had passed near the Four Lakes region (as Madison was called) in September of 1832. See *The Memoirs of Father Samuel Mazzuchelli, O.P.,* translated by S.M.M. Armato and S.M.J. Finnegan. Chicago: Priory Press, 1967. 71.

Doty was a well-known land speculator and a politically savvy promoter who urged the Wisconsin territorial legislature to establish the capital at Madison, having invested heavily in most of the lots on the isthmus earlier. Doty was an influential presence at the territorial legislature that met in Belmont, Wisconsin, in 1836, when Father Mazzuchelli served as legislative chaplain to the assembly. The assembly's debates led to the establishment of the territorial capital at Madison, largely due to Doty's successful pro-

motion. David Mollenhoff explains that in 1836 Doty had organized "The Four Lakes Company" which held 1,360 acres of the Madison isthmus between Third and Fourth Lakes (later called Monona and Mendota). Doty sold or "dispersed" many prime lots to legislators at the Territorial Legislative Assembly, and he may have offered Mazzuchelli the "promise of a lot" as described in the letter to Bishop Rosati. See David Mollenhoff's *Madison: A History of the Formative Years.* Dubuque: Kendall Hunt, 1982.

In 1838 Doty was elected to represent the Wisconsin Territory in the U.S. Congress. He returned to Madison in 1841 and served two terms as governor of the Territory. In 1847 Doty sold to Leonard Farwell land in and near the city of Madison, including the property that John Ashmead acquired from Farwell in 1854, where Edgewood would be built. In 1848 Doty donated lots in Block 67, two blocks from the capitol square, to become the site of St. Raphael's, the first Catholic church in Madison. The stone church's erection on the site in 1862 was the realization of Father Mazzuchelli 's earlier dream.

6   Atwood, David *et al.* "In Memoriam: C.C. Washburn." A collection of eulogies from the Wisconsin State Historical Society memorial service. In *Report and Collections of the State Historical Society of Wisconsin – 1880, 1881, 1882.* Vol. IX. Madison: Wisconsin State Historical Society, 1882.

7   Bicha. 106.

8   Edgar. 79-80.

9   Edgar. 87.

10   Nesbit, Robert C. and William F. Thompson. *Wisconsin: A History.* 2nd ed. Madison: UWP, 1989. 365.

11   *Ibid.* 368.

12   *Ibid.* 369.

13   *Ibid.* 371.

Excellent primary sources for a study of Cadwallader C. Washburn are located in the Wisconsin Historical Society Archives: Cyrus Woodman. *Papers, 1833-1889.* 2 archives boxes and 206 volumes. C. C. Washburn. *Papers, 1844-1877.* 2 archives boxes.

Other important primary sources are in the Archives of the Washburn-Norlands Foundation, Livermore, Maine.

Extensive primary materials regarding the Sinsinawa Dominican Sisters and the early days of Edgewood can be found in the Sinsinawa Dominican Archives, Sinsinawa, Wisconsin, and in the Edgewood College Archives, Edgewood College, Madison, Wisconsin.

2 — FROM ACADEMY TO COLLEGE

Much of the material in this chapter is taken from the Edgewood Convent Annals and other holdings in the Edgewood College Archives. Other materials can be found in the Sinsinawa Dominican Archives.

[1] Stevens, Sister Charles Borromeo. *Little Essays for Friendly Readers.* Dubuque: Hardie, 1909. 234.

[2] Mollenhoff, David V. *Madison: A History of the Formative Years.* Dubuque: Kendall-Hunt, 1982.
David Mollenhoff's book provides a rich and detailed overview of Madison's early history and its people to 1920. His discussion of the Madison Park and Pleasure Drive Association and its leaders is on pages 232-234, 324-352.

[3] Annals. Convent of Saint Regina, Madison, Wisconsin. Sinsinawa Dominican Archives.

[4] In 1915, Mother Samuel Coughlin, with her Council, engaged Cram's firm to examine the Edgewood site: "It was decided to invite Mr. Ralph Adams Cram, the Architect, to look over the Edgewood property with a view to location of future Educational Buildings. Consideration for above services, $100. Mr. Cram or a member of the firm will visit Edgewood, professionally, this summer." *Minutes of Meetings of the General Council, Book 1,* May 4, 1915. The minutes also record that the Council later reviewed a sketch of Cram's neo-Gothic plan for a college at Edgewood. Sinsinawa Dominican Archives.

Ralph Adams Cram specialized in modern Gothic design, having written books on this subject and having designed a number of famous modern Gothic buildings such as those at West Point, at Princeton University, and the Cathedral of St. John the Divine in New York. His sense of the spiritual beauty of the Gothic style and its relevance to both religious and educational institutions undoubtedly responded to the views of Mother Samuel and her council. Cram sent personal copies of his books on the Gothic ideal to Mother Samuel; several of these remain in the Library and Archives of Dominican University, River Forest, Illinois.

A copy of the Albert Kelsey plans for the new Edgewood building, including the tower, can be found in the Edgewood College Archives. Ironically, Kelsey took a dim view of neo-Gothic design, indicating to the Edgewood sisters that his own plans would be modern and appropriate for the twentieth century. (He was well aware of the choice of Ralph Adams Cram as the architect for Rosary College.) Kelsey wrote to Sister Theodosius at Edgewood, on April 7, 1919: "Much as I admire the charm and beauty of the ecclesiastical architecture of the middle ages... yet I am quite sure that it is not either an American nor a Twentieth Century manifestation of the progressive work you are now doing, and hence to reproduce the quaint cloistered buildings of the Thirteenth Century at Madison would be a decided affectation." Letter in Sinsinawa Dominican Archives, with copy in Edgewood College Archives.

3 — SURVIVING THE GREAT DEPRESSION *1930-1939*

[1] Fitzgerald, Sister Mary De Ricci. Diaries and notebooks, various. Box 1, GA 1050. Sinsinawa Dominican Archives. Other quotations from these diaries are indicated in the text.

[2] James, Sister Grace. Letter to Mother Samuel. April 8, 1928. Sinsinawa Dominican Archives.

[3] Klein, Sister Marie Aileen. "Edgewood's Fiftieth Anniversary," *Wisconsin Catholic Clubwoman,* April 1932, 24-25.

[4] Dailey, Sister Mary Hilary. "Reminiscences," March 16, 1990. Edgewood College Archives.

[5] Excerpts from junior college graduates' reminiscences in "The Way We Were," *The Edgewood Scene* Winter 1977. Edgewood College Archives.

[6] *Ibid.*

[7] Barden, Sister Marie Francis. Letter to S. Barbara Beyenka, April 30, 1977.

[8] Excerpts from graduates' reminiscences, published in *The Edgewood Scene*, Fall and Winter 1977.

[9] Green, Sister Jude. Letter to S. Barbara Beyenka, n.d. [ca. 1977].

[10] Green, Ellen Fahey. In "The Way We Were," *The Edgewood Scene,* Winter 1977.

[11] Green, Sister Jude. Letter to Sister Barbara Beyenka, n.d. [ca. 1977]. A letter from Sister Amanda Courtaux described to Mother Samuel her remarkable experience performing a shipboard concert one summer when she was returning to Europe to visit her relatives: "I was obliged to play very much on the boat, so they asked me to play on the evening of the 'Captain's dinner.' I was sorry to see my name printed as you will see it on the Program I mail to you.... But the priests on the ship told me that it would be right to show that Sisters could do also as ones in the world! I did it and every one was very pleased. Thanks be to God!" Sinsinawa Dominican Archives.

[12] Altenhofen, Sister M. Aurelia. Letter to S. Barbara Beyenka, May 12, 1977.

[13] Neumeier, Mary Kolb. In "The Way We Were," *The Edgewood Scene,* Winter 1977.

[14] "The Way We Were," *The Edgewood Scene,* Winter 1977.

[15] Green, Sister Jude. Letter to S. Barbara Beyenka, n.d. [ca. 1977]. After Sister Marie Aileen completed her work as dean of the College in 1940, she remained as a teaching member of the faculty until 1961.

16 "Madison, with its surrounding lakes, was the center of mound building in Wisconsin. Between 800 B.C. and A.D. 1200, Native Americans built more than 1,500 mounds in the Four Lakes area." Robert Birmingham. *Indian Mounds of Wisconsin*. Madison: U.W. Press, 2000. 195. He describes the Edgewood Mound Group on p. 196.

17 Marshall, Elizabeth. address to Edgewood alumnae meeting [1933?]. Sinsinawa Dominican Archives. Reprinted in *The Young Eagle* Vol. 33 (September 1933), 6 – 9. In her will, Elizabeth Marshall left her estate of $125,000 to numerous charities, and Edgewood received a bequest of $5,000.

4 — A SENIOR COLLEGE BEGINS
1940 - 1949

1 McCarty, Sister Mary Eva. *The Sinsinawa Dominicans: Outlines of Twentieth Century Development*. Dubuque: Hoermann, 1952. 429.

2 Beyenka, Sister Barbara. *A Jubilee History*. Madison, WI: Edgewood College, 1977. 14.

3 McCarty, 65.

4 Corrigan, Sister Mary Rosary. Reminiscence. Edgewood College Archives.

5 *The Edgewood Scene*, February 1977. Edgewood College Archives.

6 *Ibid.*

7 Kastenmeier, Sister Macarius. *The Edgewood Scene,* February 1977.

8 *The Tower Torch,* February 1942, 2. Edgewood College Archives.

9 *The Tower Torch*, May 1943, 3.

10 *The Tower Torch*, November 1942, 1.

11 Kress, Sister Mary Justinia. Letter to S. Barbara Beyenka, June 10, 1977. Edgewood College Archives.

12 Baadte, Sister Mary Catherine (Matthia). Letter to Sister Mary Paynter. December 12, 2001.

13 Edgewood Convent Annals II, 104. Edgewood College Archives.

14 Annals II, 128.

15 Smith, Sister Joan. Letter to Rev. Philip Henley in response to a request for information about the college, December 14, 1948. Edgewood College Archives.

16 Fitzgerald, Sister De Ricci. Letter to the Sisters of the Congregation. November 5, 1948. Sinsinawa Dominican Archives.

17 "Tribute to Sister Joan," *Signature*, 1966.

18 At a meeting of the administrative officers with Sister De Ricci, it was noted that "the revision of the catalog was taken up and it was agreed that from now on we should highlight the senior college and minimize the junior college." Edgewood College Administrative Officers Meeting *Minutes*, January 10, 1947.

    That same month, at a meeting with Mother Samuel, Sister Dunstan, Sister Joan, Sister Mary Hope, and Leo T. Crowley, "Sister De Ricci said that the building is most urgent." The meeting was to discuss the proposed fund drive for a new college building. Edgewood College Administrative Officers *Minutes*, January 25, 1947.

19 A February 17, 1948 letter, from Sister Joan Smith to D.A. Grossman, registrar of the University of Illinois, said: "In the not too distant future we hope to have membership in the North Central Association of Colleges and Universities and are working toward that end, although we have not yet made application." Edgewood College Archives.

5 — GROWTH AND EXPANSION
1950 - 1968

1 A summary of notes taken by Sister Joan Smith during Sister Evelyn Murphy's talk to the Edgewood sisters on June 10, 1950. Edgewood College Archives.

2 Edgewood College Administrators' *Minutes*, August 24, 1950. Edgewood College Archives. Hereafter called 'Administrators' *Minutes*.'

3 Administrators' *Minutes*, August 27, 1950; September 10, 1950.

4 Many discussions regarding the need for a new elementary school building had been held in the 1940s, but the hope had been that sufficient monies could be raised during the Fund Drive to provide a college building as well. See correspondence between Sister De Ricci Fitzgerald and administrators at Edgewood in the Sinsinawa Dominican Archives.

5 Smith, Sister Mary Joan. Letter to Mother Evelyn Murphy, February 13, 1955. "The fear that the city will take over our property [along Lake Wingra] grows more alarming.... We will have to put up the science building immediately to hold the property and that means more funds." Sinsinawa Dominican Archives.

6 Thompson, William. *History of Wisconsin,* Vol. VI. Madison: State Historical Society of Wisconsin, 1988. 340. Thompson also notes that in 1963 the *Wisconsin State Journal* recorded that Madison's black community counted only two attorneys, four teachers, six or seven ministers, one professor and several other university staff members, an editor of a scientific journal, and two registered nurses. 352.

7   Administrators' *Minutes*, February 1954; and letter to lay staff from the president, September 30, 1964.

8   "Financial Analysis of Operations, 1941 – 1968." March 1969. Edgewood College Archives.

9   Administrators' *Minutes*, August 20, 1954.

10 Administrators' *Minutes*, December 26, 1958.

11 Administrators' *Minutes*, November 22, 1954.

12 Letter from John Callahan, Superintendent, Wisconsin Department of Public Instruction, April 13, 1943. Edgewood College Archives.

13 Administrators' *Minutes*, March 22, 1951.
    Similarly, the administrators visited with Father Pius Barth, in Chicago in February 1956 seeking his recommendations for preparation for the North Central Association self-study. He provided very practical and specific suggestions, having been a North Central Association visitor for three colleges that year. The visit was a prudent one—Father Barth turned out to be one of the NCA visitors for Edgewood College two years later and chaired the review team! See "Report of an Interview with Father Pius Barth" by Sister Joan Smith, in EC Administrators' Minutes, February 1956.

14 Administrators' *Minutes*, January 12, 1956 and January 17, 1956.

15 "Confidential Report of North Central Examiners to the Board of Review of the Commission on Colleges and Universities, North Central Association of Colleges and Secondary Schools." January 1958.

16 Administrators' *Minutes*, May 13, 1959.

17 HEGIS Report for enrollment, 1968. Also, see *Annual Report of the Registrar for Edgewood College*. 1967-68.

18 Thompson. *The History of Wisconsin*. Vol. VI. 255.

19 Meyer, Grace. "New Horizons." *Alumnae News*. October 1965. By this date over 500 adult women had taken advantage of the "Plan for Personal Development" started in 1952.

20 "Report of First Inspection" – to the Committee on Affiliation and Extension, Catholic University of America, from Rev. James Campbell of the Catholic University of America. Edgewood College Archives.

21 Fall 1967 Compliance Report – Title VI of the Civil Rights Act of 1964. The federal civil rights acts of the sixties required enrollment reports to indicate race, whereas earlier enrollment statistics did not include racial or ethnic information. Also, students did not always choose to indicate ethnic or racial categories on official forms, so report counts do not necessarily reflect reality.

22 Letter "To Senior Resident Students," from the Office of the Dean of Women, July 20, 1964.

23 Landry, Pat Dean, class of 1951. "The End of an Era," Memorial Issue, *Alumnae News*, December 1961, 4.

24 McGreal, Sister Mary Nona. "Tribute to Sister Mary Grace Durkin," delivered at a memorial liturgy for Sister Mary Grace at Edgewood College on March 20, 1967.

25 Marik, Judy Wall (class of 1965). Letter in "Reminiscences" Supplement to *The Edgewood Scene*, spring 1977.

26 Krier, Julie Sawyer (class of 1964). Letter to Sister Mary Paynter. January 2, 2002.

6 — CHALLENGES OF A TURBULENT DECADE *1968 – 1977*

1   "Thoughts to Think Through," *Alumnae News*, June 1966.

2   *Report of a Visit to Edgewood College of the Sacred Heart*. For the Commission on Colleges and Universities of the North Central Association of Colleges and Secondary Schools. May 15 – 16, 1967. Edgewood College Archives.

3   *Edgewise*, May, 1968.

4   Lowe, Katie. "What Now?" *Signature*, spring-summer issue, 1968.

5   Blackmon, Ann. "Comment" *Signature*, spring-summer issue, 1968.

6   *Edgewise*, September 20, 1968.

7   Bennin, Lois, editor. *Edgewise*, October 1, 1968.

8   Michels, Sister Matthias. Reminiscence in a letter to Sister Mary Paynter, September 2001. During the January Winterim of 1969, a two-week symposium on "Freedom and Authority" drew large attendance.

9   Administrative Officers Meeting, *Minutes*, November 19, 1971.

10 Guilfoil, Daniel J. Letter to S. Mary Paynter. December 29, 2001.

11 "Edgewood Goes Co-Ed," *Alumnae News*, March 1970.

12 Haas, Lee. Letter to S. Mary Paynter, February 2, 2002. See the college yearbook, *The Torch—1972*, for photos of the team in uniform, their intrepid coach, and their loyal fans on a bus heading to a game and flashing "V for victory" signs.

13 *The Conifer*. 1932. 6. Edgewood College Archives

[14] McIltrot, Eileen Dhooghe. Letter to Sister Mary Paynter. February 14, 2002.

[15] Administrative Officers Meeting, *Minutes*, January 27, 1972. Actually students' requests for beer to be served on campus, particularly at "beer suppers," had been recommended during an all-campus "Think Day," in Sister Nona's time—December 7, 1965.

[16] Lesandrini, Kent. Letter to Sister Mary Paynter. January 30, 2002.

[17] The Board of Trustees, all Dominican sisters, had decided at its November 1968 meeting, that "at least three new members be elected to the Board by June 1, 1969, of whom two shall be nominated by the President's Council of Edgewood College." Edgewood College Board of Trustees *Minutes*, November 1, 1968.

[18] Board of Trustees Meeting, *Minutes* of May 16, 1972.

[19] Enrollment numbers and other college statistics for various years are taken from the *Annual Report of the Registrar of Edgewood College to the President*. Other reports indicate slightly different statistics, often due to the date of the report (September figures are different from October or later figures, for example).

[20] From *Annual Report of the Registrar of Edgewood College to the President*.

[21] Beyenka, *Edgewood College Annals*, 1974-75.

[22] *Edgewise*, May 22, 1968. This cost figure was overly optimistic; later, Sister Cecilia reported to the Board of Trustees that the anticipated cost would be more.

[23] Collins, A.B. Letter to Sister Cecilia Carey, April 3, 1973. Edgewood College Archives.

[24] Carey, Sister Cecilia. Letter to President A.B. Collins, Spitz Laboratories, April 10, 1973.

[25] In 1963, Sister Nona had appointed Greta Shetney as the college's first director of public relations. Later John Butler's appointment as director of development and public relations enlarged the work of the office.

[26] Communiqué. "Summary and Conclusions of Attitude Study, and Recommendations to the Board of Trustees of Edgewood College." December 20, 1971. Even in Sister Nona's term, at the December 1965 "Think Day," one proposal from students and faculty had been to change the name of the college "to give it an identity of its own, and to distinguish it from the high school. One suggestion was 'Mazzuchelli College.'" *Alumnae News,* June 1966.

[27] Carey, Sister Cecilia. *Report of the President to the Board of Trustees—1970-71.* Edgewood College Archives.

[28] Jill Ker Conway, *A Woman's Education*, New York: Knopf, 2001. 107. The minutes of an Edgewood College administrative officers' meeting on February 3, 1972, noted that students as well as faculty were reacting negatively to the proposals made by Communiqué. The last agreement between the college and Communiqué was a contract for a $15,000 program of TV and radio advertisements to be aired in 1978-79.

[29] Beyenka, *Edgewood College Annals, 1971-72.*

[30] Heffernan, Sister Esther. Statement to S. Mary Paynter. February 6, 2002.

[31] "College Launches New Human Issues Program." *The Edgewood Scene.* Fall 1974.

[32] *Ibid.*

[33] Carey, Sister Cecilia. *Five Year Report of the President—1970-1975.* October 4, 1975. This report points out that in 1970, 65% of incoming students were from private high schools (mostly Catholic), while in 1975, only 35% were from private high schools. Edgewood College Archives.

[34] Carey, Sister Cecilia. *Report of the President to the Board of Trustees—1970-71.* Edgewood College Archives.

[35] Continuing Education Program. *Annual Reports.* Edgewood College Archives.

[36] *The Edgewood Scene*, Fall 1976, 2.

[37] In 1970, 34% of entering students at Edgewood College were from public high schools, and 65% were from private high schools. By 1975 that ratio was almost exactly reversed. See Sister Cecilia Carey, *Five Year Report of the President—Edgewood College.*

[38] Chaplains who served at Edgewood (usually ministering in all three schools until the 1960s), from the founding of the college in 1927 to 1976, were the following: Harry Hengell (who also founded St. Paul's, the University Catholic Student Center), Leo Rummel, O.Praem., and Dominicans Raymond Kavanah, Peter Bachand, John Malone, Martin McDermott, James Connolly, John Masterson, Mark Barron, Gordon Walter, Edward O'Connor, Martin Hopkins, Neil McDermott, Richard LaPata, George Kovacec, followed by the ministry team of David Woeste and S. Clare Wagner during 1976-77.

[39] Rocca, Rae Carol. Letter to Sister Mary Paynter. January 15, 2002.

[40] See letters to Sister De Ricci Fitzgerald from Sister Joan Smith in the Sinsinawa Dominican Archives.

[41] Smith, Sister Joan. Letter to Sister De Ricci Fitzgerald, February, March 1934. Sinsinawa Dominican Archives.

Sister Barbara Beyenka states that Sister Joan "very probably" would have headed the new senior college program which began in 1940 had she not been called to work in Washington, D.C., at the Catholic University of America on the Bishops' Commission on American Citizenship. See Beyenka's *A Jubilee History.* Madison: Edgewood College, 1977. 25-26.

[42] Smith, Sister Joan.   Letter to Sister De Ricci Fitzgerald. November 26, 1945.

[43] Carey, Sister Cecilia. *President's Reports* (various years). Edgewood College Archives. The financial reports indicate the following: 1967-68: +$47,623.51; 1968-69: –($46,738.); 1969-70: –($54,143.); 1970-71: –($23,998.); 1971-72: –($37,245.26.); 1972-73: –($17,759.98); 1973-74: +$ 42,460.; balanced budgets were achieved from 1973-74 on, except for a $14,687. deficit in 1974-75.

[44] Davlin, Sister M. Clemente.   Letter to S. Mary Paynter. December 8, 2001.

[45] Letter in the supplement to *The Edgewood Scene,* Summer 1977.

[46] "Edgewood's New President: Sister M. Cecilia." *Alumnae News,* May 1968.

7 — TRANSITION YEARS   1977 – 1987

[1] Gribble, Roger. "Edgewood's new president already eyeing 5-year plan." *Wisconsin State Journal.* September 25, 1977. I, 10.

[2] Haslanger, Phil. "New leader keeps Edgewood College on course." *The Capital Times.* September 8, 1977, 1.

[3] Enrollment statistics in this chapter are taken from the *Annual Reports of the Registrar,* Edgewood College, various years. Edgewood College Archives.

[4] Financial reports in this chapter are taken from the annual *Edgewood College Budget Reports,* from the Business Officer, various years. Edgewood College Archives.

[5] *Comparative Statement of Operations.* Business Office, November 1, 1978. Edgewood College Archives. The figures for "contributed services" represent the differential between the stipends paid to the sisters and what would have been the salaries of lay employees in the same positions.

[6] Rouse, Al.   Interview with Sister Mary Paynter. 25 April 2002.

[7] "Report to the Mother General [Sister Evelyn Murphy] On Edgewood College." By Sister Joan Smith and Sister Dunstan Tucker. June 10, 1950. Edgewood College Archives. Sister Joan's own direct support and encouragement of adult women who returned to complete a degree at Edgewood during the late 1950s and 1960s was legendary.

[8] "President's Report to the Edgewood Community" quoted in Sister Anne Schaudenecker's *Edgewood College Annals — 1979-1980.* Edgewood College Archives.

[9] Pierick, Sister Carmela. *Annual Report of the Director of Continuing Education. 1982 – 1983.* Edgewood College Archives. The EPS program grew, exceeding its planners' initial hopes, and in its first two years provided the college with an income of $12,000 over and above its expenses.

[10] Beaubien, Elaine. Letter to Sister Mary Paynter. February 20, 2002. Edgewood College Archives.

[11] *Minutes of the Board of Trustees.* Meeting of February 25, 1982. Edgewood College Archives. Information in this chapter relating to the discussions and actions of the college board of trustees is drawn from the minutes of various board meetings.

[12] Dizzy, "Thank You, Sally." *Screed.* May 1981. Edgewood College Archives

[13] Keane, Lucy. *Screed.* October 1982.

[14] Beaubien, Elaine. Letter to Sister Mary Paynter. February 20, 2002. Edgewood College Archives.

[15] O'Rourke, Sister Alice. "Inaugural Address." Edgewood College Archives.

[16] [Geesaman, Claire.] "On the Cover." *Edgewood College Today.* Winter 1983.

[17] Ewens, Sister Mary. "Change is essential in meeting challenges ahead." *1984 Annual Report: Edgewood College.*

[18] *Minutes of the Board of Trustees.* Meeting of November 1, 1984. Comment on the review of the audit for 1983-84.

[19] *Minutes of Budget and Planning Committee.* Various meetings during 1983-84. Edgewood College Archives.

[20] Keane, Lucy. *Screed.* March 1984.

[21] Condron, Kerry. "What's Happening?" *Screed.* April 1984.

[22] Keane, Lucy. "Editorial." *Screed.* May 1984.

[23] Stevie [Sister Marie Stephen Reges]. "After 25 Years at Edgewood." *Screed.* May 1984.

[24] *Screed.* May 1985. Bill Duddleston was a faculty member in economics; Mike Lybarger, faculty member in history; Joan Schilling, faculty member in psychology; Tom Loden, snack bar manager; Steve Brown, residence director.

[25] *Minutes of the Board of Trustees.* Meeting of September 5, 1985. This change in responsibilities had been recommended by the

consultants who had studied the college's administrative structure—see letter to Sister Mary Ewens from James R. Morgan of Planning Professionals, Inc., a Milwaukee consulting firm, May 30, 1985. Morgan writes: "We agreed that your role would be most effective if it could focus virtually all your efforts externally as President."

26 Ewens, Sister Mary. "Dear Colleagues." Letter to faculty and staff, August 12, 1985. In *Administrative Team Minutes* 1985-86. Also see "Gift to Scholarship Fund," *The Catholic Herald*, November 28, 1985, 4. Edgewood College Archives.

27 Gribble, Roger. "Edgewood College gets $500,000 gift." *The Wisconsin State Journal, Metro.* August 13, 1985. Section 4, 1.

28 *Minutes of the Board of Trustees.* Meeting of November 13, 1986.

29 Heffernan, Sister Esther. Interview with Sister Mary Paynter. April 17, 2002. Also, see the *Minutes of the Meeting of Department Chairpersons.* November 10, 1986. Edgewood College Archives.

30 Details of the recommendations and board actions may be found in the board minutes and in the summary provided by Sister Barbara Beyenka in the *Edgewood College Annals* for 1986-1987.

8— A NEW ERA

1 Each of the first five Sinsinawa Dominican presidents of Edgewood College was principal of the high school and prioress of the convent of sisters: Sister Grace James (1927 – 1928), Sister Laurentina Boyle (1928 – 1934), Sister Marie Francis Barden (1934 – 1939), Sister Rose Catherine Leonard (1939 – 1944), and Sister Mary Hope O'Brien (1944 – 1950). They were formally the college presidents, but during these years the college was actually administered by the deans—Sister Marie Aileen Klein (1927 – 1940) and Sister Dunstan Tucker (1940 – 1950).
The succeeding five presidents served as actual chief executive officers of the college: Sister Mary Nona McGreal (1950 – 1968), Sister Cecilia Carey (1968 – 1977), Sister Alice O'Rourke (1977 – 1983), Sister Mary Ewens (1983 – 1987), James Ebben (1987 -   ).

2 "Inauguration." Selections from the address given by James Ebben on November 6, 1987. In *Edgewood College Today*, Spring 1988.

3 Rouse, Al. Interview with Sister Mary Paynter. May 20, 2002.

4 Ebben, Jim. Interview with Sister Mary Paynter. June 1, 2002.

5 "Inauguration." Selections from the address given by James Ebben on November 6, 1987. In *Edgewood College Today*, Spring 1988.

6 Murphy, S. Mary, *et al. Report of a Visit to Edgewood College, Madison, Wisconsin.* March 7-9, 1988. For the Commission on Institutions of Higher Education of the North Central Association of Colleges and Schools.

7 Members of the planning committee were Roby Blust, Sister Jane Boland, Sister Helen Dailey, Julie Hover, Doug Hutchings, Jim Lorman, Sister Mary Ellen O'Grady, Al Rouse, Judy Wimmer, John Yrios, and Jim Ebben as chairperson. The names are taken from various committee meeting notes. See *Notes from the Meetings of the Planning Committee.* September, October 1987. Edgewood College Archives.

8 *Ibid.*

9 The need for a new library had long been noted by successive North Central Association evaluators as well as by successive college administrators. Sister Nona McGreal's master plan of 1955 included a library and administration building located near the classroom building (De Ricci Hall). Sister Alice O'Rourke, in building the activities center, had planned for the new library to be built above the center in the future. After the death of Bernadine Clapp (administrative assistant to Sister Cecilia Carey) in 1984, a legacy and memorial gifts were directed by Sister Mary Ewens to establish the Bernadine Clapp Archives, dedicated on May 25, 1985. The Archives was given space in the old Regina Hall library before relocation in the new Oscar Rennebohm Library. Prior to that, archival materials were kept in the president's office or in storage in De Ricci Hall. With the establishment of the Bernadine Clapp Archives, Sister Mary Ewens appointed Sister Barbara Beyenka as first college archivist to organize and supervise the collection. Succeeding college archivists were Sister Mary Bernice Weber, Jay Hatheway, and Sister Jean Richter.

10 Golden, Ken and Napoleon Smith [Madison City Council aldermen]. *Letter to the Residents.* May 1, 1997. Edgewood College Archives.

11 Lake, Shirley. "Letter to Edgewood." May 21, 1997. Edgewood College Archives.

12 Balousek, Marv. "Ex-astronaut Sally Ride encourages local science students." *Wisconsin State Journal.* May 16, 1999. 1C.

13 Andrews, Tim. Letter to Sister Mary Paynter, June 7, 2002.

14 *Ibid.*

15 Institutional Research Office, Edgewood College.

16 Dison, David. Letter to Sister Mary Paynter, December 12, 2001.

17 Tague, Carolyn. "Edgewood Dances for Peace." *The Screed.* October 1987.

18 Kassulke, Natasha. Letter to Sister Mary Paynter. May 27, 2002.

19 *Ibid.*

20 *Annual Report of the Registrar—1963-64.* Edgewood College Archives.

21 *Report of the Registrar to the Academic Assembly.* February 26, 1988.

22 *Report of the Registrar to the Academic Assembly.* September 28, 1987.

23 Delaney, Katherine, *et. al. Report of a Comprehensive Visit..* March 2 – 4, 1998.

24 Flanagan, Scott. Letter to Sister Mary Paynter. June 6, 2002.

25 Leonard-Rock, Pearl. Letter to Sister Mary Paynter. June 7, 2002.

26 *1987-88 Financial Statement.* Summarized in *Edgewood College Today.* November 1988. 13.

27 Annual reports of the college auditors. 1990, 2001.

28 Delaney, Katherine *et. al. Report of a Comprehensive Visit.* March 2 – 4, 1998.

29 Uselman, John. Letter to Sister Mary Paynter. June 11, 2002.

30 Vernon Sell served as director of the Study Abroad Office during the 1990s. In honor of his long service in promoting Finnish culture in this country, Professor Sell was awarded a knighthood—the Order of the Lion—by the government of Finland through its U.S. ambassador who made the award on the Edgewood campus April 18, 2002.

31 *Report of the Registrar to the Academic Assembly.* Various years. Also information from the International Student Advisor and from the file re: "International Students" in Edgewood College Archives.

32 Schintz, Sister Mary Ann. Fifteen area specialists taught workshops about Africa, East Asia, India, and Middle and South America. The co-directors conducted follow-up workshops at Madison and Milwaukee schools during the following two years, and they also served on a joint Edgewood-University of Wisconsin global education committee headed by Michael Hartounian, Wisconsin Department of Public Instruction.

33 Naughton, Sister Sarah. Letter to Sister Mary Paynter, June 6, 2002. The quotation describes the purpose of the Center as stated in a letter to James Ebben from Steven F. Skolaski, president of the Oscar Rennebohm Foundation. July 30, 2001.

34 Members of the committee were Judy Wimmer, academic dean; Maggie Balistreri-Clarke, dean of students; Raymond Schultz, director of graduate programs; Jane Wilhelm, assistant financial officer; faculty members Bill Duddleston, Mary Mercier, Sister Mary Paynter, Steven Post, Virginia Wirtz; and students Heather Hansen and Tracey Scott.

35 Delaney, *et. al.* By the time of this NCA evaluation visit, the administrative team had been stable for some years, in contrast to the situation at the time of the 1988 visit. This time, the only new member of the administration was Dan Klotzbach, who had succeeded Al Rouse as Chief Financial Officer in 1997 when Rouse was appointed Special Projects Coordinator.

36 *Ibid.*

37 Bennion, Donald H. and Barbara Ann Barbato. *Report of a Focused Visit to Edgewood College, Madison Wisconsin.* For the Higher Learning Commission of the North Central Association of Colleges and Schools. June 3 – 4, 2001.

38 Kimball, Richard. President of The Teagle Foundation. Letter to James Ebben, President of Edgewood College. May 25,1999.

39 In 1965, Gordon Moore, co-founder of Intel, observed that the number of transistors per square inch on integrated circuits had doubled every year since the integrated circuit was invented, and he predicted that this rate would continue. In more recent years, he explained "Moore's law" as the doubling of data density approximately every eighteen months, a definition currently used.

40 Harty, Sister Marian. Letter to Sister Mary Paynter. May 27, 2002.

41 The first two courses at Edgewood College to use Web-based materials were *Medieval History*, taught by Sister Jean Richter, and *College Writing III*, taught by Sister Mary Paynter. These courses were designed by the two instructors using MS *FrontPage*, and made available on the college Web site. Syllabi are in the College Archives.

42 *Notes from the Meetings of the Planning Committee.* September, October 1987.

43 The years of Jim Ebben's presidency saw the passing of many beloved members of the campus community. The news of the deaths of Sister Alexius Wagner and Sister Anthony Daniel Reidy (business), Sister Mary Claude Flanner (library), Sister Catherine Cordon (philosophy), Sister Mary Clare Gilligan (registrar), Sister Joan Leonard (religious studies), Sister Mary Rosary Corrigan (education), Sister Elizabeth Devine (art), Sister Jeannette Feldballe (biology), Sister Marie Stephen Reges (religious studies), Claryce Dierschke (continuing education), Sister Catherine Moran (foreign languages), Sister Alice O'Rourke (president), Laurie Ellen Neustadt (art therapy), Sister Isabelle Mary Sauer (education), Sister Calasancta Wright (financial officer), Sherri Zirk (assistant to the president), and Sister Jerome Heyman (library) brought not only a feeling of loss but also a deep sense of gratitude for all that these people had contributed to creating the enduring values and traditions alive in today's Edgewood College community.

Index